Volume 2

iPad App Directory™
★★★★★

Welcome

In this second edition of the ultimate guide to iPad apps we plunder the App Store still further for the most essential, ground-breaking apps that you need to install on your device, as well as warn you off some over-priced tat. The real beauty of apps is that there truly is something for everyone. Need something to entertain and amuse yourself? Take your pick. In search of an app to speed up your productivity at work? We've got it covered – and then some, right here. Enjoy the read and happy downloading.

Ryan Butt – Editor

Our top five

 **iBooks**
Free
Still the best way to read books on your iPad. Page 10

 **Infinity Blade**
£1.79/$3.99
A truly incredible game that you will never tire of playing. Page 59

 **OMGuitar**
£1.79/$2.99
An amazing guitar synth that looks and plays amazing.. Page 90

 **Read It Later**
£1.99/$2.99
The best way to store pages to read offline in your own time. Page 100

 **Theodolite HD**
£2.99/$4.99
Augmented Reality on your iPad 2 with hundreds of practical uses. Page 145

iPad 2 App
Directory™
★★★★★

Imagine Publishing Ltd
Richmond House
33 Richmond Hill
Bournemouth
Dorset BH2 6EZ
☎ +44 (0) 1202 586200
Website: www.imagine-publishing.co.uk

Editor in Chief
Aaron Asadi

Production Editor
Ryan Butt

Design
Danielle Dixon, Annabelle Sing

Printed by
William Gibbons, 26 Planetary Road, Willenhall, West Midlands, WV13 3XT

Distributed in the UK & Eire by
Imagine Publishing Ltd, www.imagineshop.co.uk. Tel 01202 586200

Distributed in Australia by
Gordon & Gotch, Equinox Centre, 18 Rodborough Road, Frenchs Forest,
NSW 2086. Tel + 61 2 9972 8800

Distributed in the Rest of the World by
Marketforce, Blue Fin Building, 110 Southwark Street, London, SE1 0SU.

ISBN 978 1908 222 114

IMAGINE
PUBLISHING

Contents

Your guide to the best apps for the iPad

78
Lifestyle
Here's how your iPad can be beneficial in every day life, helping you shop and so DIY.

90
Music
The iPad evolved from the humble iPod, so there are loads of apps to kick out some tunes.

100
News/ Weather
With iPad you no longer need to sit through news bulletins to catch the latest headlines.

114
Photography
Bring your photos to life with this fantastic array of creative apps for your iPad.

124
Social Networking
Stay in touch with your friends and family with these essential apps for blogging and tweeting.

134
Sports
Catch all the latest live scores and improve your own skills and techniques with your iPad.

144
Travel/ Navigation
Learn how your trusted iPad can become your essential travelling companion with these apps.

156
Productivity /Utilities
Use your iPad to make life easier and speed up your productivity with some truly innovative apps.

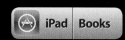

Books

Your iPad can store an entire library's worth of literature, ensuring that you always have something on hand to read whenever the fancy takes you. The following pages are dedicated to the latest book and comic apps that can be added to your virtual shelves and read whenever you want.

Top Paid Apps	Top Free Apps
Guiness World Records: At Your Fingertips ★★★★	**iBooks** ★★★★
Gems and Jewels ★★★★★	**Kindle** ★★★★
The Wasteland ★★★★★	**Sesame Street: The Playground** ★★★★

Staff pick of the section	
War In The Pacific ★★★★★	**SciFi Now** ★★★★★

■ Amazon's Kindle Store is about as straightforward as they come…

■ With thousands of books on offer, there is something for everyone on Kindle.

Price: Free   **Developer:** Reinke LLC

Kindle
The popular iBooks alternative

 Amazon's Kindle offers users the chance to purchase, store and read thousands of books. It enables over half a million works to be browsed utilising the popular retailer's website, using the simple standard interface of either flicking horizontally or tapping a page's edge to read text.

From a convenience angle, Kindle's online store offers customers a complete chapter of paid-for works by way of a sample, and naturally employs a file format that can be read across all of the service's platforms. To be clear, that's the Kindle reader itself, PC, Mac, BlackBerry and Android phones. When agonising over that crucial purchasing decision, you'll be glad of the chance to glance over Amazon's helpful customer reviews that, though occasionally irrational, offer a far preferable option to making blind purchases. All of which, incidentally, are handled through a quick dip into Safari and the retailer's mobile website itself; your purchases refreshing on the following home screen visit.

As far as user-friendliness goes, *Kindle* adopts a policy of simplicity over beauty of design, which, seeing as it's an app to view predominantly plain text, seems perfectly reasonable. Simple to navigate and easy to read, Kindle isn't ambitious but delivers on its promises.

Rating ★★★★★

Price: £2.99/$5.99 **Developer:** Guinness World Records

Guinness World Records: At Your Fingertips

If you want to be a record breaker, this is what you need…

Spread across a handful of extreme categories (including Tallest, Craziest and Most Expensive), *Guinness World Records: At Your Fingertips* offers users an interesting insight into what it takes to become a legend amongst generations of drunks. This may occasionally require doing a little more than withstanding the pain of a needle or forgetting that falling causes death, but oh well.

Each category contains perhaps half a dozen or so separate entries chronicling various individuals' life work, making good use of the device's features through a range of interactive elements. These are often as simple as dots placed upon items of note that will bring up small portions of text thereon, but stretch to reveal a potential record attempt, no less. Using the constant connectivity of Apple's devices, the Guinness World Record for typing the alphabet backwards could very well be yours by the middle of next year. Sure, that hardly matches the 100 metres for prestige, but it's a start.

Aside perhaps from three-dimensional diagrams to manipulate, offering that additional level of presentational pizzazz, it's difficult to claim value for money isn't present here. Although the stuff covered is only a fraction of what you will find in the printed book,

■ There is loads to see and do on each page, make this a far more engaging prospect than the printed edition.

■ With so much going on each page the size of the app is pretty large compared to most books.

the way in which it is presented and the way in which you engage with it makes this feel like a whole new voyage of discovery. More bulk and even more innovation would be welcome in future editions but for now this a good, solid read.

Rating ★★★★☆

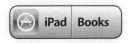

Price: Free Developer: Apple

iBooks

The future of reading, now!

 The first and most obvious advantage *iBooks* holds over its peers is its virtual bookshelf. Like much of Apple's work, this app boasts an elegance of design (and extended feature list) that only the most miserly could bring themselves to detest. Sharing the same basic navigational commands as its main rival, *Kindle*, *iBooks* distinguishes itself with greater customisation, from a range of available fonts to the fact both PDF and ePub documents can be imported. Factor in instant brightness adjustment to soothe weary eyes and you'd be forgiven for thinking that Apple has the contest pretty much sewn up.

Sadly though, the two main drawbacks iBooks suffers from involve elements any successful reader must eventually overcome, namely prohibitive unit cost and poor selection of texts. In order to provide a fair and equitable test of value and variety across the respective apps, we took the top ten fiction bestsellers, checking each of our two contenders for the level of value offered. Expecting a negligible difference, we were surprised to find that five of the researched works didn't feature on the iBookstore at all. Over the remaining five that were present, users could save over 11 pounds in total shopping via Amazon's service, running to around a 40 per cent difference overall. We're certain a gap of this size would lead even consumers who can afford the luxurious design of Apple's offering to consider how much harder their money could work. There will come a point, after all, at which handheld readers will be old hat, and people won't be prepared to pay extra just for their novelty. Beautifully designed, yet undeniably expensive on a unit-cost.

Rating ★★★★☆

■ There are lost of in-app options that allow you to alter the font, create bookmarks, highlight key words and browse via category.

■ Your purchased books are displayed in an attractive bookcase for easy selection.

SciFi Now

Price: £1.19/$1.99 **Developer:** Pixelmags

The world's leading science fiction magazine comes to the iPad

■ The content is presented exactly as per the magazine, you just swipe to turn pages.

■ All the goodness of the magazine minus the hassle of finding a place to store all of your old copies. Let's all switch to digital!

The debate as to whether the internet or a handheld magazine is better is never going to die. Both boast positive and negatives that the other would love to include/exclude and it's unlikely one will ever ride out on top. What will, however, is a mix of both.

Giving you a free issue of the magazine when you purchase the app, *SciFiNow* opens up the ability to buy every back copy released and gives you instant access to the monthly publication as soon as it goes on-sale. Reading it on iPad is a treat. Flicking through the pages with your fingers or zooming into a particular article, which is heightened thanks to the iPad's slick resolution and speed, is effortless and makes the experience as good as having the actual print magazine. In some instances it's even easier as bookmarking a page or searching for a particular feature is as simple as a touch of a button. You can even share an issue with a friend who also has the app installed, making the App as close to its real-life counterpart as possible.

Rating ★★★★★

Stanza

Price: Free **Developer:** Lexcycle

It's a library, bookstore, text book and portable PDF reader all in one!

You may be wondering why you would need *Stanza* when *iBooks* comes free with the iPad. Well, while *iBooks* is a perfectly good eBook reader, albeit with overpriced books to download, *Stanza* offers so much more flexibility and customisation and a choice of online bookstores to visit. There are links in *Stanza* to more than 100,000 books, covering all subjects and genres. As they come from a variety of bookstores, there is competition on pricing, so costs are kept reasonable. Once you have downloaded a selection, you can view them in a cover flow style, giving the true bookshop feel to your experience as you flick through. That's not all, though; you can customise the font sizes and colours, read in portrait or landscape, adjust line spacing and there's a full-screen option so you can fully immerse yourself in a book.

What impressed us though was the ability to drop eBooks and PDF files onto a tab in iTunes and have these files pop-up to be read within *Stanza*. This means that you are no longer tied to only downloading on the iPad, and you can copy over your library of books from any PC or Mac.

Rating ★★★★★

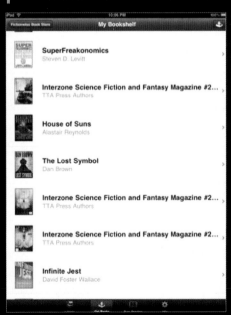

■ Have international best-sellers in your hands at the touch of a few buttons…

■ Text can be customised in many ways, adjusting colours, sizes and spacing to suit your preferences.

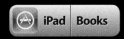

Price: £2.99/$4.99 **Developer:** Gameloft SA

War In The Pacific

Immerse yourself in history

With shows like *The Pacific* and *Band Of Brothers* giving World War II's most prolific campaigns a lick of Hollywood gloss, it's no surprise to see historical texts receiving the same treatment. War in the Pacific is an engrossing history lesson for anyone looking to learn more about the Pacific Theatre. It's an app that will appeal even to those with an in-built aversion to reading books on the subject, thanks to the rousing orchestral soundtrack and the abundance of striking photography from the frontlines.

Throughout each of the 20 in-depth chapters, you will find well-documented first-hand accounts of each significant event throughout the campaign, surrounded by photos complete with captions, leaked documents from war officials and boxouts that elaborate on some of the more detailed elements. Page presentation is delivered in razor-sharp HD, and thanks to some neat menu design any user can flick through pages and jump to specific sections with ease. Chapters can be viewed in a simple playlist menu, or can be charted on an intricate map of the Pacific region to follow the flow of the greatest battles.

Rating ★★★★★

■ The bombastic score and poignant photography complement the book.

Price: £0.59/$0.99 **Developer:** pixelmags

Go Run

Thinking about running? This will help you every step of the way

We all pledge, often in an alcohol-induced haze on New Year's Eve, to rid our bodies of toxins and get fit for the forthcoming year. Granted, such resolutions are usually swiftly forgotten about, but if you're serious about improving your fitness then the *Go Run* app provides the perfect springboard for your ambitions.

This digital magazine is geared towards runners of all abilities, offering useful tips that can be read on the move and practical advice on training and nutrition. When you download the app you will get part one of 'The Beginner's Guide To Running', which is the first of many in-app books that will steadily help you enhance your running skills. In fact, the app pledges to help you train for your first 5K run from scratch in just 12 weeks!

The pages of this eBook are informative and eye-catching without constantly bombarding you with text. Everything is kept waffle-free in bite-sized segments, providing only the essential information you need to get going, which is generally friendly and encouraging.

Rating ★★★★★

■ The app will get you ready for your first 5K.

■ The app manages to be both educational and fun.

Tidels Rapunzel

Price: £0.59/$0.99 **Developer:** Tidels

Let your hair down with this classic follicular fable

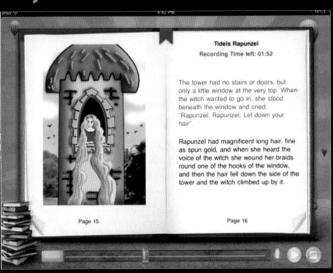

■ Recording is done one paragraph at a time.

Thanks no doubt to the recent hit Disney movie *Tangled*, Rapunzel is the current fairytale du jour among the under-10s, and this app contains Tidels' take on the story.

Represented on the iPad screen in the form of a book open on a table, the reader can elect to have the text read aloud by a narrator, or they can select the 'I Will Read' mode. It's this mode that uncovers the app's unique selling point: a recording function where you can record yourself narrating the story, which is great for absent parents, as they can record the story for their child to enjoy while they're away.

Operation of the recording process is a little clumsy, and the play and record buttons are so close together that it's all too easy for little fingers to over-record a section by accident, but overall this is a great feature that personalises the app and works well.

The prose is a little dated, and some of the English constructions could do with reworking, but the recording feature alone makes this a worthwhile purchase.

Rating ★★★★★

Price: £0.59/$0.99 **Developer:** Stepworks

The Emperor's New Clothes – A Kidztory Classic Animated Interactive Storybook

Another classic tale from the Kidztory Collection Interactive Storybook

The 11th adaptation in the Kidztory series of animated interactive storybooks from Stepworks, The Emperor's New Clothes continues the traditional combination of enchanting animation, charming narration and fun sound effects. The winning formula shows no signs of letting up, as the vain Emperor's foolish pride is ultimately deflated by the precocious common sense of one small boy.

The Read To Me / Read By Myself feature is here, each page providing a new character or object for children to prod and laugh at the resulting sound effect. The narration is clear and funny, with Stepworks' regular narrator, noticeably a bit more grown up since the days of The Little Red Hen, handling different accents with aplomb. The developers have even been creative enough to bag a 4+ age rating in spite of the mandatory nude scenes.

There once lived an **emperor** who cared only about himself.

■ Graphics are bright, colourful and amusing…

Rating ★★★★★

Price: £7.99/$13.99 **Developer:** Touch Press

Gems and Jewels

Captivating visuals enhance this guide to precious stones

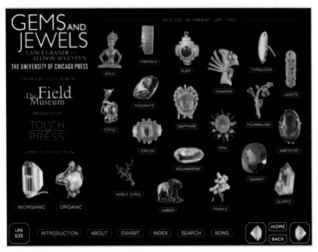

When the iPad was launched back in spring 2010, one of the apps that showcased it was a stunning interactive version of the periodic table called Elements, used because of the way it harnessed the iPad's capabilities and showed it off to be the show-stopping gadget it really is.

Gems and Jewels comes from the same developers, Touch Press, and works in a similar way, presenting a dazzling array of over 300 3D renditions of precious stones, shown in their naturally occurring states as well as jewelled settings, that can be spun, pinch-zoomed and generally messed with against a classy black background.

The download comes in at a jaw-dropping 1.66GB, so you know before you've even launched the app that it's a serious piece of work. Each item can be viewed from multiple angles and perspectives, and is accompanied by authoritative captions that tell you what you're looking at. A beautifully presented treasure trove of information, *Gems and Jewels* represents another perfect showcase for the iPad's capabilities.

■ The app's interface is just beautiful; there's no other way to describe it.

Rating ★★★★★

Price: £7.99/$13.99 **Developer:** Touch Press

The Waste Land

A content-rich version of TS Eliot's greatest work

Hailed as one of the seminal works of poetry of the 20th century, TS Eliot's The Waste Land is undeniably a complex work of great depth and vision. This app is a comprehensive collection of reference materials, interviews, video clips and audio readings that lifts the lid on many of the references and allusions found in the poem. It includes a specially-filmed video performance by Fiona Shaw synced to the text, two readings by Eliot himself, other readings by Viggo Mortensen, Alec Guinness and Ted Hughes and over 35 video perspectives from respected contributors.

The app is beautifully produced and the light, airy interface style makes it a joy to use. A must for students of literature and poetry fans, this is a shining example of how today's technology can breathe new life into the classics.

■ Includes full video performance by Fiona Shaw.

Rating ★★★★★

Price: £1.19/$1.99 Developer: ScrollMotion Inc

Sesame Street: The Playground

4 waddling penguins   5 slow turtles

It's one for younger kids, but that doesn't mean the app is condescending. In fact, after you've read and scrolled your way through all 16 panes, the cast takes you through some of the words they used throughout, with definitions and pronunciation, giving the app some great educational value. A well-presented and brilliantly put together interactive package.

Rating ★★★★★

Price: £1.79/$2.99 Developer: Octopus Kite

Bartleby's Book Of Buttons Vol 1

Designed with both young and older children in mind, this beautiful interactive storybook will keep your kids glued to your iPad. Your child will help Bartleby in his quest to add to his button collection by flicking switches, rotating the iPad and pushing buttons. It's easy to use and children will soon pick it up thanks to the colourful interface.

Rating ★★★★★

Price: £2.99/$3.99 Developer: Ghostwriters Ent

The Frog King HD

THEN SHE TOOK HER FAVORITE PLAYTHING, A GOLDEN BALL, AND THREW IT UP ON HIGH AND CAUGHT IT. BUT ONE TIME THE BEAUTIFUL PRINCESS'S GOLDEN BALL DID NOT FALL BACK INTO HER LITTLE HAND BUT INTO THE WATER.

Turn your iPad into a high-definition storybook with this app. The presentation is superb with beautiful illustrations and the ability to either read the story yourself or have it read to you. While it's aimed at youngsters it's not too useful as a teaching guide due to the small text. It's also pricey for a story that lapsed out of copyright years ago.

Rating ★★★★★

Price: Free Developer: Sesame Workshop Apps

Sesame Street eBooks

"Help Elmo keep those monsters busy so the monsters won't chase the puppy."

Elmo, Ernie and Big Bird et al take part in dozens of adventures with full-screen illustrations. As you would expect, it combines fun with learning, and is sure to captivate and enthral younger users. It's a shame, then, that it uses a subscription service of either £2.39 a month, or beyond the £20 mark for a year. It's galling that individual purchases aren't allowed, to be honest.

Rating ★★★★★

Price: £4.99/$9.99 Developer: Callaway Digital Arts

Miss Spider's Bedtime Story

It was bedtime, but the Cozy Hole was still abuzz!
"We have to speed up this routine," Holley sighed.
Miss Spider agreed. "Maybe a wishing web would help!"

This charming digital story book may seem expensive but you're getting a lot for your cash. In addition to a story that can be read on your own or narrated, there are puzzles to make, pictures to colour in, a matching pairs game and even a 13-minute episode to watch. The story is well presented and features treats that trigger interactive sections when touched.

Rating ★★★★★

Price: Free Developer: Imagine Learning, Inc

Bookster

had an elephant's nose?

Bookster aims to speed up literacy learning by giving an interactive edge to a spoken word and visual image book. The interface is simple: each page has a child's voice reading out the words, and by pressing a button in the corner the user's voice can be recorded. Simple but effective. The real question is whether mimicry in itself is education.

Rating ★★★★★

Price: Free Developer: Angela Patchell Books

VIZeBooks

Working in much the same way as iBooks, the VIZeBooks app offers a selection of award-winning visual art books to purchase and download. Aimed at designers, artists, illustrators and photographers, the interface is clean and easy to navigate, and can be customised with downloadable palettes. Disappointingly, at the time of writing there were only 11 books available and we would like to see full-size previews of the books on offer. Has the potential to be an excellent resource, but is currently too bare in terms of content.

Rating ★★★★★

Price: £0.59/$0.99 Developer: Marcus Wilhelm

Jannie & Luis: Chalkboard

Perfect for letting children express themselves, Chalkboard offers seven chalk colours, unlimited undo and redo possibilities and a sponge for deleting. Creations can be saved and then shared. Despite being developed for children, the realistic re-creation of a chalkboard could even have adults creating their very own masterpieces.

Rating ★★★★★

Business/Finance

Aside from playing games, reading books and enjoying other forms of entertainment, your iPad also functions brilliantly as a tool for helping manage your finances, run your business and keep you well organised. Here we take a look at the apps that can save you time, energy and even some money.

Top Paid Apps	Top Free Apps
Documents To Go Premium – Office Suite ★★★★★	**James Caan Business Secrets** ★★★★★
Quickoffice ★★★★★	**BT Fon Wi-Fi** ★★★★★
BluePrint Sketch ★★★★	**WebEx for iPad** ★★★★

Staff pick of the section

Wealth Manager ★★★★	**nCloudbox** ★★★★

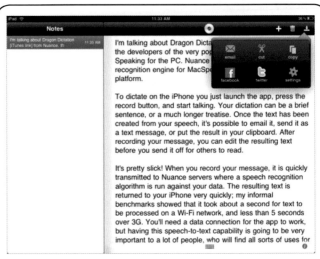

Price: Free **Developer:** Nuance Communications

 Anything you say will be recorded and translated into text.

Dragon Dictation

Dragon Dictation is a free app that lets users record audio, which is instantly converted into text. Simple is the best adjective to describe its inherent qualities; the opening screen offers nothing more than a three-word instruction and a button on a one-colour background. Tap, as instructed, and it's time to talk. When the talking is over hit the 'Done' button and wait for the audio to be converted to text. This is where *Dragon Dictation* starts to show cracks. The conversion is often less than 100 per cent accurate. For a better success rate a user needs to speak clearly and precisely. For this very reason a keyboard icon is included. This offers the backup option of being able to edit text via the keyboard.

Completed text has several outlets, as it cannot be saved to the device. 'Text' adds it to the body of a message ready to send. 'Email' is self-explanatory, while Facebook and Twitter lovers can post directly to an account. Its simplicity is there to be admired, but the same can't be said of its core feature – text conversion. So while the app is undoubtedly useful, it needs to be more accurate and reliable if it is to be deemed truly essential. Mercifully, it's free so you can afford to take the chance, but there are other – though admittedly, paid for – apps out there, such as *Audio Memos*, that do the same thing far better.

Rating

Price: £9.99/$19.99 **Developer:** DataViz, Inc

Documents To Go Premium – Office Suite

View, manage and edit your documents on the move

Trawl through the App Store, and you'll come across a countless stack of apps that allow you to transport files and edit them on your iPad, but *Documents To Go Premium* is hands down the best of the bunch. Admittedly, one glance at the price is enough to deter most casual app buyers, but if you require a means to bridge the gap between home and office, then this is perfect. The app works in tandem with a desktop app that you can download from the Dataviz site, enabling you to drag documents into a desktop folders, synch your desktop to your iPad, and then view and work on the same documents on your portable device. It is capable of syncing more than one desktop to the app, making it a convenient means of porting documents between home and work while using your commuting time to work on them.

The app supports the Microsoft Word, Excel and PowerPoint files, and any changes you need to make can be applied to the iPad versions of the documents, saved, and then with a quick synch back to your desktop the amended and updated files will be transported back to where they originated from.

The effectiveness of *Documents To Go Premium* isn't confined to just synced folders either, as you can also view and manipulate supported attachments sent via the default Mail app, MS Exchange and Google Mail. Additionally, you can also pluck documents from a wide range of supported cloud storage devices – enabling you to work virtually whenever and wherever you see fit.

Despite such a seemingly relentless gush of positivity however, *Documents To Go Premium* isn't perfect. Conspicuous by its absence is a spell checker, and we did experience some syncing issues (the desktop and iPad just seemed to lose their connection to each other periodically), but certainly the latter problem seems to have been addressed with the 4.0.2 update. A simple and effective solution for your data transfer needs, *Documents To Go Premium* will undoubtedly help you work remotely.

■ After downloading the app, go to the DataViz website at www.dataviz.com and download the desktop app.

Rating ★★★★★

■ To get started, open up the app on your device, tap on the 'Settings' option at the bottom of the page and then tap 'Add'.

■ You can access the contents of your desktop folder through the app. If you make any changes then hit the 'Sync' button to update the changes on your computer.

Price: £11.99/$19.99 **Developer:** Antecea Inc

Cloud Connect Pro

Manage files, desktop computers and more with this app

If there's one limitation of using an iPad for regular work, it's the file system. To put it simply, there isn't one. In many ways, it's a positive move by Apple, simplifying how users interact with the system and removing the need to manually manage files. But if you were hoping to plug your iPad into a Mac or PC and drag files back and forth between machines, then you'll be disappointed.

Thankfully, *Cloud Connect Pro* is here to help. It enables you to transfer files from any computer, and access a Dropbox account, iDisk or WebDAV/SFTP/FTP server. Launch the app, and you'll see a sidebar with options for viewing shared documents, accessing bookmarks, connecting to a Gmail account, viewing saved places (such as Dropbox), and accessing network places. At the bottom of the screen is a dock with icons for playing media, settings, file transfers, documents and a trash can.

So far, so good, but *Cloud Connect Pro* also has a few aces up its sleeve, the most impressive of which is the ability to remotely log on to your Mac or PC, and interact with it via MultiTouch. As a result, you can log into your home computer over a 3G or Wi-Fi connection, drag files into the *Cloud Connect Pro* documents folder, and see them appear on your iPad seconds later. Some of the other clever features packed into the app include wirelessly

printing to an AirPrint printer, the ability to play music, watch videos and view photos, open iWork and Office files, zip and unzip files, open files in other apps (for example open a word document in Pages), transfer multiple files and folders, wake a computer remotely, and many more. It's an exhausting list of features, more than we can fit into this review.

The price is considerable when compared to similar apps. Whether you can justify the price depends on which features you'll use. This app will certainly enable you to easily manage files between your iPad and desktop computer, and it's great being able to remotely access a desktop computer.

If there's one problem we have with this app, it's the custom-built interface. It's not ugly by any means, but the large icons and blue colour scheme feel out of place on an iPad, with a desktop computer feel to them.

Despite this though *Cloud Connect Pro* is certainly one of the most feature-packed office apps we've seen on the iPad and is truly outstanding at managing large numbers of files on your device. If you work remotely often or just need to get out of the office once in a while then this comes highly recommended.

Rating ★★★★★

■ The app allows you to manage high volumes of files on your device.

■ Once you are all connected up, using this app is incredibly easy and seconds mere minutes to master.

Price: Free **Developer:** The App Business Ltd

James Caan Business Secrets
Straight from the Dragon's mouth

James Caan is best known to British audiences as one of The Dragons from *Dragon's Den*, where he would help budding entrepreneurs by financing their product if he deemed it worthy. However, this free app has got to be the second-best assistance a young businessperson could receive.

The Secrets section of the app consists of eight 'volumes', from 'People & Hiring' in the beginning to your 'Exit Strategy' at the end, and each of these volume consists of several downloadable tips delivered by Caan in audio form, and also in easy-to-read text. These clips only last for a couple of minutes, but they work well, and Caan mostly uses plain English to get his points across. Cringeworthy business speak is kept to a minimum, especially in the early chapters. When terms like 'liquidity' are used, Caan usually offers a relatively simple explanation and definition.

Caan's style throughout delivering these secrets is quite anecdotal, and while some chapters may sometimes veer into self-indulgent arrogance, his personal examples lend more credence to his tips. This is a man who is clearly knowledgeable about the subject matter, and the content spans into the modern era, with advice on how to market via the internet and traditional methods. But these secrets are only half the app. Caan's autobiography The Real Deal is on here in its entirety – you simply download each chapter to the Playlist section of the app, which is alongside the Secrets and The Real Deal. The book is read by Caan himself, and while it is perfectly listenable, his delivery is a little slow, and we would have preferred the option to read it. But maybe that's

■ You also get James' audio book, The Real Deal for free.

■ James Caan appears in the app frequently to deliver advice personally…

asking a bit too much.

The Playlist, while functional, is the weakest section of the app. The design is where it suffers most, as it takes a good few presses to hit the play button without messing the volume, and even when you're listening to The Real Deal audiobook, a large button still implores you to 'Read This Secret'.

But such grievances don't matter, because *Business Secrets* is the perfect app for those seeking to start a new organisation.

Rating ★★★★★

Price: £0.59/$0.99   **Developer:** David Detry

Audio Memos 2

The quick and easy way to record your thoughts

The full title of *Audio Memos 2* includes the extension The Voice Recorder, which perfectly describes what it's all about. The interface gets straight to the point with a red 'Record' button, which you tap to start recording. It sounds simple and it is, but delve deeper and there's more than meets the eye. There's the date and time, a volume slider and a playback button. Tap the 'Add' button to start a recording and choose quality, volume and whether to use mono or stereo.

A completed recording makes its way onto the home screen list where users can take control of it. Delete with a single swipe and tap or simply tap to get a summary, and tap 'Send' to email a recording. The fun doesn't stop there – tap the information icon to reveal an IP address. Add this to a browser and the iPad is connected with all recordings listed in the browser. Click a link for playback or right-click to download and save to the desktop for future reference. Intuitive interface, good quality recordings, and expansive options make this app a winner.

Rating ★★★★★

■ The app comes with a direct link to Facebook and Twitter for almost instant publishing.

Price: Free   **Developer:** British Telecommunications

BTFON Wi-Fi

Opening up free Wi-Fi, wherever you are

This app is ideal for anyone currently in a 3G carrier contract that doesn't include unlimited internet use. Open to BT internet customers only, *BT FON Wi-Fi* allows free, unrestricted use of almost two million BT hotspots across the UK. Setup is as simple as entering a valid BT internet username and password then either searching for hotspots by location or entering a postcode. Syncing with Google Maps, *BT FON Wi-Fi* highlights areas with active BT FON hotspots using a blue overlay, complete with a specific number of points available. By tapping an available connection, users can view information on where the point is housed, be it a hotel, bar or cafe. The execution is flawless, although the app will scan for access points every time Google Maps is scrolled, making very specific searches slow but accurate.

As a free app, *BT FON Wi-Fi* comes highly recommended to anyone with a BT internet account.

Tap Forms HD – iPad Database

■ You can record audio using the iPad's built-in microphone…

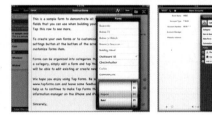

■ Location specific info is appreciated, particularly in bustling cities with an overwhelming number of access points.

■ The interface is clean and simple to navigate, while setup is a minimal process…

Rating ★★★★★

Price: £5.49/$8.99   **Developer:** ClickSpace Technologies Inc

Keep your life in order with this essential forms app

Tap Forms HD is like a 21st century digital Filofax, enabling users to organise their lives with sections for notes, bank details, contacts, loyalty cards, audio dictation and more. It's an incredibly convenient app for storing masses of personal details, and is a doddle to use. A record tab (called Forms) stories entries, and can be accessed with just one tap of a finger. When adding new forms, it's possible to choose from custom templates that include email accounts, insurance details and serial numbers, although it's not possible to add fields from within a template, which has the effect of limiting their usefulness considerably.

As would be expected, the app includes a passcode lock, and the ability to add an encryption key and auto-lock after a set number of minutes. Forms can also be exported via email, Dropbox, Bluetooth, web server or Wi-Fi connection.
This is the perfect app for anyone with a busy life to juggle. The inability to add entries from within a form is an inconvenience, but this is a minor niggle in an otherwise feature-packed app.

Rating ★★★★☆

Price: £2.99/$4.99   **Developer:** ITCreate

BluePrint Sketch
Sketch all of your bright ideas onto blueprint paper

We have to admit, there's something magical about blueprints. After all, the rockets that took mankind to the moon and back were designed on blueprint paper. Don't raise your hopes too high, however, as this is more of a sketching tool with the ability to create quick drawings and design layouts.

The intuitive interface makes it easy to manipulate objects. At the bottom of the screen is a tab bar with buttons for adding symbols, signatures and fonts; in total there are 36 objects to be used. With just a tap of a finger, objects can be re-sized and edited. It's also possible to edit the fill colour and borders to give objects a unique appearance.

It's easy to whip up a sketch in mere seconds, but by digging further into the interface, more additional features appear. It's possible to group and copy objects, move them via a virtual control stick, and share them with friends via email. Sketches can also be saved to the iPad's gallery for later viewing.

Great for brainstorming and object-based sketching, but not suitable for those looking to actually blueprint an idea.

Rating ★★★★★

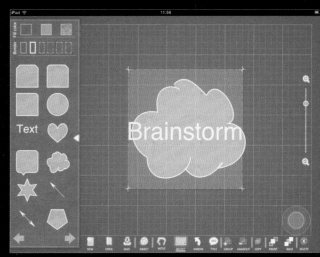

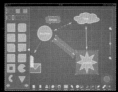

■ This app is great for sketching out any ideas that pop into your head, but its extensive feature make it useful for a variety of purposes…

■ The interface allows you to quickly email sketches directly from the app.

Price: £0.59/$0.99 **Developer:** Prosperity Financial Services PTE Ltd

Wealth Manager

Worried about the future? This might make things better, or worse…

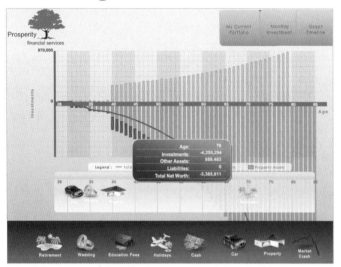

■ This app allows you to track your cash and see if you have enough to see you right.

If you want to find this financial planning software In the App Store, then you'll obviously have to search for the words 'Wealth' and 'Manager', but we'd like to think that there are a couple of other search terms that would work just as well. How about 'The app that that'll make you lose all hope for the future'? Or, 'The graph of inevitable depression'? Doesn't sound so tempting a download, does it? But depending on your mood, that's what *Wealth Manager* is.

In all seriousness, *Wealth Manager* is all about ensuring you can live to a ripe old age (assuming you do), with enough money to keep you going. And it does a fairly good job of this. It allows you to plot your age, how long you intend/expect to live, how much cash you're willing to put away per month, and exactly when you hope to retire. Sprinkle in extra cash vacuums like marriage, cars, holidays and homes, including exactly how expensive you'd like them to be, and the app will then produce a graph showing how long (or not) your cash is likely to last. It's all perfectly simple drag and drop stuff, with some easy to understand pop-up menus. And though there's no tutorial, we got to grips with it within minutes. Depressing affirmation of life's realities aside, it's really quite useful, and at this price it shouldn't affect your retirement fund too much.

Rating ★★★★☆

Price: £5.99/$9.99 **Developer:** Atlu Mantri

AgileBoard

It's your own whiteboard, only smaller

The *AgileBoard* app replicates your own personal whiteboard, complete with sticky notes. The app allows you to create columns of specific business, add notes, change their colour, and customise them according to your needs. It breaks down big tasks into a visually manageable form, but requires that you have a very hands-on approach with it. Unfortunately, it doesn't act like a calendar, or 'talk' to your iPad's calendar, and won't remind you about timed events. You have to keep referring to it, which is perhaps the reason it allows you to screenshot your board for ease of access.

Simplicity is probably *AgileBoard*'s greatest asset. While keeping track of your progress can lead to a mess of information in almost any other form (particularly written, our handwriting is terrible), *AgileBoard* keeps things tidy and clear.

■ It might look simple, but keeping things clear is the best way to use this app.

Rating ★★★☆☆

■ The high-tech password system is a 4x4 grid of coloured blocks…

Price: £2.99/$4.99 **Developer:** Davide Pirola

Color Password for iPad

Eye-catching security

Color Password does pretty much exactly what the title suggests, using combinations of colours instead of standard letters and numbers. The app uses a 4x4 colour grid, giving users an almost endless number of combinations. However, creating a colour password for the first time immediately reveals just how difficult a colour combination is to remember.

Once inside the app, it is all a matter of adding an entry – which is effectively information or notes typically related to passwords. There is the option to choose a type, which includes website, credit card, code, note and custom. A collection of icons can be added to help visually categorise an entry. Entries are then placed into an alphabetically sorted window displaying the icon, the title and other related information. A single tap opens an entry ready for editing or deletion. This effectively is the extent of the app's functionality, with the colour-coded password being its unique selling point. This is not enough to justify the high price.

Rating

■ Users can switch a window to notes and copy and paste content from the opposite window.

Price: £1.19/$1.19 **Developer:** BL

Side by Side Pro

Go multi-screen, and start multi-tasking while on the Web

The iPad offers nearly 10" of screen real estate. What is doesn't provide is the option to split up the screen to accommodate more than one window. However, this is exactly what *Side by Side Pro* does. The app is a multi-window reader/browser with offline reading and note-taking capabilities.

The split window scenario is nothing new to desktop users, but having the choice on the iPad is definitely a plus point. By default, the start page screen is split into two columns, with a host of links to the left and more in-depth info to the right. The first instinct is to tap an option on the left and see the right panel update. Obviously, this doesn't happen, as the windows operate independently. However, the side-by-side stance is still perfect for picking a topic left, and investigating further via the right.

Switching orientation from portrait to landscape also opens up the window content, making it easier to read. A button sits between the multiple screens, and a quick tap allows the user to resize a column to give it more – or less – screen space.

Rating

Price: £0.59/$0.99 **Developer:** Zhejiang Dahua Technology Co Ltd

DMSS-PRO

One of those apps that feels like it should only exist in the far-flung future, *DMSS-PRO* allows you to access remote security cameras so that you can view and control them from the comfort of your iPad, as long as you're connected to the net. You just input your camera's IP address, DNS number and login details, if it has them, and then you're away. It works a treat.

Rating ★★★★☆

Price: £0.59/$0.99 **Developer:** Zhejiang Dahua Technology Co Ltd

2Screens: Presentation Expert

Screens is a fully-featured document manager, file viewer, web browser and whiteboard with VGA-out to a TV, LCD monitor or projector. You can switch between screens containing web content, PDFs, PowerPoint slides and photos/images, all within the same app. Not every app is compatible with the optional VGA adapter, with Safari a notable example.

Rating ★★★☆☆

Price: £1.79/$2.99 **Developer:** Wei Hong

MyNotePad HD

There are hundreds of digital notepads available, but this at least attempts to do something different by providing a decent array of additional features. In fact, *MyNotePad HD* is something of a Swiss Army notepad – giving you an on-hand calculator as well as a voice recorder. The pad feature comes with an assortment of pencil widths and colours.

Rating ★★★☆☆

Price: Free **Developer:** Mellmo Inc

Roambi – Visualizer

Roambi is an innovative app that transforms business reports and data from your existing CSV, HTML and Excel spreadsheets into secure, interactive mobile dashboards to display on iPad. It's a great way of turning your company information into eye-catching, colourful charts that are ideal for presentation purposes. The fact that it's free makes it all the better.

Rating ★★★★☆

Price: £2.99/$5.99 **Developer:** adnX SARL

FlexTeam

This app works in tandem with the Mac version to allow you to sync your working schedule from your computer to your iPad. You start by creating a schedule on the desktop app, and then with one tap you can port it across to your device. It's especially handy if you manage a team and want to keep track of their movements throughout the day.

Rating ★★★☆☆

Price: Free **Developer:** Kishore Tipirneni

Sign-N-Send Free

If you receive email attachments that require you to use an online signature – such as press NDAs – this free app provides an effective method of speeding up a process that would have previously required some degree of printing and re-scanning. You simply highlight the attachment, open it in *Sign-N-Send*, then write directly onto the digital document.

Rating ★★★★☆

Price: £1.19/$1.99 **Developer:** Guangbing Liu

HandySign

Handy Sign is an app designed to speed up the process of signing off PDFs and applying comments to email attachments. It supports pretty much any form of text entry you could imagine – keyboard text, hand-drawn – and the documents are exported easily via email. It's simple to use, and features an extensive range of options to customise your work, be it how you view the PDFs, to colour selection, but as it only supports PDFs we would probably favour Sign-N-Send instead. Works well and is easy to use, but its focus is primarily PDFs.

Rating ★★★☆☆

Price: Free **Developer:** Raizlab Corporation

Whiteboard Free

The clue is in the name. This is a virtual whiteboard that allows users to sketch pictures, add ideas and share them. The app itself is basically a red pen which can be used to sketch on the whiteboard. One tip size, one colour, and an eraser or a trash icon to wipe the board clean – that's it. This might be free, but there's very little of value here to keep you coming back.

Rating ★☆☆☆☆

WebEx for iPad

Price: Free **Developer:** Cisco

WebEx is all about creating an online meeting experience by getting users to simultaneously view the same data, just like in a real face-to-face meeting. The app is simple with an intuitive interface that gets right into the action. Users get invited to a meeting, typically via email, pop in the meeting number and join in. It's easy to use and optimised for iPad 2.

Rating ★★★★☆

DejaOffice 2010

Price: Free **Developer:** CompanionLink Soft

This app is all about getting organised on the move, managing contacts, tasks, expenses and more. The interface is the key player, giving one-point access to all the components of the app. Contacts scours your contacts and gives the option to add more, ie colour-coded categories. Then it's back to the Home screen to check out dates on the five-views calendar and add tasks, notes and expenses. All standard fare, but the option to sync with Outlook, Notes, Contacts etc via a collection of methods (Wi-Fi, USB, etc) is what we liked.

Rating ★★★☆☆

iRemote Desktop

Price: Free **Developer:** Hana Mobile LLC

The premise of iRemoteDesktop Free is simple: get direct access to a Windows desktop via your iPad. That's the last time the word simple is going to be used in this review. There's only support for Pro/Business versions of Windows, set-up is convoluted, and help is found via a link to a webpage. Plus, third-party software needs to be installed and a Gmail account is required. Once past all the set-up shenanigans, It's easy to use, if not a little limited on the features front. This app might be free, but it offers too many barriers for the user.

Rating ★★★★★

Quickoffice Connect Mobile Suite for iPad

Price: £8.99/$14.99 **Developer:** Quickoffice Inc

For sheer functionality, Quickoffice is hard to beat. Not only can it create, edit and save Word and Excel files, but it can also open and sync files via Wi-Fi, Dropbox, MobileMe, Google Docs, Box, Huddle and SygarSync. Documents can be moved, emailed and deleted by dragging them to the icons, and a number of page layouts make editing documents easier.

Rating ★★★★★

SecuMail

Price: £29.99/$49.99 **Developer:** On-Core Software

If you're worried about privacy when sending files, *SecuMail* lets you encrypt and decrypt text with algorithm-based key pass phrases, and send it via email or SMS. For corporate users who want to protect their files with OpenPGP v4, this is a decent app. However, for such a high price we'd expect more features, like the ability to encrypt other formats.

Rating ★★★☆☆

Business Insider

Price: Free **Developer:** Wyse Technology Inc

This is the companion app for the popular news site that features real-time news, analysis and original commentary. Everything you read can be saved and stored offline to read as and when you want and new feeds are delivered regularly to ensure you stay well-informed on the big stories in the business world. As an app it is functional rather than innovative – there is nothing here to excite beyond the subject matter itself, although it is easy to navigate and provides a decent service for you to dip into during your commute.

Rating ★★★★☆

nCloudbox

Price: Free **Developer:** Neovisture.

Cloud storage apps are fast becoming ten a penny these days, so it's important to keep up to speed with the best ones. *nCloudbox* is similar to the popular *Dropbox*, offering storage and transfer of files online. You can log into the app via your *nCloudbox* account, and share data between two or more users, regardless of format or file size. Connection is simple, and the transfer speed is decent enough to allow for quick access to files. As competent and polished as *Dropbox*, this is another functional and simple cloud storage app.

Rating ★★★★☆

Wyse PocketCloud Pro

Price: £8.99/$14.99 **Developer:** Wyse Technology Inc

Wyse PocketCloud Pro enables anyone to edit and transfer documents. While other apps simply transmit a video signal from your computer to an iDevice, this re-encodes the video and streams it over four bandwidths. As a result, you can interact with applications on your work PC with little to no lag, watch video content, and more. It may be expensive but this app is worth every penny for the amount of features it provides.

Rating ★★★★☆

Thomson Reuters Marketboard

Price: Free **Developer:** Thomson Reuters

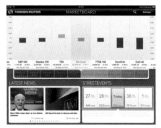

A rival to the Bloomberg app, this one features news, events and stock market performance on the home page, all presented very nicely. Tap on the Briefcase to search for companies to add, but you can't select which exchange. Although performance can be assessed between dates, you can't track prices of your investments. Not as useful as Bloomberg.

Rating ★★★☆☆

Calculator HD

Price: Free **Developer:** Liying Liu

A financial calculator with a ticker tape showing your calculations that can be saved. The interface is utilitarian and there's a modest number of bog-standard calculations that can be performed. Works on both orientations, filling the screen with its bland display. Not really inspiring and because it's free you have to suffer advertising support.

Rating ★★★☆☆

Stock Wars

Price: Free **Developer:** Continuous Integration

Interesting stock trading game that uses real stocks and shares on the NYSE, AMEX and NASDAQ, feeds in news and provides real-time quotes. Analyses your positions with purchase history, performance and trends. Display is busy and informative and your performance is ranked against other traders. Very useful for those looking to invest.

Rating ★★★☆☆

Easy Books

Price: Free **Developer:** Geode Software

Although this bookkeeping and invoicing package is available for free, it's better to look at it as a demo because it is restricted to 100 transactions. After that, an in-app purchase of £11.99 removes that limitation and £9.99 adds invoicing. It's a full package for P&L, balance sheet, auditing, VAT returns and invoicing. A clear interface makes things simple.

Rating ★★★★☆

Currency Convert Free

Price: Free **Developer:** Kory Hearn

This is an advert-supported free app that converts every currency in the world from one to another. It's easy to use: simply select the two monetary units to convert from and enter the amount. In practice, it feels like a blown-up iPhone app with lots of wasted space, which is no surprise as it's a joint device app. For shoppers on the go, the iPhone version is probably more practical. Pay 59p and you can remove the ads, but they aren't intrusive.

Rating ★★★☆☆

iiTV

Price: Free **Developer:** Capital Accumulation

From Interactive Investigator, the UK's online leader for investments, comes six channels of video, from money saving tips for the hard up, to market analysis and to interviews with CEOs. All packaged with some fairly dubious comedy (yes, really). Something of a work in progress as a few items are well out of date, but lots of good advice can be found amidst the tat. It will need updating regularly to keep your interest, and ensure your fiscal decisions are current.

Rating ★★★☆☆

Investment Guide +

Price: Free **Developer:** Forbes Digital

Essentially a magazine on your iPad from the Forbes investment group, offering investment ideas, words of caution and tax strategies. The layout is dreary and typically corporate American, but get past this and you'll find a decent amount of good advice. It is all American-orientated though, and the interface is actually pretty poor. The random pop-up adverts are especially annoying. So, much more work is needed by the developers to appeal to the masses.

Rating ★★☆☆☆

Mobile Trader

Price: Free **Developer:** Advanced Currency Markets

Want to make trades, purchase stocks and check the markets, on your iPad. That's the promise of Mobile Trader which offers practice trading, using live data, but no money, or if you're feeling brave enough, actual trading. Create an account in order to register for a practice trade but unfortunately after doing so, selecting almost any function crashes the app on version 1.4. A shame, it would be great to see if you have the potential to make money.

Rating ★☆☆☆☆

FOX Business

Price: Free **Developer:** Fox News Digital

The clammy tentacles of the Fox network reach the iPad with this app that's based on the FOX Business TV channel. There's live news at lunchtime, but that's in the US, so tea-time for us, or video on demand is available. The best bits are not the market news and stock movements, but the portfolio tracking where you can get notifications if the stock hits a specific low or high. Slick presentation, it's like Bloomberg but a bit more interactive and personal.

Rating ★★★☆☆

Wonga

Price: Free **Developer:** Wonga.com Ltd

You've probably seen the TV adverts from Wonga, offering short term, payday type loans to those with poor credit ratings, at astonishingly high APRs. This app let's you apply on the move. It's simple, works well and quickly, but you do need to be in a job, and you do need to pay the loan back on time. The morality of it, I leave to you. It seems to make it far too easy to get your hands on money. We urge you to read the small print before signing up.

Rating ★★★☆☆

Price: £3.49/$5.99 **Developer:** Todd Barnes

StockWatch – iPad Edition

Track your stocks, bonds, mutual funds, futures and more. The app is like the Bloomberg one but more orientated towards tracking your stocks, without the glitz of Fox Business. It also has news, technical charts, research tools and the ability to sync between your iPad and iPhone. Supports both UK and US investments and includes a low stock warning.

Rating ★★★★☆

Price: £0.59/$0.99 **Developer:** Adam Williams

Expense Tablet

Yet another app for the business person on the go. Keep track of your expenses and spending, without going to the effort of running a full budgeting program. The clear and attractive interface and simple operation are plus points as are the ability to set budgets, view graphs and track by category and account, but needs to add recurring expenses to make it more useful. Now there should be no excuse for handing your expenses form late!

Rating ★★★☆☆

Price: £2.99/$4.99 **Developer:** iBear LLC

Pay-Off Plan

As the name suggests, this app is there to help you pay off your loans, from interest-free parent loans to the mortgage. Input the details and see how long it's going to take to clear. Less helpful for fixed mortgages, this is much more useful for credit card debts and shows exactly the shocking amount of interest you'll be paying.

Rating ★★★★☆

Price: £0.59/$0.99 **Developer:** Graham Haley

Meter Readings

Gas and electric prices have literally doubled in recent years, so keep tabs on them and lower your carbon footprint with Meter Readings. It tracks electric, gas and water from your readings, shows rates, charges and three separate time of day readings, which is useful for things like Economy 7. All the data can be displayed as graphs and checking since the last bill shows how much you're going to be fleeced for next time.

Rating ★★★★★

Price: £1.79/$2.99 **Developer:** Kory Hearn

Gold Tracker

Given the current mania for gold, the prices being at record highs, what better than an iPad to track the price of it and other precious metals. There are up-to-date prices and the ability to calculate the value of scrap metal – for dealers and pawn shops – while hiding what you pay for metals from the public. Calculations are possible in foreign currencies as well. Version 2.1.2 had issues, so make sure you purchase a newer one than that.

Rating ★★★★★

Price: £11.99/$19.99 **Developer:** iBear LLC

Money for iPad

Manage your money by setting up multiple accounts, credit cards, bank accounts, cash and budgeting. A nice feature is the re-occurring bill feature which is created via a calendar. OFX import is supported for bank records supplied in that format. The presentation is first class although it's a little garish and the calculation side is lacking.

Rating ★★★★☆

Price: £0.59/$0.99 **Developer:** J. Lane

Payslip UK

Worried your boss isn't paying you the right amount? Or wonder exactly why you have to pay so much tax? This app complete with updates for tax and NI plus forthcoming budget changes Payslip is your one-stop shop for calculating PAYE. It covers tax codes L, P, Y, and T and has the ability to start mid-year with P45 pay and tax to date logged in. This is really for employees who have extras like overtime, bonuses, cash for car, student loans etc.

Rating ★★★★☆

Price: £0.59/$0.99 **Developer:** Peit Jonas

Lottery

Don't resort to typical numbers chosen from birthdays where multiple winners share the prizes, pick numbers at random with this. Define how many numbers from what scope and click on draw. Also pick a bonus number. Misses a trick by not logging drawn numbers from actual lotteries and specific machines. Not worth paying for.

Rating ★☆☆☆☆

Price: £1.19/$1.99 **Developer:** Piet Jonas

Mileage

If you spend a lot of the time driving on business, keeping track of mileage expenses and what it is costing you is vital. This app will track distances and rates, and also let you know how much you can drive for on a tank of petrol. With history charts and logs of your claims, you'll know exactly where you are up to with your business mileage.

Rating ★★★★☆

Price: £3.99/$6.99 **Developer:** Practicalproject

TapInvoice

Invoicing for your work, time and supplies is a vital part of running any kind of business and this iPad app has a raft of features to do just that. It can issue invoices, receipts, credit and debit notes, cash sales and PDF invoices. It can also log sales and produce analysis showing top clients. You can send the documents directly by invoice, importing information directly from your contacts. The interface is clean and simple but also very dull and uninspiring.

Rating ★★★☆☆

Education/ Reference

With access to an entire world of information at your fingertips, your iPad can be an essential learning tool. From looking up quick facts to fully immersing yourself in the many thousands of educational apps available, it has never been easier to learn something new.

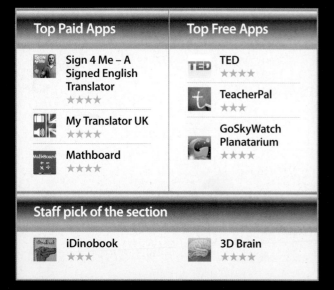

Top Paid Apps	Top Free Apps
Sign 4 Me – A Signed English Translator ★★★★	TED ★★★★
My Translator UK ★★★★	TeacherPal ★★★
Mathboard ★★★★	GoSkyWatch Planatarium ★★★★

Staff pick of the section

iDinobook ★★★	3D Brain ★★★★

■ The app keeps track of all your entries, making it easy to recap on stuff you have already learnt.

■ Once you enter the text your wish to sign then the app may take a few seconds to process it…

Price: £7.49/$12.49   **Developer:** Vcom3D

Sign 4 Me – A Signed English Translator

If you want to learn sign language, look no further

If you've ever thought of learning sign language, then *Sign 4 Me* is perfect, coming with a broad lexicon to help you along with the whole process. Using it is quick and easy. Just type in what you want the avatar to sign, and he'll act out each word for you, with subtitles letting you know which one he's doing, while you can also alter the speed and camera angle to get a better look at the gestures. There's a limited selection of stock phrases to use, but if you want to learn sign language rather than just getting him to repeat swear words (which he won't do), you'll probably be writing your own stuff anyway.

However, our main grievance is that the avatar often spells out unnecessary words, and doesn't stick to the conformities of modern sign language, which can be confusing.

Rating ★★★★★

Price: Free **Developer:** Willflow Limited

TED

Inspirational videos whenever you need them

While YouTube will forever be the place to indulge in all your video-related fantasies, *TED* offers a fine alternative. Based around a group of educational, inspirational and inspiring videos, this app allows you to search through TED's catalogue and watch talks and seminars from a range of different speakers for instant inspiration. There's a tremendous amount of content to be explored, and although a number of videos aren't as good as others, overall there's something for everyone, as long as it fits into one of the app's predetermined categories.

These set groupings are varied, though, incorporating everything from lectures on humour to culture. The search function also stretches this further, with elements that may not be directly associated within a certain type still existing within the app. It has to be said that the download itself can be a little fiddly. It's far to easy to get stuck in a menu, and it can often take far too long before a video starts playing, but given the detailed information for each presenter and the quality of each video, this is a tremendous app with plenty to offer in numerous areas.

Tailor-made for the iPad (and now available on iPhone and iPod touch), you have full access to the full back-catalogue of TEDTalks

from some of the world's most fascinating people, including education radicals, tech geniuses, medical mavericks, business gurus and music legends. There are more than 900 videos to view (and more added each week) and these can be viewed in both high or low-res formats depending on your current network connectivity or stored to view offline later.

Options include the ability to curate your own playlist of inspiring speeches, share your favorites with friends and even tell the app how much viewing time you have available and it will hand-pick some videos to suit your needs. You can even stream the videos onto the big screen via AirPlay – which is handy for the boardroom or the classroom when attempting to inspire young and impressionable minds.

There's even a subtitled version offered by TED, meaning that regardless of what your situation may be, this is an app you should, at the very least, try out. A huge database of inspirational, information and humorous videos, *TED* makes you realise just how good the App Store is. As a free download, you really have nothing to lose by downloading it, but everything to gain.

Rating ★★★★☆

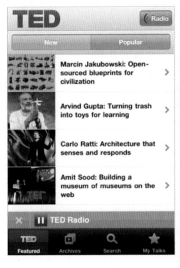

■ You can jump straight to the most popular videos or search for something specific…

■ The app draws on an impressive database of speakers from the very pinnacle of their respective professions…

Price: Free **Developer:** NASA Ames Research Center

NASA App HD

A free app from NASA that's out of this world

This official app from NASA offers users an almost overwhelming amount of content for nothing and covers everything from space and the universe to NASA and its various missions.

Launch the app and you'll be greeted by the NASA Launch Schedule and an A-Z list of current NASA missions. The layout on the main screen is similar to the iPhone's Contacts app, making it incredibly easy to navigate. Everything from the Hubble Space Telescope to the International Space Station is listed and clicking on an entry will give you more details about it.

Each listing comes with an introduction and facts about the mission, with one of the coolest features being the ability to check the current location and path of missions via Google Maps. There are also gorgeous images of space taken from the missions and videos and interviews from the excellent NASA TV, while there are pleasingly regular news updates and you can even find out how long missions have been in orbit for. It really does give a remarkable insight into the workings of NASA and its various missions throughout the years.

It would be wrong to keep your newfound knowledge to yourself so sharing it has been made very simple and can be done through Facebook and Twitter or via email. For a free app, the amount of content on offer here is incredible, so much so that we would almost be happy to pay for it. Whether you're interested in NASA's projects yourself or you have a child or sibling who is

■ The app is packed full of information from NASA's proud history of space travel.

■ One of the best features is the ability to check mission paths via Google Maps.

learning about space exploration then this is a brilliant learning tool that provides great insight into the missions past and present. It is also packed with great special effects – such as launch information and countdown clocks that really engage the user.

A great app packed full of valuable information, there is no reason not to download this immediately and enjoy an entire universe of information at your fingertips – regular updates keep things running smoothly too.

Rating ★★★★★

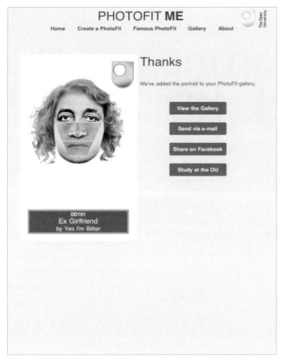

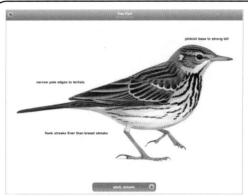

■ The picture quality of the birds varies from good to noticeably low-res…

■ Have you seen this person? No, probably not… except in your nightmares!

Price: £2.99/$4.99 **Developer:** Theo Harisk

Price: Free **Developer:** The Open University

PhotoFit Me

Make yourself and others into a photo fit, if you can

To promote its Social Sciences course, the Open University has produced this app to show the general public just how hard it is to produce an accurate photo fit to identify crime suspects. By touching on parts of the drawing of a face you are given, you can easily switch out features for alternatives. The idea is to create a photo of yourself or someone famous from given options.

It does prove nigh-on impossible to get an accurate fit for the people. You can tweak the width and height of the feature, as well as move it up and down the face to find the correct position. You can darken the skin colour, and add hair styles, glasses and facial hair. There's also the option to email or share on Facebook.

This is a pretty basic app, with some novel value. It's entertaining momentarily, but short of using it to try out how a new goatee may look on oneself, it has very little longevity. It's an effective advert for the need of proper training for this kind of skill, however. A simple and well-presented app with one task, but it holds limited appeal beyond the initial intrigue.

Rating ★★★☆☆

Bird Encyclopedia+

Packed full of info on all of our feathered friends

Bird Encyclopedia+ is a searchable database of birds around the globe. You can leave your books at home, and just carry this around with you; that is, if you have enough storage space on said iDevice. *Bird Encyclopedia+* requires over 1GB of space: 1.35GB to be exact. So we had to clear a large portion of space off our hard drive in order to even be able to install it.

Still, despite it taking an age to download and install, the app itself starts up quickly. Straight away you're launched into a search bar and screen with species listed in alphabetical order. It's is very easy to use, simply type in the name of the breed to be presented with its vital statistics. Alternatively, a downwards swipe of the digit will result in a 'pot luck' selection.

The information, while detailed, is presented poorly in a long list form. There is an option to increase or decrease the font size, but the button is constantly present and obscures the text. Additionally, the picture quality of each breed of bird varies substantially from the good, through to the pixellated. For an app that costs £2.99, it's just not good enough.

Rating ★★☆☆☆

Price: Free **Developer:** ITWorx

TeacherPal

Is this app top of the class?

 Teachers are the target market for this app and it sets about its business with a tidy and promising UI. But, creating with *TeacherPal* isn't the instant hit it should have been.

Creating classes is easy: one tap, add a name, choose an icon and the first class is added. Tap again and another is ready to go. As more classes are added it soon becomes obvious that the accompanying icons are in short supply, resulting in doubling up. And there is no option to add your own either. Then it's time to move on to adding students. In essence this is a breeze: tap and add their details. However, students need a picture, so a photo of every single student needs to find its way onto the iPad. Adding grades, creating attendance records and noting behaviour is easy, although the attendance option is not so obvious, and creation and population is a time-consuming task just for one class. So, what is really frustrating is that the whole process needs to be repeated for each new class, an issue that needs some work done to improve it and make life a lot easier for you.

However, this is version 0.1 of *TeacherPal*, and while at some points it shows, with a few rough edges, the signs are encouraging. Try it and get ready for the upgrade.

Rating ★★★☆☆

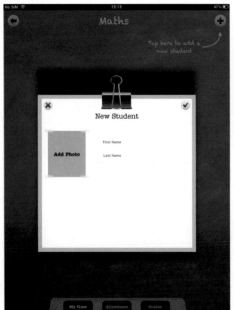

■ Using the app is relatively easy but there are definite issues to iron out…

■ In terms of functionality, this app must try harder.

Price: £1.19/$1.99 **Developer:** Boram Kim

Apartment Bible HD

View what you'll never have

 We've used some pointless apps in our time, but this effort from Boram Kim is easily one of the worst. You'd think that something called The *Apartment Bible* would be the ideal way of deciding how to decorate your room. In fact, it's little more than a slideshow of high-resolution pictures.

Once the app has loaded you're presented with six different categories: Living Room, Bedroom, Kitchen, Bathroom, Jacuzzi and Kids Room. Simply select one of the above and you're transported to a slideshow of (admittedly) lush looking pics. That's all you get, though, and while the pictures are easy on the eye, they perform no actual use.

None of the pictures are highlighted or annotated, so you have no idea what an item is called, the colours of the paint used or even if the items are available for sale in your country, which makes the entire thing as useful as a chocolate ashtray. If the app linked you to places where the featured items could be bought, or even gave you names, it would at least have some purpose, but as it stands it's just a collection of very pretty pictures and nothing more.

Not so much a bible as just a collection of pretty high-resolution images of some nice rooms. It's pretty pointless.

Rating ★☆☆☆☆

■ The apps shows off loads of nice rooms, but it's lacking any sort of information on the products.

■ The Puzzle Map works fine up to a fashion but things get trickier when you start getting to the tiny European countries…

Price: £1.79/$2.99 **Developer:** Daniel Wickremasinghe

Montessori Approach To Geography HD – Europe

Teaching kids geography

The latest in a long line of Montessori method apps, *Geography HD* aims to teach children about nearly all the different countries of Europe… or their names and shapes, at least. The app itself is split into three sections: Names & Locations, Puzzle Map (shapes) and Puzzle Map (names). The Puzzle Map parts are where the app strays into frustration. The app highlights a country on the map, and asks you to find its shape on the board behind it. With the larger countries this is a piece of cake, but as Europe contains so many small countries/principalities, the activity soon devolves into the most haphazard photohunt game imaginable. Sure, the Names & Locations may help you work out your Moldovas from your Macedonias, but there aren't many people who can differentiate between the shapes of Andorra, Monaco and Liechtenstein.

Rating ★★★☆☆

Price: £2.99/$4.99 **Developer:** MYUNGJONG LEE

ReplayNote

Notes needn't worry

This purports to be a business aid, enabling you to record voice messages and write down important notes at the same time, but then it can also convert these notes into YouTube videos, which hardly seems appropriate. Outside of creating sub-Microsoft Paint drawings and writing notes (something that the native iPad app handles just as well, if not better), there isn't much else that *ReplayNote* can do.

Admittedly, as there is no built-in recorder app on the iPad like there is on the iPhone, the voice recording function is a neat idea, but the microphone isn't powerful enough to pick up a voice when drawing, and the iPad's form factor hardly lends itself to being used as a discreet dictaphone, so it's not very useful. If it's important, using an optional stylus will help your drawings' fidelity immensely, but with only four backgrounds each with four non-changeable colours there isn't that much you can alter. If *ReplayNote* had committed to being either an efficient note-taking app with voice recording, or a fun, creative doodler, then the chances are that it would have had a greater chance of success. As it is, these two ideas don't really come together in any sort of useful way and the app suffers because of it.

Rating ★★★★★

■ Much of what's here can be done in Notes, the rest isn't worth bothering with…

■ Yes, you actually have to pay good money for this app – save it as many of the features are superfluous.

Price: £2.99/$4.99   **Developer:** Alberto Polo Rolodan

iDinobook: Encyclopedia of Dinosaurs for iPad

Concrete information on everything you wanted to know about dinosaurs, trivia and education combine in an app that will attract the most ardent of dinosaur anoraks. Its dossier is packed with prehistoric knowledge, making you every bit the natural explorer.

Here, app users will find well over 200 species. You can choose to categorise them alphabetically, or by weight, length, age or diet. Interactivity is simple yet effective, utilising finger swiping to access the Data page. Here, users discover a fact file that tells you the meaning of your favourite Sauropsida's name, its dimensions, eating habits, history, detailed anatomy, habitat, date of discovery, and fossil record.

This all seems straightforward, but isn't without charm. Clicking on the attached image will access the album, where you can flick through photos and illustrations, with entertaining animations included. Extended factfiles have fun interactive elements, allowing you to compare your dinos with modern species, and has an operational digital ray view to examine skeletal structure. It's not just a history lesson you're getting, but also one of geography, with the additional Map page. Here, users can discover dinosaurs that lived in their continent, country, and even local region, linking straight back to the Data page. Great for little monsters.

Rating ★★★★★

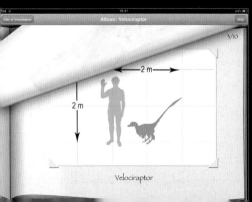

■ All of the info is well-presented and engaging.

■ The app delivers loads of interesting facts

Price: £0.59/$0.99   **Developer:** Milad Fakhr

My Translator UK

A world of languages in the palm of your hand

With so many translators available to choose from in the App Store, it can be difficult to sort the wheat from the chaff, and on first impressions, you'd be forgiven for thinking that *My Translator UK* was yet another run-of-the-mill example. Its basic look and design, however, do a disservice to the amount of content on offer here, with 57 languages, covering everything from French and Spanish to Haitian Creole and Swahili.

Enter words or phrases, and the text will instantly translate as you type thanks to the auto-complete system, which is invaluable when you need results fast. Also, unlike some other apps, there's no need to struggle with pronunciation thanks to the excellent text to speech feature. Your translated text will be read aloud by a native speaker, giving you the option to either practice until you've got the pronunciation perfect, or use the app to do the speaking for you.

You'll need internet access to translate new words and phrases, which could lead to costly roaming charges when abroad.

Rating ★★★★★

■ Think of a language and this app will translate.

■ The app comes loaded with phrases…

Body Parts

Price: Free **Developer:** Mujitha Bai K

Learn all about the human body

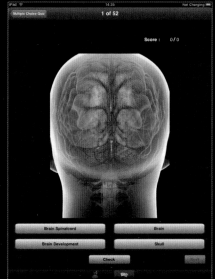

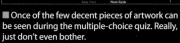

■ A checklist of the parts using poor-quality artwork.

■ Once of the few decent pieces of artwork can be seen during the multiple-choice quiz. Really, just don't even bother.

On the face of it this is a great idea for an app, one that shows the various body parts, where they are, what they are called and how they link up. Great for kids and students studying the basics of human biology, or even if you're intrigued by what happens in your body. The *Body Parts* app is split up into two systems: that of imagery of body parts and the other that deals with flash cards.

In reality, the first has illustrations, the second one photos, drawings, scans and 3D artwork. The body parts side has either a test or learning option. On the learning side there's the illustration of the body area with number annotations. Stupidly, the descriptions aren't all on screen, you have to tap through them one by one. When it comes to the test, it's the same illustration and the student needs to enter the number and the body part. It's absolutely dismal. The body parts section is better, although the artwork varies wildly in quality from excellent to rubbish. The entire package is underwhelming, lacks any useful information or options and is likely to put anyone off biology for good.

Rating ★★★★★

Mathboard

Price: £0.59/$0.99 **Developer:** Marco Mazzoli

Competitive counting on iPad

The prospect of practicing maths is one to fill any student with dread, especially the younger age range that this app is aimed at. It offers addition, subtraction, multiplication, division, squares, cube and square roots. Okay, here's the clever stuff, you can have questions up as a quiz, both timed and untimed, or as problems to be solved. The answers can be set so that the user has to enter them, or select from multiple choice answers.

It's all presented on an old-school style chalkboard format, and you have enough space on the board to do your workings out. The quizzes can be saved so you can test different students later and the scope of the questions is completely configurable from the number, to the range of variables and type of mathematic problem. Getting kids to complete the quizzes in the fastest time certainly introduces an element of competition that makes learning more fun, but whether the option to have an expiring clock to race against is a slightly more cruel way to get them to learn we're not sure.

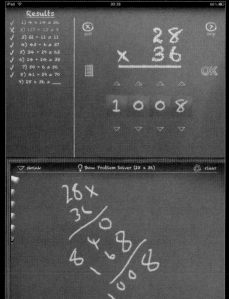

■ For more complex questions there's a neat bit of chalkboard for workings out.

■ The timed element enables students to compete against each other, even if the questions are easy.

Rating ★★★★★

Price: £0.59/$0.99 Developer: Dean Lefor

Learning Game Pack

This interactive educational game pack offers children and toddlers eight different games to help them with their matching and counting abilities, and recognise numbers and letters. One game offers a letter, prompting your child to correctly identify the picture beginning with that letter. A great early learning app that will teach your child basic literacy.

Rating ★★★★☆

Price: £1.19/$1.99 Developer: Alexandre Minard

Find Me! For Kids HD

This enjoyable app invites kids to look for hidden objects within pictures. With five grid sizes and three levels of difficulty (the last one has similar, but subtly different objects), this game will help develop the visual skills and observational senses of your child. Though it's designed for small kids, children up to the age of ten will enjoy trying to pick out highlighted objects from the grids. Enjoyable for children of all ages, but it could do with more variety.

Rating ★★★★☆

Price: £1.19/$1.99 Developer: Galen Tingle

Times Tables Warp

Making times tables fun is always going to be a challenge, but this app actually manages to pull it off. Using a selected character, tilt the device to move your character, and tap the screen to fire. Each level starts off with the player having to destroy asteroids to reveal multiplication facts then, as the level progresses, players must show what they have learnt. Great fun for kids.

Rating ★★★★★

Price: Free Developer: icity2r Mobile

Please Touch The Exhibit

A fun app from The Melbourne Museum brings out the inner tyrant in you. Ever wanted to step beyond the rope, or lift up the glass cabinet to examine museum exhibits further? This app positively encourages it, albeit in a virtual digital way. Using the best attributes of the iPad, you can shake and tilt it to look at the ten different themes covering science.

Rating ★★★★☆

Price: £2.99/$4.99 Developer: Dear Panda LLC

Course Notes

As the name may suggest this app is a virtual notebook that provides pages for taking notes. For simple note-taking there is a quick session. This presents a neat clean page where users can add text notes, to do notes and even a sketch note. This is a winner, where users can choose a paintbrush and modify brush size, hue, saturation and brightness.

Rating ★★★★☆

Price: £0.59/$0.99 Developer: James Knibb

It's Learning Time

This delightful app is designed to help children tell the time, and it does so via a series of fun and intuitive mini-games on both analogue and digital clock faces. After choosing the level of play, your child has to drag the hands around the clock face to match the time that is spoken by the app. If correct, a then cuckoo shoots out of the clock to offer praise. There are four difficulty levels that progress from hourly times to half-past the hour, quarter past the hour and eventually individual minutes. A cool learning tool for youngsters.

Rating ★★★☆☆

Price: £0.59/$0.99 Developer: RumbleApps

Paper Helper

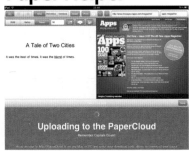

There's quite a few writing apps available, but PaperHelper stands out from the crowd with an in-built browser alongside its word processor. For those who work on the go, this app is perfect. It's easy to type with, and there's the standard sending and saving options, in addition to the ability to upload your document to an online 'cloud' for retrieval.

Rating ★★★★☆

Price: £6.99/$11.99 Developer: United Soft

Redshift – Astrnomy

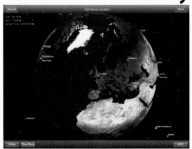

Ever wanted to soar through outer space? Well, Redshift allows you to do just that. With 100,000 stars, 30 asteroids, and 10 comets, every major star is displayed in a 3D model, and you can pan around them with a swipe of a finger. The feeling of flying though space and manipulating what you see with your fingers is impressive, even if it's a little tricky to navigate.

Rating ★★★☆☆

Price: £1.79/$2.99 **Developer:** Vito Technology

Solar Walk

From the people who brought you the superb *StarWalk* comes a guide to the solar system. For that reason the interface and features such as time machine feel familiar. There's a modest amount of detail on each planet and a fly-view straight to the planet of choice. The various moons are supported, and the best feature is the graphics with a 3D option.

Rating ★★★★★

Price: Free **Developer:** GoSoftWorks

GoSkyWatch Planetarium

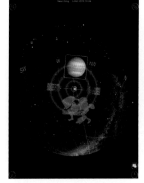

Clearly you can't keep a good idea down because this app could be the twin of *StarWalk*. It does exactly the same thing of locating your position and displaying the night sky, but with a poorer display and more jerky animation. The planetary highlighting is nice, but lacks much data. Better is the ability to find constellations, for those armed with telescopes. Pretty good for free but *StarWalk* is the better app.

Rating ★★★★★

Price: Free **Developer:** Chromatic Arts

Colormixer

Good job this is a tool/toy for colour and not spelling, as it's all American. Mind you, after ten minutes you won't care either way, as standard colour theory information is mixed with pretentious and at times, ridiculous, waffle with a faint hint of being translated from a language that is not of an English tongue. If you want to see how colour works in reality, try the Photoshop Express app. You have to pay for it, but it's worth it. Sadly, you get what you pay for with this. It delivers some degree of useful info but it is presented badly.

Rating ★★★★★

Price: Free **Developer:** Cold Spring Harbour Laboratory

3D Brain

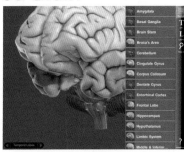

Who could refuse to see the brain in 3D along with 29 interactive structures that you can look around. It's packed with interesting information such as how each region works and what effect mental illness and brain damage has on its operation. The only flaw is that the graphics suffer when zoomed in, but it's a good app for students.

Rating ★★★★★

Price: £5.99/$9.99 **Developer:** Innovative Language

Beginner French for iPad

The iPad is well suited to language apps thanks to the Mic. Here there's a raft of features from different French voices and 25 storylines to follow, to reading, pronunciation, vocabulary and grammar, though the ability to rate your efforts is missed. The app is pricey, and the interface is unrelentingly grim, but it is effective as a language lab.

Rating ★★★★★

Price: Free **Developer:** Brad Larson

Molecules

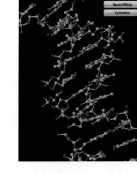

You may remember this models from GSCE physics. A more accurate title would be protein molecules because that's what this little piece of software is about. It's an app to view and manipulate molecular structures with your fingers. New molecules can be downloaded from the RCSB data bank directly to the iPad and viewed, or can be added via filesharing. The latest update adds .pdb and .pdb.gz file extensions. There's no denying the information provided, but this is perhaps one for the science students only.

Rating ★★★★★

Price: Free **Developer:** Dr Tony Phillips

3D Sun

Ideal for fans of the Nic Cage film, *Knowing*, or just those with a desperate need to know when a major flare is erupting on the surface of the sun. Using data from the orbiting pair of NASA satellites, you get a digital version of what's happening on the surface of our closest star. Track sunspots and flares and enjoy the spectacular gallery. The irony is, if they're right about flares affecting equipment it won't work! A decent and insightful app but the presentation could be better to really engage the user with the subject matter.

Rating ★★★★★

Price: £1.79/$2.99 **Developer:** Kelvin Beecroft

UK Driving Theory Test

Really, is the UK driving test hard enough? Some say no, especially the theory test that negates having to read The Highway Code. Happily the government is doing its best to make it tougher. That's where this guide to getting through the theory comes in with over 900 questions from the official DSA question bank and everything you need to spot hazards.

Rating ★★★★★

Price: £1.79/$2.99
Developer: Penguin Books

Happy Babies: Ladybird Baby Touch

In this virtual game of peek-a-boo, babies from as young as six months can touch the animal parents on-screen to reveal their babies and play animal noises, developing great hand/eye co-ordination in the process.

Overall Rating ★★★★☆

Price: £0.59/$01.99
Developer: Bonnier Digital Services AB

Paint My Wings

Keep little ones entertained, while at the same time teaching them colours. This finger-painting app is based around butterflies. Touch a shade from the palette, then touch a part of the butterfly's wings to fill it in and the same colour appears on the other wing. Delightful.

Overall Rating ★★★☆☆

Price: £2.99/$4.99
Developer: Chillingo Ltd

Big Trucks: Rough and Tough HD

The modern world wouldn't be what it is without supersize machinery. Learn all about these macho machines in this app that comes complete with sound effects and features cranes, wrecking balls, bridge layers and more.

Overall Rating ★★★☆☆

Price: £1.19/$1.99
Developer: Chillingo Ltd.

Ant Work

Presented as a game, this educational app actually presents a series of logic tests. For players young and old, Ant Work gets the grey matter working over 24 levels (6 in the free versions) by asking you to move and sort barrels around a playing area.

Overall Rating ★★★☆☆

Price: £1.19/$1.99
Developer: Chillingo Ltd

Money Origami HD SET 02

Learn how to fold your money into interesting shapes with this fiscal origami app. The shapes are designed for dollar bills, and the step by step instructions will take you through a diamond ring, heart in a heart and nine other projects.

Overall Rating ★★★★★

Price: £0.59/$0.99
Developer: M E & E United Worx.

Cute Baby Flash Cards

Flash cards have long been the staple way to present information and teach youngsters various imagery and words. This app has 200 flash cards arranged in different categories such as transport, food and animals.

Overall Rating ★★★☆☆

Price: £0.59/$0.99
Developer: Innovative Investments

Montessori Matching Board

Matching games are a great way to help develop a child's intellect and recognition skills. This simple, yet bright game not only allows toddlers to pair up shapes, but it is possible for mums and dads to record in their voices too.

Overall Rating ★★★★☆

Price: Free
Developer: Nth Fusion LLC

A Basic Time App – iPad Version

Using an analogue clock face, this app aims to help children to learn how to tell the time. Designed to be used with adult supervision, narration helps youngsters understand the concept of hours, minutes, quarter hours and more.

Overall Rating ★★★★☆

Price: £0.59/$0.99
Developer: David Tillotson

Build A Car HD

For little boys and girls who love to cars, trains and other vehicles. This brightly coloured app allows you to create and build images of wheeled transport from an array of parts. Think of it as virtual Fuzzy Felt. While it's aimed at kids, you'll find your inner toddler and have a go.

Overall Rating ★★★☆☆

Price: £5.99/$9.99
Developer: Theo Harisk

Birds Dictionary

This app is packed with 1.35Gb information on birds from all over the world. Read about migration, feeding patterns and species information. Great for twitchers and those with an interest in nature. It has a great search feature and doesn't require internet connection.

Overall Rating ★★★★★

Price: £8.99/$14.99
Developer: Berlitz Publishing

Berlitz Mi Profesor de Espanol for iPad

Learn the basics of the language before heading to Spanish-speaking countries. This app aims to pass on the basics of vocabulary and conversational sentences, via bite-size lessons that last for ten to 15 minutes a day.

Overall Rating ★★★☆☆

Price: £1.19/$1.99
Developer: Chillingo Ltd

WhyKids Poo Lite

From an early age children are interested in poo and farts. Food goes in one end looking lovely, and comes out the other looking decidedly different. This app, based on a cartoon book series, is designed to be educational via bright animations and fun music.

Overall Rating ★★★★☆

Price: Free
Developer: Michael Britt

PsychGuid

Ensure your pampered pooches will be given a great welcome in America and Canada by firing up Dog Friendly, tapping into the app's website to find out which destinations will allow dogs. You can discover off-leash parks and a variety of dog-friendly attractions.

Overall Rating ★★★★☆

Price: £11.99/$19.99
Developer: Motionics LLC

iAlignCalc

This technical addition to your iPad is worthy of note for mechanical students and workers. Put simply, you can calculate machine shaft alignments, using various methods, calculate thermal growth for different materials and used for combined misalignments.

Overall Rating ★★★★☆

Price: £1.19/$1.99
Developer: Nicole Firnhaber

KidsAbacus – and other calculating aid

The ancient method of calculation gets a 21st Century overhaul. When your children run out of fingers, show them how to use the sliding beads to help with homework. Also on the app are money counting tasks in various currencies.

Overall Rating ★★★☆☆

Price: Free
Developer: Innovative Investments

Reading for Kids – I Like Reading

Make learning about words exciting with this app. As it reads a story to your child the words are highlighted in red, while a child can touch any word and hear it being pronounced. Or simply record the story in your own voice.

Overall Rating ★★★★☆

Price: Free
Developer: Language Systems Limited

Chinese Writer for iPad

Learn the art of writing Chinese characters in simple to follow steps. The free version offers the user the basic 25 characters. Once you've registered you'll be able to try out up to 1,000 different characters.

Overall Rating ★★★★☆

Price: Free
Developer: Dream Corte

Kids World Map

Start exploring the world on this app and your kids will learn that geography can be fun. Bright pages relay information about the countries such as capital cities, the culture, national dress, national anthems, famous landmarks and so much more.

Overall Rating ★★★★☆

Price: £4.99/$6.99
Developer: Encyclopaedia Britannica Inc

Britannica Kids – Knights & Castles

Covering curriculum favourite topics such as The Middle Ages and Key Arthurian figures, you can navigate your way around via the maps and learn through jigsaws. Finally test what you've learnt on the quiz.

Overall Rating ★★★★★

Price: £1.79/$2.99
Developer: Chillingo Ltd.

ChemJuiceGrande

The handy thing about the VOX app is that you don't need an internet connection in order to make a translation. But what else do you get for this pricey app? You can view all sorts of phrases placed in categories but there are just over a thousand words overall.

Overall Rating ★★★☆☆

Price: £2.99/4.99
Developer: SIS d.o.o.

Wrecks of the Adriatic Sea

 This is a fascinating insight into the wrecks of boats and planes that lie on the sea bed just off Croatia. The stunning photographs by Danijel Frka, facts and stories of each rotting hull and fusilage is an intersting look back in history.

Overall Rating ★★★★☆

Price: £0.59/$0.99
Developer: Wolfram Alpha

Wolfram Tides Calc

 Whether you fish, surf or love spending time on boats, the habit of the tides can dominate your day and determine what you do and where you go. With this app you can plan ahead around high and low tides, use your current location and refer to historical data.

Overall Rating ★★★☆☆

Price: £1.79/$2.99
Developer: Sutro Medi

Freshwater Flyfishing Tips From the Pros

 If you're having trouble reeling in the Big One, take a look at this app. With 100 tips from top experts including Harry Murray and Skip Morris plus hundreds of photos, you're bound to learn a thing or two.

Overall Rating ★★★★☆

Price: Free
Developer: 57Digital Media

RBC New Wild Garden

 See how to create an award winning garden by one of the entrants to 2011 Chelsea Garden show. Revealed are early plans, philosophy of the garden, planting schemes, gallery and explanations of how this garden was created.

Overall Rating ★★★★☆

Price: Free
Developer: Sebit Educations

Building Parallel Circuits

 A great way to introduce the world of electronics to children. Here, using a combination of 3D graphics and 2D symbols you can recreate circuits that include light bulbs, batteries, switches and wires.

Overall Rating ★★★★☆

Price: £0.59/$0.99
Developer: David Tillotson

Angry Bird Maker HD

 Angry Birds is still a favourite game for many and now you can make your own grumpy tweeter. Choose from a selection of bodies, add suitably menacing eyes from the library and top your bird off with a beak and other accessories. Pointless, but fun.

Overall Rating ★★★☆☆

Price: £2.19/$4.99
Developer: Multieducator Inc

Revolutionary War

 Get to grips with US history and learn all about the American Revolution in this app. With first-hand accounts, paintings, documents and more, you'll understand what it was like to live through the period, and view videos on TV via Air Play.

Overall Rating ★★★★★

Price: £1.79/$2.99
Developer: Sutro Media

World War One Posters

 This app pulls together an array of posters that were produced by different governments throughout World War One. Look through the archives to view the propaganda and motivational adverts from over 400 pieces.

Overall Rating ★★★★☆

Price: Free
Developer: Adalberto Rivera

The Year You Were Born Lite Edition

 Discover what happened the year that you started life on Earth. Using this app you'll discover who won the Oscars, Top songs of the year, what shows were playing while your parents tried to soothe your screams and more.

Overall Rating ★★★★☆

Price: Free
Developer: Eric Rayne

PianoBird

 Presented in the form of a game, the aim of *PianoBird* is to help the player to sight read music on the piano keyboard. The better you are the more cheers and applause you receive. The app can be tailored towards different skill levels and for different lessons.

Overall Rating ★★★★☆

Price: £0.59/$0.99
Developer: Otto Chan

Glossary of Astronomical Terms

 Most of us can identify the Plough and Orion's belt, and at a push name all nine planets of the solar system, but beyond that we're at a loss. If you want to know more this app contains over 1,500 terms and definitions.

Overall Rating ★★★★☆

Price: £14.99/$19.99
Developer: Edward Baxter

Baxters Database of Violin Makers HD

 If you're into violins, you'll love this app. As the author rightly states, books on the subject are very expensive. Here the main information such as maker, maker's workplace and value as been collected for over 21,500 instrument makers.

Overall Rating ★★★★☆

Price: £59.99/$98.99
Developer: Wan Chi Lau

One Thousand Characters Reference

 Learning Chinese characters is more than simply mastering a language. It's an art form. Here you'll discover 1,000 characters and over 250 phrases of four characters each which are arranged to make learning them easier.

Overall Rating ★★★★☆

Price: Free
Developer: Claudia Cassidy

USA Map Puzzle

 With 50 states in making up north America, remembering all their names, let alone their positions is a huge task. With this fun and colourful puzzle you'll soon become familiar with their shapes as you slot them into place. The grid is quite easy to follow for children.

Overall Rating ★★★☆☆

Price: Free
Developer: Radslaw Gasecki

English Irregular Verbs Lite P

 Get your mind around the confusing English language in this simple testing app. It's easy to use: you're presented with a list of common words, and you must enter the various versions of each word into the empty boxes next to it.

Overall Rating ★★★☆☆

Price: £1.79/$2.99
Developer: Daniel Munk

Wedding Floral Basics

 Wedding flowers can cost an absolute fortune if you go to a professional florist. There's no reason why you can't do your own though. With this app you can learn how to create button holes, corsages and bridal hair adornments.

Overall Rating ★★★★☆

Price: £2.39/$3.99
Developer: Packard Technologies

US Supreme Court Cases

 Over 1,000 landmark cases that were heard in the US Supreme Court since 1793 can be found within this app. Features include the ability to create multiple tabs so that you can compare several cases and bookmark interesting ones.

Overall Rating ★★★★☆

Price: Free
Developer: Wine Growers Diredt

Wine Growers Direct

 Some people just like to down a bottle of fermented grape juice with their meal, taking little care over choice or flavour. If you want to learn more, take a look at this app. You'll discover about food matching, how to taste wine and what to look for in a good bottle.

Overall Rating ★★★☆☆

Price: Free
Developer: Susan Koshy

TideIsColors

 This is a simple app is presented in the form of a colour wheel to help children learn the different colours, Click on a colour and you're presented with a block of that shade and the written word, it's also possible for a voice to say the colour out loud.

Overall Rating ★★☆☆☆

Price: Free
Developer: Xing Wei Zheng

Colouring Book Like Real

 A very simple app that will keep the kids amused. Here you're given outline drawings that are out of copyright and a simple brush tool. Select your colour then use your finger to shade in the characters and background.

Overall Rating ★☆☆☆☆

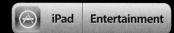

Entertainment

Okay, so the iPad has many practical uses as a work tool, but it's predominantly a fully portable entertainment system on which you can watch TV and movies, get creative with paint and generally be transformed into an unblinking zombie with a wealth of cool apps. A lot of which are featured here.

Top Paid Apps	Top Free Apps
Animation Creator HD ★★★★★	Comics ★★★★
Sketchbook Pro ★★★★	VEVO HD ★★★★★
iSpy Cameras ★★★★★	Tap TV ★★★★★

Staff pick of the section

Pocket Devil HD ★★★	Fluid ★★★★★

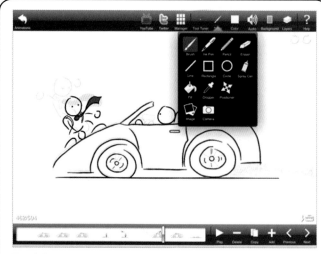
■ With this app you can create your own animations in minutes.

Price: £1.19/$1.99 **Developer:** Red Software, LLC

Animation Creator HD

Create animations on your iPad with just a flick of your fingers…

This app is very easy to use. Once you've created a new project and tapped the toolbox button to show you the options you are ready to get cracking. You can select backgrounds, change painting/drawing tools and, of course, colours. Once you've started your animation you can use the '+' button to add the next frame with onion skinning or you can copy the frame to add to it. For more ambitious users there is the option to add layers like a Photoshop document. The colour palette is a little disappointing but you can use a sliding scale of colours to create more desirable tones. The brush choices are cool, as is the ability to easily alter the brush size and get to work on your creations quickly and easily.

If you are artistic then you will undoubtedly get some enjoyment from this app – hell, even if you aren't then it's a cracking app to while away the hours. It's simple, easy to use and a great deal of fun, not to mention great value for money. Well worth a download.

Rating ★★★★★

Price: £1.79/$2.99 **Developer:** Freeze Tag Inc

Etch-A-Sketch HD

Try it yourself – have an impromptu art attack!

Anyone remotely familiar with the operation of a Space Hopper or Marathon bar will be fully aware that memories of the past don't always match up with their inevitably disappointing real-world realities. Creaking bones will inevitably give way – leaving their owner in a painful heap.

With this in mind, we come to *Etch-A-Sketch HD*, a drawing program programmed for one of the most sensitive touch screens ever devised, that allows its users to draw using only two directions of motion – vertical and horizontal. Aping the properties of its childhood toy inspiration exactly, the app allows users to draw simulated magnetic iron filing drawings using the two movement dials. Advanced users can amaze friends and family with their single stroke portraits, while most will just end up opening Photoshop instead.

An array of equally fake 'stamps' can be dragged and dropped into each picture, while an actual photograph can be laid 'behind' the magnetic layer, allowing users to trace the image.

Ultimately though, diluting the retro experience familiar from all of our childhoods with a suite of 'helpful' features feels a little like seeing a printing museum using an inkjet. Sometimes, we like the misery… In practice, it's as obsolete as the retro fad it mimics. This isn't the same as the real thing, and not half as fun.

Rating ★★☆☆☆

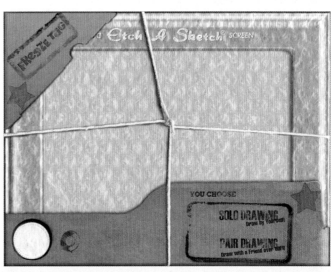

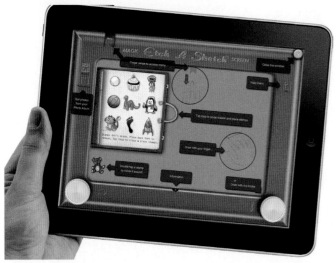

■ Apart from the retro feel, this app has very little going for it as there are infinitely more advanced drawing apps out there.

■ A drop-down menu gives access to a range of quaint stickers that you can drag and drop onto the screen.

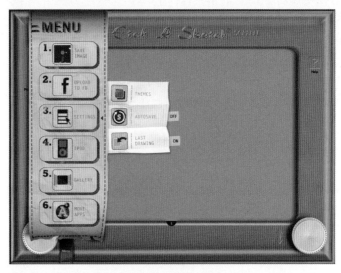

■ Images can be posted straight to Facebook with just a few screen taps. You can also instruct your iPad to play music in the background while you draw.

Price: £0.59/$0.99 **Developer:** One Result Ltd

Magic Drawing Pad

Turn your iPad into a colouring book from the future

The Magic Drawing Pad is a digital colouring book app that's been designed for the iPad. Once it's loaded up you can select from stickers, stamps, and pens to decorate your Magic Whiteboard with. The stamps consist of various shapes and objects, while the sticker designs vary from campervans to sea creatures. Simply pick from the Small, Medium or Large options, and you can dab your décor all over the page. And if you make a mistake, don't worry, simply select the Eraser tool and rub away.

There's no doubt that kids and adults of all ages will be amused by this app. However, while the controls are pretty responsive, there are a couple of issues. The first of which was the colour selection: the green actually turned out to be a mustardy shade of yellow – not quite the fern shade that was expected. Secondly, in the 'Import Photo' function the pictures appear in the wrong orientation.

Rating ★★★★★

■ If you make any mistakes, just use the eraser tool. If your kids are on it, you may need it quite often!

■ There are a couple of issues with changing orientations.

Price: £1.79/$2.99 **Developer:** Robot Wheelie LLC

FaceGoo HD

Turn your photos into hideous works of art

FaceGoo enables you to bend, stretch, rotate and generally apply bizarre new effects to a host of pictures, as well as letting you import your own pictures. By calling up a photograph, you can then tap and drag portions to hideously deform it beyond recognition, and then add special effects.

Such effects include stickers. Tap on the glasses icon to call up a drop-down menu, pick a sticker, and when it is pasted onto the photo you can pinch or expand the size, rotate it, and then stick it into position. What's more, if you want you can then animate these stickers and assign goofy sound effects before sharing your final, distorted composition with your friends.

It's all nonsense, but you'll be surprised at how addictive it can be. When you apply the 'Bouncy Goo' effect to your pictures, then you'll see what a technically impressive showcase app this actually is. A bloody enjoyable waste of time.

LOVEFiLM UK

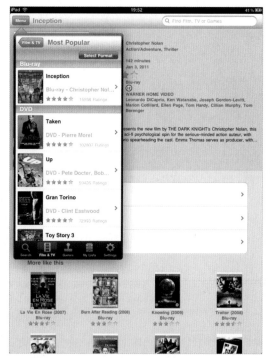

■ LOVEFiLM carries all sorts of games. Even, as you can see, ones from nearly six years ago.

■ The portrait effects in *FaceGoo* can't exactly be described as 'subtle'.

■ Your altered pictures will work well on your friends' birthday cards.

Rating ★★★★☆

Price: Free **Developer:** LOVEFiLM

Browse over 67,000 titles and manage your lists on the move

 LOVEFiLM is the UK's most notable, and usable, online movie rental service, and this app is almost the perfect companion. In what is surely a smart move, the app is not totally inaccessible to non-registered users. The app allows anyone to browse the LOVEFiLM library, tempting users to sign up.

The initial interface is a typically text-driven list split across New Releases, Most Popular, Coming Soon, and a comprehensive list of genres. Flip up and down, find a genre and a single tap presents a list of relevant releases. The problem here is that the list doesn't seem to have any type of logical order and there is no option to filter anything except format. The options are Blu-ray, DVD or the default Show All that's useful if you don't want a specific format.

Selecting a release reveals a host of information, including director, runtime, release date and an expandable summary. Add in the format, certificate and cast and it's almost too much to take in. For good measure there are three reviews, if available, and a long list of recommended similar rentals.

Rating ★★★★☆

Price: £1.19/$1.99 **Developer:** MYW Productions

Eye Illusions HD

A picture tells a thousand words, but can you trust what you see?

 Your eyes are incredible organs, constantly processing the world around you and feeding the information to your brain so you can make some kind of sense of your surroundings – but you can easily trick them with a couple of straight lines. Think of *Eye Illusions HD* as a kind of covert hacking tool for your grey matter! This app gathers together a wonderful selection of stills and videos to play tricks on your eyes. Within the well-laid-out menus, you will find colour tests, disappearing objects, optical illusions, crazy patterns, impossible objects and weird lines that you will find yourself staring at, unable to work out what you are seeing. You will convince yourself that an image is moving when it's completely still.

Eye Illusions HD is just a still and video viewer, but it's the way the database is kept regularly up to date – keeping the app fresh beyond its initial download – that makes it worthwhile. It's a must-have app for any self-respecting fan of optical illusions. A weird and wonderful gathering of the best illusions known to man, with new additions being added every day.

Rating ★★★★★

■ Even though they're just still images, they can still mess with your mind!

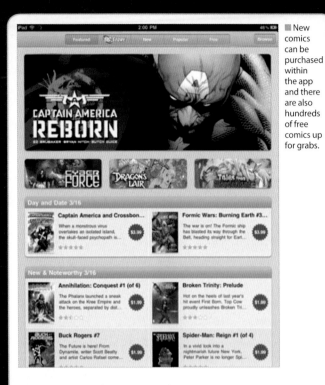

■ New comics can be purchased within the app and there are also hundreds of free comics up for grabs.

Price: Free **Developer:** ComiXology

Comics

Enjoy classic comics on the move

Anyone who's spent time with the Marvel or DC Comics apps will feel right at home with ComiXology's *Comics* app. It's exactly the same technology except that it features comics from all kinds of publishers plus ones from the big two.

The app features a very slick and user-friendly interface that is easy to navigate and never buries any of its content out of sight. Just like the aforementioned apps, its best features are that it has a section dedicated to free comics, which is updated regularly and it uses 'Guided View Technology' to make the reading experience as pleasant as possible on the small screen.. Intelligently panning and zooming around the comic page, it's a great solution to the problem of small-screen viewing.

The only slight niggle was that the app was occasionally prone to unexpected crashes, although we suspect that this was just a minor glitch that has since been eradicated by an update. A polished product for comic fans everywhere, this makes reading comics on the move a real pleasure. Highly recommended to everyone.

Rating ★★★★☆

Price: Free **Developer:** VEVO LLC

VEVO HD

Music videos come alive on iPad

VEVO is an online entertainment platform dedicated to bringing you the latest music videos. Directed at music lovers, the quality and variety of videos is something to boast about. With over 25,000 videos from 7,500 artists, there is plenty of choice on offer.

You can browse the feature section, search for artists, or filter your search. This is all standard, but *VEVO* also lets you know if that artists is on tour, allows you to buy gig tickets and purchase songs. You can also share videos on social networking sites, bring up info about the artist, view their Twitter feed and more.

The videos vary from live performances, interviews and music videos. The introductions to each video are annoying, but it disguises the loading time, so this is not too much of a problem. The ability to leave comments or ratings would be nice, but all in all this is a comprehensive app that could provide music fans with that little bit beyond what you get with similar established apps. *VEVO HD* is an excellent app that is packed with a variety of useful options and features a wide range of artists to suite all tastes. Unfortunately it's just lacking user interactivity.

Rating ★★★★★

■ VEVO brings you easy access to gig tickets for your favourite artists.

■ Choose from a wide variety of videos from over 7,500 artists.

Price: Free Developer: TapMedia Ltd

Tap TV

Watch classic movies and cartoons plus the best of YouTube

There are many different ways you can watch video on the iPad, but the truth is that videos are only as good as the source they come from. What *Tap TV* offers is the ability to 'tap' into an extensive archive of videos to watch via Wi-Fi at any time you see fit. As you might expect, the app is split into a diverse range of channels: movies, cartoons, documentaries, App TV, audiobooks, Magic TV, Best of YouTube and Silent Classics. Unfortunately, when it comes to movies or cartoons you're unlikely to find anything particularly new, but it's a great source of ancient classics that you can educate or just plain torture your kids with, or watch on your own for pure nostalgia value (and the inevitable swell of mild disappointment that accompanies returning to your childhood favourites).

We found some excellent old Warner Bros cartoons lurking in the lists, and some great Charlie Chaplin movies that you probably won't have seen for years! There are new videos too though, particularly on the documentaries and App TV channels.

The app is well laid out with easy-to-navigate menus, the only downside is that some videos are a little slow to load.

Rating ★★★★☆

■ While you'll find some new stuff on the system, most of the content is old and grainy…

■ The interface is attractive enough.

Price: Free Developer: Fabien Sanglard

Fluid

Turn your iPad into your own personal pool

Fluid does nothing more than turn your iPad into a pool of rippling water. It sounds pointless and in a way it is, but there's something compelling about Fabien Sanglard's app and we'd be lying if we didn't admit to wasting a good hour of our time messing around with *Fluid* when we first discovered it.

The concept simplicity in itself. There is no game, no real point to it; you simply drag your fingers across the water's surface in order to manipulate it. And yet despite this *Fluid* is actually a hell of a lot of fun and surprisingly absorbing, simply because the physics for it are so damned good. It's utterly mesmerising to watch the swirling patterns as you drag your fingers through the water, and even though there's not really a lot to it, you'll still discover it to be an entertaining time-waster.

A slider adjusts the speed of the water, there's the option to turn the soothing background music off and it's even possible to import your own images to use as your pool's base (which is more than a little disconcerting if you've chosen a photo of a loved one).

Yes it's little more than a tech demo, but Fluid remains an impressive one.

Rating ★★★☆☆

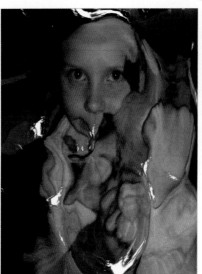

■ The app is fairly pointless, but if can be a great tool to relieving stress as you swish the water.

■ You can import photos into the app and then move them around as if they were made of water.

Price: £2.39/$3.99 **Developer:** Autodesk

Sketchbook Pro

SketchBook Pro is a fully-featured, fun artists' app that can also have a place in the professional environment for Graphic Designers. The app has a 1024x768 canvas and a multitude of brushes, pencils, and pens that can be used to create multi-layer drawings and paintings, and it's very good. Initial attempts will be sketchy and you gradually learn the various techniques, but it gets easier in time and before too long you'll be creating eye-catching art that you'll want to show off. Just another fine example of how great the iPad is for drawing.

Rating ★★★★☆

Price: £1.79/$2.99 **Developer:** EYEDIP

Pocket Devil HD

While *Pocket Devil* is similar to *Pocket God* in many ways, and has received harsh criticism in the comments on iTunes because of this similarity, we think there is certainly room for both games on the App Store. In this game, the goal is simply to kill your minions in the most gory, gruesome and depraved way possible.

Rating ★★★☆☆

Price: £0.59/$0.99 **Developer:** SKJM, LLC

iSpy Cameras

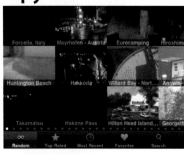

They say that everyone has a voyeristic side, but rather than twitching the curtains at your neighbours, give *iSpy Cameras* a try. This app links your device to thousands of webcams from all around the world, in real time. It works as well as can be expected, with some glitchy cameras and unfocused pictures, but it works well enough from what we have seen.

Rating ★★★★☆

Price: £0.59/$0.99 **Developer:** Dan Bradeanu

Music Bubbles

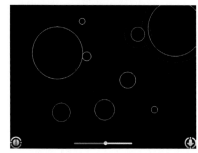

This effort from Dan Bradeanu is a good idea in practice, but fails due to poor presentation and execution. Touching the screen creates a circle that continually pulses a sound. Up to 30 can be added at one time, which will build a cacophony of noise that, with practice can be made quite tuneful. Unfortunately, you're hindered by a massive lack of options.

Rating ★☆☆☆☆

Price: £0.59/$0.99 **Developer:** Jason K Smith

Uzu

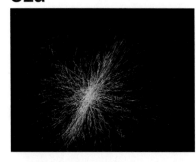

If you want to show off the iPad's multi-touch capabilities then you should definitely show off Uzu to your friends and family. While it's a fairly straightforward particle visualizer at heart, it remains a compelling experience and a great time waster. Touch the screen and the on-screen particles will move around, being easily directed by swipes and taps.

Rating ★★★☆☆

Price: Free **Developer:** Leonardo Cantelmo

XKCD

Written by a physics graduate, this pulls no punches in its brainy approach to humour, poking fun at science, technology and their integration into human relationships. The app itself is presented like an email inbox, giving you a message on the UI when a new comic is delivered. *XKCD* is a long-running and consistently amusing comic, sample it through this app.

Rating ★★★★☆

Price: £1.19/$1.99 **Developer:** Matthew Booth

Crayate

The way *Crayate* works is reasonably straightforward. It allows you to pick one wild animal and one background, and then uses them to create one single outlined image that you then colour in. There's a wide range of coloured crayons to use, and the really neat part is that they behave a lot like real wax crayons. At first they leave a diffuse mark on the paper, with lots of white bits showing through, but the mark will grow darker and more solid the more you draw over it. This makes it pretty difficult to make a consistently coloured picture.

Rating ★★★★☆

Price: £1.79/$2.99 **Developer:** MotionPortrait Inc

PhotoSpeak

PhotoSpeak, as the name may suggest, brings photos to life and makes them speak. It promises to transform a portrait photograph into an animated three-dimensional person, and make it repeat anything you say. But what it actually delivers doesn't quite live up to this promise. The voice recording and playback works well enough, as long as you eliminate all background noise, but there is no noise cancelling functions, which means if a TV is playing in the background then it will pick up random noises from the broadcast.

Rating ★★☆☆☆

Price: £0.59/$0.99 Developer: Robert Paul Neagu

Gravitarium

Fun relaxing app that requires you to do nothing more than manipulate a star field into all sorts of strange shapes. Coded in under 24 hours by Robert Paul Neagu, it's a mesmerising piece of work that's enhanced by some truly beautiful music and the ability to make subtle little tweaks via the options. Not earth-shattering but still good fun.

Rating ★★★☆☆

Price: £2.99/$4.99 Developer: COM2US USA

Ocean Blue

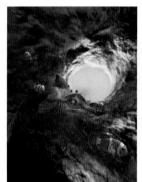

Go find your own Nemo. This entertaining underwater app allows you to recreate an ocean environment and populate it with a variety of different fish and mammals. While there aren't many species of aquatic life on offer, those that are available are exceptionally animated and look incredibly lifelike. In addition to featuring handy information about each marine animal it's also possible to synch two pads together to create an even larger aquarium. Great fun but the long term appeal is limited.

Rating ★★★☆☆

Price: Free Developer: Metaversal Studios

Shave Me

It's the app your iPad has been crying out for! If you've ever fancied yourself as the next Sweeny Todd then give *Shave Me!* a try. With this app, your pad is turned into a sheet of overgrown bristles and you use the supplied razor to craft it into whatever patterns take your fancy. Shave too fast though and you'll end up drawing blood. If shaving's enough effort in real life, would you really be bothered to play this? It's possible to upgrade a get more tools though. Designer stubble was so Eighties! For for five minutes tops!

Rating ★★☆☆☆

Price: Free Developer: Stuart Palmer

Annoying Fly

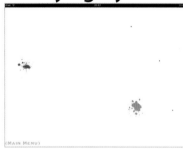

Got a thing against flies? Then you'll love Stuart Palmer's new app. You're presented with a white screen and a buzzing fly. Swat it and you get the joy of revisiting the menu again so you can swat another. There are two types of fly on offer and the option to take out a swarm, but it's all fairly pointless stuff that is designed to occupy for a short amount of time.

Rating ★☆☆☆☆

Price: Free Developer: bitapoly

Toy Ball

This is a simple toy app where you drop a set amount of balls into available holes. It's a decent enough idea but is let down by rather lousy and unconvincing physics. Yes it's free, unlike similar releases, but why settle for what is effectively an inferior app? Save up your cash and get something decent and more engaging like *Labyrinth* for the money instead.

Rating ★☆☆☆☆

Price: £3.99/$5.99 Developer: Eiji Nishidai

iFont Maker

Bored of Helvetica and Times New Roman? Now you can spice up your documents with your own unique style. This truly excellent app allows you to create any type of font you wish. Once you've created your font of choice – something which is surprisingly easy to do – you're able to save it as a TTF file and use it in all manner of applications such as those from Adobe and Microsoft Office. An extremely useful app that's easily worth its low asking price –just think of the hours of fun you can have exploring new fonts!

Rating ★★★★★

Price: Free Developer: Andrew Griffiths

Cloud Text

Got a thing for clouds? Then why not download this app from Andrew Griffiths and feel all fluffy inside. *Cloud Text* allows you to type anything you like and turn it into a soft, cloudy looking font. It's a smart enough idea and even lets you upload your creations to the likes of Facebook and Twitter, and send cute, cuddly messages to loved ones. Beyond that though, there's not much else you could use it for. But will you really want to? It's free so give it a try and lose yourself in the clouds, there is definitely some enjoyment to be had here.

Rating ★★☆☆☆

Price: Free Developer: Mark O' Flynn

Score This

Play lots of games but never have any pens or papers handy to keep your score? Then why not download *Score This* and never have to worry about keeping a tally again. This free app lets you keep results for up to six players on a variety of games, from darts to Scrabble. A straightforward app, but still highly useful – you'll be surprised just how useful!

Rating ★★★☆☆

Price: £1.79/$2.99 **Developer:** Pavel Dichev

Art In Motion

Now here's a bizarre art package. Rather than draw new picture you take pre-existing ones and manipulate them by adding orbs and cause it to move. It takes a while to get to grips with, but the concise controls and unique styling makes it worth persevering. An interesting app that provides hours of entertainment, but there are better for the price.

Rating ★★★★☆

Price: Free **Developer:** Sam Meech Ward

Hypno Digit

Impress your friends and relatives with these simple number puzzles that allow you to predict the numbers they're thinking of. There are six different puzzles to try out and while there are pop-up ads – as you would expect in a free app – they're not intrusive in the slightest. You won't continually return to it, but it's a fun way of showing off at parties and you can almost see the brains of small children shrink into their skulls when you try it out on them! Download it for free, have some fun and then delete it and forget about it forever.

Rating ★★★☆☆

Price: £2.99/$4.99 **Developer:** Infinite Dreams

Let's Create! Pottery

Use a virtual potter's wheel to create some virtual clay works of art without getting your hands dirty. Once you've created something, fire it up in the kiln, sell it for a nice profit then use the money to buy more materials so you can create even more extravagant pieces of work and build up your coffers. In fact the only thing that lets this great app down is that it doesn't play *Unchained Melody* while you're making your creations! It's a little expensive for what is essentially a throw-away app, but it's decent enough fun while it lasts.

Rating ★★★★☆

Price: £1.19/$1.99 **Developer:** Brandon Bogle

Koi Pond HD

Turn your iPad into a virtual pond with this relaxing little app. While there are only four backgrounds to choose from it's possible to change them in a variety of different ways thanks to a really useful level editor. In fact it's almost as much fun creating elaborate pondscapes as it is relaxing and enjoying your completed work. A nice, relaxing app.

Rating ★★★☆☆

Price: Free **Developer:** Krzysztof Rutkowski

Best of YouTube

Yes we know there's already a YouTube app available for your iPad, but this is still worth a download, as you immediately have access great movies. Nicely presented and with a huge selection of categories to choose from it's a decent app that's only let down by the fact that there's only currently around 800 videos to choose from, but they're mostly crackers.

Rating ★★★☆☆

Price: Free **Developer:** Webworks

10,500+ Cool Facts

Although identified with Scotland, bagpipes are actually a very ancient instrument, introduced into the British Isles by the Romans.

Are you one of those people who retains random snippets of information in your head? This is the app for you. Did you know that men are six times more likely to be struck by lightning than woman? Or that kissing can play a part in tooth decay? Well you do now and this handy app will fill your head with so much useless trivia you're never unlikely to lose at a pub quiz again. The free pop-ups annoy –but you must expect them in free apps – but this is still fascinating stuff that will enthrall you for several hours at least.

Rating ★★★★☆

Price: Free **Developer:** Amy Faulkner

Paint Animals

It's almost like painting by numbers. Here you have to fill in the shape with your own details. *Paint Animals* is an entertaining app that presents you with a blank space and lets you paint the missing animal. It's possible to create a variety of different colours with the included palette and you can even change the transparency to view the finished article. There are far better painting apps available, but this is nevertheless A charming little gizmo that will go down well with young artists; or those just too lazy to try the real deal.

Rating ★★★☆☆

Price: £1.79/$2.99 **Developer:** Lianxing Zhu

Colourful Aquarium

Rather dull virtual aquarium that features plenty of unrealistic fish and, for some reason, a huge digital clock. While it's possible to clean your tank, adjust the flow of bubbles and feed your fish, stodgy controls and no incentives give you little reason to return to the virtual world that Lianxing Zhu has created. Go for *iQuarium* instead.

Rating ★★☆☆☆

Price: £0.59/$0.99 Developer: Hunted Media

Music Hunter

Bored of your tired old music collection? Looking for a new artist to inspire you? This is where Music Hunter comes in, allowing you to explore different musicians within chosen genres and styles. Via a simple interface, you are presented with a selection of songs and can hear previews of any track that takes your fancy. A great musical interlude.

Rating ★★★★☆

Price: £0.59/$0.99 Developer: Software Logix

OmniSketch

Clever little art app that has a procedural brush (which uses mathematical algorithms) to create all sorts of special effects. They cleverly draw shapes and patterns with each stroke. It's certainly not as accessible as some of the artistic packages we've used and it's a little fiddly to get to grips with, but it's amazing what you can eventually achieve after a few practice sessions. It's not an essential art package, but it's very hard to moan when it's this cheap.

Rating ★★★★☆

Price: £1.19/$1.99 Developer: Hansol Huh

ARTREE

Art, it seems, is no longer about splodging paint on paper with a brush. These days a basic knowledge of maths is helpful. Use algorithms to create beautiful digital trees. Once you've created your masterpieces it's possible to send them to friends and create high-resolution PNG files of them. You don't really have too much control over what you're creating, but that's the nature of algorithms. Just be glad that they don't take as long to grow as real trees.

Rating ★★☆☆☆

Price: Free Developer: Channel 4

4oD Catch Up

TV on demand is one of the greatest inventions to come to the fore in recent years. While before we were slaves to the schedule, now we simply press a few buttons and see what we missed whenever we want. Now Channel 4 has got in on the iPad action and brought 4oD to our tablets, a slick viewing portal that is loaded with fantastic shows.

Rating ★★★★☆

Price: £0.59/$0.99 Developer: Rutland Games Inc

Movie Mogul

Movie Mogual is like Game Dev Story, but for the movie industry. Tasked with creating a movie from the ground up, you're forced through screen after screen of poorly drawn cartoons and genuinely terrible celebrity puns as you hire scriptwriters, directors and actors. While the game is fun at first, it is let down by poor production and a idea that lacks execution.

Rating ★★☆☆☆

Price: £4.99/$7.99 Developer: Plasq LLC

Comic Life

This is a great app for transforming your photos into eye-catching comic strips. Setting up is easy, you simply import an image from your photo gallery and then then pinch it to scale into one of the selected page templates. You can then crop and rotate you image before applying all kinds of snazzy effects such as captions, speech bubbles and sound effects. You can share your creations with others and save them to your device to view or modify later. Although the price is rather high, we highly recommend this app.

Rating ★★★★☆

Price: Free Developer: Synsion Radio

TuneIn Radio

It seems like such a simple idea, yet it's one that we can see being loved by many users across the world – an app that lets you connect to digital radio stations. A quick download later and you're presented with around 40,000 music, chat and whatever else stations from all over the globe. It's probably not surprising that with those numbers being thrown around, all manner of topics are being covered at any one time, anywhere in the world. Basically, you get to listen to the whole world easily and for free. Very highly recommended.

Rating ★★★★★

Price: £2.99/$4.99 Developer: Ngo Vinh Hoang

YoFilm

This is a curious little app that gives you direct access to hundreds of movies. As long as you're really into films that have long since seen their licenses expire and are available for free online, usually via YouTube, this is perfect. It offers the weirdest selection, including some of the biggest travesties of recent cinema, but it's strangely compelling.

Rating ★★☆☆☆

Price: Free
Developer: Sprite Labs

Talking Anya

Talking Anya is an app that will surely appeal to your doll-kids. They can dress Anya up and interact with her as she dances around the screen, or record a voice message for her to repeat to friends over Facebook and email. Not bad for a free app.

Overall Rating ★★★★☆

Price: £1.79/$2.99
Developer: October Films Ltd

Rude Tube

Are you a fan of the popular TV show *Rude Tube*? If so then this app is for you. Featuring a host of the best and funniest clips, there's a variety of content to keep you amused. However, with only 120 in-built clips, you'll probably get bored pretty soon.

Overall Rating ★★★☆☆

Price: Free
Developer: SPARK LABS

Tour Wrist

This is a brilliant app that lets you virtually explore a surprisingly large array of venues using the tilt functionality on your iPad. The presentation is brilliant, and you'll be exploring certain areas in style in no time at all. A great download.

Overall Rating ★★★★★

Price: Free
Developer: JamPot Technologies Ltd.

Slangatang

Originally created on the UK version of *The Apprentice*, the developer has added to the previously limited array of sounds to include a whole variety of sayings and phrases from various regional dialects. Amusing in short bursts but ultimately a waste of time.

Overall Rating ★★★☆☆

Price: Free
Developer: University Joseph Fourier

i3D

This app is a neat concept idea that requires the iPad 2 to work. The in-built camera tracks the position at which you view the screen and adjusts an image accordingly, making it look 3D from every angle without glasses. Works well, although limited.

Overall Rating ★★★★☆

Price: £1.19/$1.99
Developer: Jim VanDeventer

Film Classics

Film Classics includes an impressive array of – you guessed it – classic films watch on your iPad. You can stream or download 30 famous movies, from Faust to Snow White. Our only gripe was the slightly dodgy quality of some of the content, but otherwise it's great.

Overall Rating ★★★★☆

Price: £1.19/$1.99
Developer: Hien Ton

Crazy Symon

Based on the popular memory game, *Crazy Symon* has you matching colours as they appear on-screen. But what starts off as a relatively simple exercise soon becomes extremely taxing with later sequences being fiendishly difficult to match.

Overall Rating ★★★★☆

Price: £1.19/$1.99
Developer: 22learn, LLC

Abby's Magic Laptop for Preschool

If you don't mind your kids playing on your expensive iPad, then this is a great app that mimics a toy laptop. With large interactive buttons and a variety of educational games, your toddler should get a lot of enjoyment out of this.

Overall Rating ★★★★☆

Price: £0.59/$0.99
Developer: PiVi & Co

Fatbooth HD

The popular iPhone app makes its way to the iPad, complete with the same face-fattening silliness that made the original so popular. Snap a picture of a mate with the in-built camera or select one from your gallery and watch as the app piles on the pounds.

Overall Rating ★★★★☆

Price: £0.59/$0.99
Developer: Kuda Software

Full Auto

This fun first-person-shooter lets you roam around some impressive 3D environments and have a blast while you're at it. It controls with touch input only, and while it's somewhat fun there's very little to do after a few minutes. Which defeats the object somewhat.

Overall Rating ★★★☆☆

Price: Free
Developer: Outfit7

Talking Tom Cat 2 for iPad

This interactive critter mimics your voice is own amusing way, while also responding to a variety of inputs. The animation is great and it's good fun for a while, but the novelty will probably wear off after a few minutes.

Overall Rating ★★★☆☆

Price: Free
Developer: Fox Interactive Media

IGN Pro League

If you're interested in the professional gaming circuit then you might want to check out this nifty free app. You can watch highlights and streams of ranked matches or current competitors going head to head. Works well, but there's not a huge amount of in-built content.

Overall Rating ★★★☆☆

Price: Free
Developer: Boto Media Limited

Flying Monsters 3D

Read and learn about a variety of dinosaurs in this somewhat brief but entertaining app. With an added interview with David Attenborough and some interesting facts about a whole host of dinos, this app is certainly short and sweet but well worth downloading.

Overall Rating ★★★☆☆

Price: £0.59/$0.99
Developer: Tayasui

Talking Carl HD

Talking Carl HD is a brilliant distraction for your kids, with some high-quality visuals and amusing interactivity creating a bright and colourful app. Carl is incredibly cute and the app works very well. It actually manages to excel in its own simplicity, which is remarkable in itself.

Overall Rating ★★★★☆

Price: Free
Developer: William Alexander

3D Eye Free

3D Eye Free is a collection of 'magic eye' images for you to enjoy, with simple instructions given on the best way to view them. The effect works well for the most part, but these things are probably a little dated in today's age of true 3D. Worth a look, though…

Overall Rating ★★★☆☆

Price: Free
Developer: iBear Story

Coin Push HD Pro – iBear Story

This app lets you play a variety of light hearted and entertaining slot-machine-esque games. Unfortunately, while the app is free, the high cost of the in-game purchases to get playable coins is high. It's just not worth it.

Overall Rating ★★☆☆☆

Price: Free
Developer: Lynx Labs

Epic Pranks for iPad

At first glance we didn't have high hopes for *Epic Pranks*. With an unappealing layout and slightly odd premise, we were soon laughing at some of the prank suggestions on offer and might even pull off a few around the office. Does what it says with plenty of humour.

Overall Rating ★★★☆☆

Price: Free
Developer: Bloom Studio, Inc.

Planetary

This visually stunning app is a wonderful way to enjoy the cosmos around us, but it's main feature is the ability to listen to music as the 3D camera swoops around planets and galaxies. It's a whole new way to listen to music on the iPad, and one that we love.

Overall Rating ★★★★★

Price: £0.59/$0.99
Developer: WTF Apps

#1 Cheat Words With Friends Edition

If you're a fan of the popular *Words With Friends* app, you might be tempted to pay for this. Our advice: don't. It attempts to scan your playing board and suggest words, but half the time it doesn't work. Buy a dictionary instead.

Overall Rating ★☆☆☆☆

Price: Free
Developer: END Games Entertainment

Click! The Game: Lite Edition

Do you enjoy repeatedly clicking a button, and comparing scores with friends who have also clicked the same button? It's designed as a tongue-in-cheek game, and while we were laughing initially the humour quickly wore off.

Overall Rating ★★☆☆☆

Price: Free
Developer: Deja

Deja

This app is a fun and intuitive way to share videos you've found online with friends. It's laid out in a montage style and you can click on different videos to view them. However, the app is temperamental at times and occasionally fails to load.

Overall Rating ★★★☆☆

Price: Free
Developer: Moov Corporation

PhoneFlicks

This free app lets you browse a catalog of over 100,000 movies, find all the hottest releases, view streaming movies, find your favourite TV shows and more. It's useful for keeping track of your rental history and you can add and remove movies in your Netflix queue easily.

Overall Rating ★★★★☆

Price: £0.59/$0.99
Developer: NextApps Inc.

Booooly! HD

This puzzle app reminiscent of games of old has you attempting to line up and match colourful critters in a confined 2D space. With features including OpenFeint and Online Leader Boards, there's plenty of fun to be had here for puzzle enthusiasts.

Overall Rating ★★★★☆

Price: £1.79/$2.99
Developer: Mobobo

Talking 3D Lab Mat HD

The graphics and animation on offer from these interactive characters really doesn't compare to other apps available on the App Store. What does set it apart though is the 100s of characters and voices on offer.

Overall Rating ★★★☆☆

Price: £1.79/$2.99
Developer: Outfit7

Talking Lila the Fairy

Bearing a striking resemblance to Tinkerbell form Peter Pan, kids will surely go crazy for this interactive fairy that sports some decent graphics and fun interactivity. It's a bit pricey when you consider the multitude of similar apps on offer, though.

Overall Rating ★★★☆☆

Price: £1.19/$1.99
Developer: SixClick Inc.

Cube It 3D

This puzzle app has you shifting shapes around to try and get the required design in a limited number of moves. It's been done before but it's presented well, and there's a scaled difficulty level for both adults and kids. Not bad and fairly good fun.

Overall Rating ★★★☆☆

Price: Free
Developer: Feedtrace LLC

InstantPulp

InstantPulp brings all the latest and greatest celebrity gossip together into one status-update-esque page, with the option of searching popular stories and tweets from celebrities. If the lives of stars is your thing, you could do worse than this app.

Overall Rating ★★★★☆

Price: £0.59/$0.99
Developer: Appdicted

Make A Monster HD

This app does exactly what you would expect, really. Use a variety of colours, appliances and silhouettes to create your perfect monster and share him with your friends. With thousands of possible combinations, there's a lot of fun to be had here.

Overall Rating ★★★★☆

Price: Free
Developer: Marcus Scherer

Make An Animal

This app lets you – you guessed it – create your own animal and share it with friends. The cartoony visuals are somewhat appealing but there's not much fun to be had after a few minutes. Somewhat cute but ultimately fairly limited in its appeal.

Overall Rating ★★★☆☆

Price: £0.59/$0.99
Developer: Diatom Studio

Flowpaper

Flowpaper lets you draw some visually cool effects and create some neat abstract art. While the features on offer are somewhat limited it's quite good fun drawing in this image style, and certainly offers something different from other similar apps.

Overall Rating ★★★☆☆

Price: Free
Developer: Zappar Limited

Zappar

This augmented reality app pops out a 3D image and provides image when pointed at certain promotional material. It works in a similar manner to QR codes, and if more companies get on board in future we can see this proving quite popular everyone.

Overall Rating ★★★★☆

Price: £1.19/$1.99
Developer: Color Monkey

VinylLove™

Browse through your album collection and play them in that old, familiar vinyl style. It's a novel and fun way to listen to your music, complete with spinning vinyl as you listen to your favourite tune, but could do with a few more features to broaden its appeal.

Overall Rating ★★★☆☆

Price: £1.19/$1.99
Developer: blackpawn.com

Sketch Club

This drawing app lacks the presentation and appeal of some other apps available for a similar price. There's a decent array of features and some neat drawing techniques on offer, but it didn't quite pack the 'oomph' we'd hoped for. Spend your cash on *Sketchbook Pro* instead.

Overall Rating ★★★☆☆

Price: Free
Developer: Apalon

Magical Images Free

Magical Images Free is a fun little app that uses an animation trick that you control yourself (by moving a slider back and forth) to make some images seemingly come to life. It's a neat trick and one that's enjoyable, albeit in brief spurts.

Overall Rating ★★★☆☆

Price: £1.79/$2.99
Developer: SunSpark Labs

Morfo 3D Face Booth

This is a great idea for an app, letting you take a picture of a person or pet and apply computer graphics to animate the head to say words and make facial expressions. It's very enjoyable and there's plenty to do, but the appeal won't last beyond a few hours.

Overall Rating ★★★★☆

Price: Free
Developer: FIPLAB Ltd

Talking Baby Monkey HD

The central monkey character of this app is incredibly cute and is sure to appeal to kids under about six years old. Like many other similar apps he'll repeat your voice in his own amusing manner and there's also plenty of fun interactivity.

Overall Rating ★★★☆☆

Price: £2.99/$4.99
Developer: Savage Interactive Pty Ltd

procreate

Procreate's incredibly advanced drawing tool lets you create some visually stunning images on your iPad. The minimalist interface lets you get on with drawing and there's a whole host of features on offer.

Overall Rating ★★★★

Price: £0.59/$0.99
Developer: Two Teeth Technologies

Mood Camera

Mood Camera proclaims that you can visualise the 'mood' of people and objects around you by pointing your iPad 2 camera at them. In reality it seems to simply add some cheap visual effects to the images. We weren't really that impressed. Overpriced rubbish.

Overall Rating ★★☆☆☆

Price: £0.59/$0.99
Developer: Paul Soft

Artwork Evolution

Unfortunately this app doesn't really let you control the artwork it creates. Instead, it takes pictures from your gallery or otherwise and randomly assigns abstract effects to create a new image. They all look pretty similar, and it's not very fun.

Overall Rating ★★☆☆☆

Price: £0.59/$0.99
Developer: Digital Bananas, LLC

Stupid Test

There's a variety of somewhat challenging and entertaining questions here to keep you and your friends amused for a few minutes. Unfortunately there's not much content and you'll be done with it quickly, so here's hoping for some decent updates.

Overall Rating ★★★☆☆

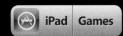

Games

This iPad is rapidly becoming a well-respected mobile games console with software to rival anything you'd find on the Nintendo DS. This can be a bad thing though as you stare despairingly at your screen, hooked on the latest puzzle game while your productivity goes out the window. But, hey, who cares?

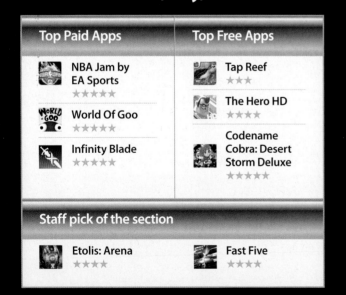

Top Paid Apps	Top Free Apps
NBA Jam by EA Sports ★★★★★	Tap Reef ★★★
World Of Goo ★★★★★	The Hero HD ★★★★
Infinity Blade ★★★★★	Codename Cobra: Desert Storm Deluxe ★★★★★

Staff pick of the section

Etolis: Arena ★★★★	Fast Five ★★★★

■You have a certain number of goo balls to rescue on each level, so build those structures well.

Price: Free   **Developer:** Idea and Design Works LLC

World Of Goo
We get our hands dirty with this slick iPad game

 World Of Goo made its iPad debut amid a blaze of critical acclaim. First released for PC and Nintendo Wii in 2008, it immediately garnered top review scores, won tons of awards, and went on to sell by the bucketload, all without an expensive marketing campaign. Made by independent developers Kyle Gabler and Ron Carmel, it's a true indie success story and feels right at home on the iPad. Though fundamentally unchanged from its original incarnation, there's something about the way it plays on the iPad; it feels like it was supposed to be played on the iPad's touch screen all along.

The idea is to build a bridge or tower by stringing together a series of sticky goo balls in order to reach a pipe at the end of the level. All remaining goo balls then move along the gooey structure and into the pipe. There's a minimum number of goo balls you have to rescue, meaning you have to build the structure as efficiently as possible so as not to waste any. This is easier said than done, given the way in which bridges and towers are susceptible to swaying in the wind and collapsing under gravity. It takes a sharp and creative mind to overcome some of these challenges, particularly on the later levels, but it's never anything less than great fun.

Rating ★★★★★

Price: £1.79/$2.99 **Developer:** Electronic Arts Nederland BV

Dead Space HD

In space no one can hear you scream with frustration

You have to hand it to Electronic Arts. Rather than adapt the excellent and vastly underrated *Dead Space: Extraction* to Apple's iPad, they've instead created a brand-new title that fans of the franchise are bound to lap up.

Set three years after the events of the original game, and nicely setting up the story for the recently released *Dead Space 2*, The iPad version proves to be every bit as atmospheric as its forebears. This in part is due to some truly phenomenal lighting effects, and sound design that has allows the game to truly immerse you into the onscreen action. It's undoubtedly an impressive achievement, further helped by some well-staged set pieces, which, while not quite on par with those of *Dead Space 2*, nevertheless showcase the game's strengths brilliantly. Unfortunately, while *Dead Space* is an impressive technical achievement, its controls aren't up to the same high standards. Movement is relatively straightforward, but things become a little more difficult upon drawing your weapon. Tapping the right hand side of the screen draws your gun (further taps fire it), tapping a number near the gun switches through its different modes (the alternative is a cumbersome tilt method), and tapping on your protagonist's back activates stasis mode, which is handy for slowing down approaching necromorphs. It sounds relatively straightforward on paper, but is a lot trickier in practice, particularly on the iPad, and once you start adding in movements like swiping downwards to stomp enemies, or double-tapping your character's back to spin him through 180 degrees, it becomes even more cumbersome to play.

You do of course get used to it, but there'll always be moments, particularly when you're under attack from numerous necromorphs, that you just can't respond quickly enough to what's happening onscreen. This makes for some very frustrating deaths, and ruins the game's fantastic atmosphere.

In-app purchases also rear their ugly head (although they aren't essential to complete your quest), while the pacing lacks the legs of its bigger brothers. *Dead Space* is still an enjoyable game that fans of the genre will certainly like. It's just far too ambitious for its own good. Beyond the fantastic presentation and visuals, it's let down by the cumbersome controls. Recent updates have gone a small way towards rectified such issues, but the touch screen is still no substitute for a meaty joypad in this particular instance.

■ Extra ammo and credit chits can be found by searching each room thoroughly. Beware the odd shock, though…

Rating ★★★⯪⯪

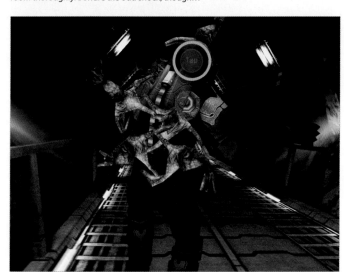

■ It is the visuals that make this game a truly appealing prospect. It is one of the best-looking games on the iPad. Shame the gameplay doesn't quite match up.

■ Its when quick movements are required to avoid to combat enemies that the game starts to fall apart. A shame considering you will be doing this a lot.

Price: £2.99/$4.99 **Developer:** Gameloft

Fast Five

Fast, furious and packed full of high-octane mayhem

 Drawing heavily from the mechanics of its Asphalt racing games, Gameloft's *Fast Five* is a hefty title that delivers more content than its small asking price suggests. It follows ex-FBI agent Brian O'Conner – played by Paul Walker in the movie – as he pulls off a seemingly small heist, and unknowingly triggers a larger, more deadly chain of events that leads him and his crew to Rio de Janeiro.

Fast Five is purely a racing game, so all of the on-foot action and shooting from the movies are nowhere to be seen, and only mentioned in mid-chapter conversations between O'Conner and other characters. On-foot shooting sections would have certainly mixed up each chapter, as they are essentially all just a string of similar race types that quickly become a tad too familiar after only a few events.

You can unleash a nitro burst by tapping the icon on the left for a speed boost, or to give yourself more ramming power for taking out other drivers. Rewind power-ups can also be used up to three times in most races, letting you undo misjudged turns or devastating crashes. The rewind skill is helpful given how perilous some tracks can be.

Drifting, however, isn't. Tapping the brake lightly while turning is supposed to result in a drift that rewards you with bonus cash at the end of each race. However, it tightens your turning arc so severely that cornering effectively becomes a real pain. Drift events that demand you slide round bends as often as you can quickly become an irritating slog as a result, and may have you reaching for the quit icon fast.

The Underground Market menu lets you select one of many race modifiers that can give an advantage on the tarmac, such as bursting the tyres of another racer, swapping around grid positions before the start of a race, and more. Some of these are big gambles, but when they pay off, they pay off big.

You can also spend your winnings on new cars, or tune up your existing rides, as well as modify the appearance of any vehicle with new body kits. Money and experience can be either won or bought with actual money via the in-game storefront, but progressing through using this method waters down the replay value somewhat.

Fast Five is a huge game at a modest asking price, and while the controls may feel slack and erratic at the outset, practising to get a feel for the tilt sensitivity is to be advised. That aside, this is another solid racing title from Gameloft.

Rating ★ ★ ★ ★ ☆

■ The graphical filters are pretty cool, and aren't something that you'd expect in a game at this price point.

Couldn't tell ya. But two of 'em went down when the shooting started. That ain't good.

Continue

■ The story's kind of nonsense, but what else would you expect from a *Fast Five* game?

■ There are many physics-based puzzlers about, but this is one of the best.

Price: £0.59/$0.99 **Developer:** Chillingo Ltd

Mummy's Treasure
A jewel in the rough

Puzzlers of this ilk are ten-a-penny on the iPad, each reworking that age-old standard of completing a goal by using the constant tug of gravity in myriad new and different ways.

The new and different way here is to discard the mummified cubes to leave only the treasure safely stationary on screen, using the weight of each object to knock others away. This may be managed by destroying sand platforms, throwing weaker stones aside to cause a tower to tumble, or simply dropping bricks on top of one another.

Earlier puzzles start off simple enough, asking that a block is removed in a specific order to relinquish the treasure. Later on, however, tasks become a little more difficult, requiring pinpoint precision or timing to ensure you hit your target. You'll be scored for each level completed, depending on how many moves you've used under or above par, the time it took, and how many of the hidden gems have been found, so there's plenty of replayability.

Rating ★★★★☆

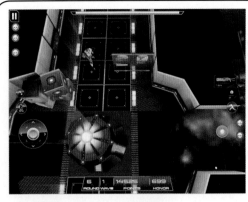

■ If you were looking forward to something similar to Angry Birds, you may be disappointed.

■ It looks stunning, probably only third to *Rage HD* and *Infinity Blade*.

Price: £1.19/$1.99 **Developer:** Chillingo Ltd

Etolis: Arena
Chillingo steps it up a notch

Ever since *Angry Birds*, Chillingo has moved from strength to strength. *Etolis: Arena* is its latest high-quality offering, but the cracks are beginning to show in the renowned developer's armour.

For the most part, *Etolis: Arena* repeats much of the quality that has gone into its past titles. The first thing to note is the effort that's gone into making this a good-looking game. Though it doesn't answer to *Infinity Blade*, it is another example of how capable the iPad is as a games console.

The object is to eliminate wave after wave of increasingly difficult enemies by navigating the level and blasting away with whatever weapon you have to hand. Auto-aim is enabled by default, but it should be turned off if you hope to get more precision from your attacks.

Problems arise when trying to switch weapons, throw a grenade, use your special ability or sprint away from danger – due to the small, awkward buttons. This is an issue a developer as experienced as Chillingo should have spotted. Despite this, there's plenty of gameplay here for those who can overcome the control issues. A single interface issue means that *Etolis: Arena* falls short of yet more greatness from Chillingo.

Rating ★★★★☆

Price: £2.99/$4.99 **Developer:** Logic Factory Int

Ascendancy
Control the universe from the comfort of your iPhone

Ascendancy was a classic PC strategy game from Logic Factory, released in 1995. 16 years later, and it's now been updated for iOS, and the end result is an utterly absorbing title that's just as addictive.

Playing one of 21 distinct races, the aim of Ascendancy is to become the dominant life force. This is achieved by building up your planet's population, deciding what technologies your race will learn, and much more. As your race grows in power, you'll be able to build shipyards, create spaceships, and eventually move on to colonise other planets. Colonisation can be done peacefully by simply settling on unoccupied planets, or you can attempt to declare war on the other races.

It's a truly addictive experience thanks to the sheer number of options that are available, as well as the challenging AI, but it's not without a few issues. Our biggest concern with *Ascendancy* is that the tutorial is a real mess, making it really hard to initially make any progress. Get over this massive roadblock, however, and you'll discover an incredibly satisfying strategy title that just keeps giving and giving.

Rating ★★★★★

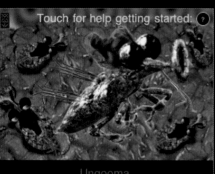
Touch for help getting started:

Ungooma

We are Ungooma. Please do not hurt us!

We look forward to many interesting encounters.

■ The only thing that really scuppers Ascendancy is a lacklustre tutorial.

■ Even though it was originally released 16 years ago, Ascendancy hasn't aged one bit.

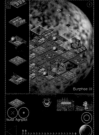

Price: £2.99/$4.99 **Developer:** Electronic Arts

Ultimate Mortal Kombat 3
Sadly, there's nothing 'ultimate' about this…

There are many things that the iPad can emulate brilliantly, but if there's one thing that touch screen will never perfectly replicate, it's the tactile precision of a quality arcade stick. Despite the excuse that *Mortal Kombat* has never really been a series where such precision is important, you'd still like to be able to say you feel in control. And sadly for *UMK3*, this isn't really the case.

This is *Ultimate Mortal Kombat 3* in name only, an ugly polygonal cast replacing the campy retro charm of the original's digitised combatants, with only half of the fighters being bothered to show up. Those that did decide to turn up look terrible, with the poorly animated, budget 3D models doing even the most iconic characters no favours whatsoever.

Back To The Future Episode 1 HD

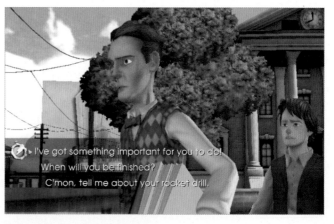
I've got something important for you to do!
When will you be finished?
C'mon, tell me about your rocket drill.

■ You're often asked to choose from three or more responses in typical adventure game style.

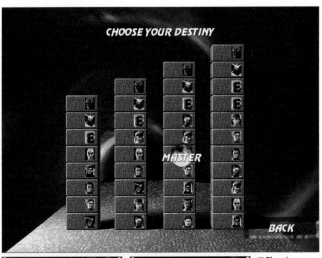

CHOOSE YOUR DESTINY

MASTER

BACK

■ The absence of Sektor & Cyrax, as well as house favourite Cabal, is strange.

■ As with most fighting games, the iPad's on-screen controls disappoint.

Rating ★★☆☆☆

Price: £3.99/$6.99 Developer: Telltale Games

Great Scott, or, er, just plain regular?

From *Wallace & Gromit* to *Monkey Island*, Telltale has gained a reputation for breathing fresh life into a beloved yet inactive series. Though occasionally workmanlike in nature, its releases have consistently captured the essence of each subject licence, throwing in references aplenty to keep seasoned veterans entertained.

And so that formula is resurrected through this first of five nostalgia fests featuring Doc Brown and Marty McFly, which opens as trusty hound Einstein becomes a time travel pioneer on a dusky parking lot.

Troubles begin to arise, however, when rather than going on to play the role of loveable eccentric through our hero's existential crisis, Christopher Lloyd's character instead disappears into thin air as the iconic DeLorean fails to dematerialise, offering his friend and confidant an apology before disappearing into thin air.

As ever, a solid app is ensured by adequately designed gameplay and high production values. However, those hoping execution might match expectations should prepare to be slightly disappointed.

Rating ★★★☆☆

Price: Free Developer: Namco Networks America

Ridge Racer Accelerated HD

Nought to £6 in thirty seconds…

Nothing in life is free. We've not spent our collective years on Earth without learning that one hard and fast rule, and yet even still, no one likes feeling tricked. Disheartening it was to boot up *Ridge Racer Accelerated HD* for the first time, only to learn that to get any amount of content, you first need the £5.49/$8.99 unlock fee.

Do so, and the game's 50 vehicles and 12 tracks will become available across the varying new modes. Initially this will overwhelm, giving plenty of choices where previously there were none. However, without a central arc of progression, the content feels lacklustre – as though you've been handed a sandbox but no bucket. You're free to play with the grains and build your own makeshift castle, but without the proper tools it feels wasted.

As far as arcade racing goes, *Ridge Racer* is unrivalled, but feels too flat to recommend. The content is there, but poor design and a high price tag will leave many underwhelmed.

Rating ★★★★★

■ Aside from the necessary on-screen D-pad, the HUD will be familiar to fans.

■ The trademark drift-heavy *Ridge Racer* gameplay is in full effect.

Price: £0.59/$0.99 **Developer:** Minoraxis Inc

Fruit Juice Tycoon 2

Enron looks positively saintly in comparison

We've never set up a lemonade stall, but we imagine it to be a harmless, character-building and endearing experience. Not so in *Fruit Juice Tycoon 2*. Here, the juice industry is defined by hostile takeovers, political backstabbings, dirty tricks and even kidnapping. Don't let the bright colours fool you – we're surprised the corner stalls aren't ran by gangs.

It's the RPG elements that set this sequel apart, seeing you purchase stock, manage stalls and level up. For the most part, it plays as a business simulation/time management sim as you attempt to expand your business into new neighbourhoods, but the actual juice-selling part takes the form of a match-three game that's so simple you won't have any trouble satisfying customers.

The business and micromanagement aspect can actually feel quite involving, but it's the simplicity and repetitiveness of these more 'gamey' elements that let it down.

Rating ★ ★ ★ ★ ☆

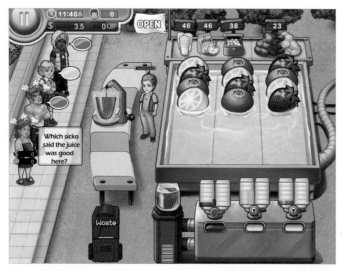

■ The match-three gameplay is slightly disappointing compared the business side.

Price: £1.79/$2.99 **Developer:** Electronic Arts

NBA Jam by EA Sports

Still slamming strong after all these years

Back before phones barely had the technology to manage a call, and mobile gaming meant getting a bus to the nearest arcade, an unusual sports title was quickly becoming a smash hit. *NBA Jam* brought something new with its fast-paced action, over-the-top manoeuvres and hilarious commentator.

Now on the iPad, the new version seeks to relive that charm with the same mix of caricaturised players and frenetic action. And it does, in every possible way.

There are a number of abilities available. For example, block is used with a tap of the left button, yet hold down the central run button and swipe left, and your player will push their opponents. While this can be cumbersome at first, the controls eventually become second nature.

With 36 matches in each division, not to mention unlockable characters, basketballs and special modes, there's plenty here. NBA Jam manages to bring the playability and joy of the original into a neat and stylish package. A must-have game for your iPad, whether you're old enough to remember the original or not.

Rating ★ ★ ★ ★ ★

■ Fans will be please to see the customary *NBA Jam* big heads are here in full force.

Although its graphics are insane, the controls deserve equal acclaim.

You will probably face the God King many times!

Price: £3.49/$5.99 **Developer:** Chair Entertainment

Infinity Blade
So much more than a pretty face

Infinity Blade by Chair Entertainment – under the watchful eye of Epic Games – is the latest developer to jump onboard the iPad, and the end result is one of the best-looking iPad games ever.

Visuals are only half the story, however, as Chair has created a title which is just perfect for playing on the go. Taking control of a Knight, your goal is to defeat the God King, an impossible task that will see you die on your first attempt, only to take on the role of your child, eager to avenge the family bloodline.

Infinity Blade is all about repetition. You face the same enemy, walk through the same parts of the castle and will eventually die by the God King's hand until you finally develop the skills to defeat him. And yet for all its repetition and grinding gameplay, it's never boring to play.

This in part is due to the control system that has you parrying sword swipes and dodging and blocking blows with simple swipes and taps of your finger. It's a delightfully elegant control system that still requires a large amount of skill due to the different enemies that you face. Truly stunning stuff.

Rating ★★★★★

Price: £3.99/$6.99 **Developer:** Electronic Arts

Tiger Woods PGA Tour 12 For iPad
Not quite a hole in one

This is more of an update than a sequel to previous games, although in fairness it doesn't deviate especially far from the controls of its predecessors. The touchscreen swing mechanic returns, requiring the player to draw their finger down a meter and swipe to swing. You can draw and fade the ball by curving your finger's movement, and add spin by swiping during its trajectory.

The bulk of the play takes place in the PGA Tour, which sees you compete for cash prizes, which can then be used to enter tournaments or buy equipment. Smaller modes come in the form of the Tiger Challenge and Closest To The Pin. The latter mode is self-explanatory, but EA's decision to limit this multiplayer mode just to Facebook is odd.

The disappointing multiplayer decisions don't end there. While multiplayer is included, it's confined to Bluetooth and Wi-Fi, which is a shame as online play would have made the app a more tempting proposition.

Rating ★★★★★

While there are better-looking sports games out there, Tiger's visuals can hold their own.

The familiar Tiger controls are back – if it ain't broke and all that.

■ Don't expect any typical *Tomb Raider*-style action here – there isn't any.

Price: £3.99/$6.99 **Developer:** ideaworks

Lara Croft And The Guardian Of Light

Lara goes portable for her latest adventure

Dispensing with the traditional adventures that were so popular on the PlayStation, *Guardian Of Light* takes a more arcade-style approach in the form of an impressive twin-stick shooter. There are still tombs to plunder and puzzles to solve, but the emphasis is placed on action and destroying as many enemies as possible.

It's a concept that works surprisingly well thanks to the solid controls, well-placed button layouts and some cleverly designed stages. Another huge bonus is the excellent multiplayer mode that can be played via Wi-Fi or Game Center, which adds massively to the core game.

Graphically it's highly impressive, with glorious-looking locations, excellent lighting and well-animated characters, but it's the satisfying gameplay and the multi-tasking required to complete each level that will keep you coming back for more.

Rating ★★★★★

■ It doesn't feature the most original of ideas, but Monster Trouble's a decent game.

■ The *Warcraft*-inspired graphics are a definite plus point.

Price: £2.99/$4.99 **Developer:** Magic Dream Games

Monster Trouble HD

Yet another tower defence game…

The App Store isn't exactly lacking in tower defence games, so it takes a lot in order for one to stand out. *Monster Trouble HD*'s method for doing this is to take what was already an offshoot of real-time strategy, and then try to take it back to the source a bit, playing more like a *Command & Conquer*-style top-down game than the more static likes of *Fieldrunners*. The fully 3D visuals, which bear more than a slight resemblance in style to Blizzard's *Warcraft* series, are fairly impressive, and the fact that you can use the iPad's full range of pinch, zoom and pan gestures to zip around the map makes it feel quite involving, especially when the action heats up.

It really doesn't feel much like what you might expect from tower defence, though. While the enemies will always spawn from predetermined entrances, the layouts feel organic and open, while still allowing you to spot chokepoints where you can maximise the impact of your defences. You'll need to as well, because it's quite easy to spread your defences thin, leaving you desperately shifting your misplaced garrisons as the enemies gang up on a lone troop and quickly exhaust your supplies.

As solid as *Monster Trouble HD* is, though, it doesn't do much that genre fans won't have seen before, and it lacks the depth of some of the iPad's better strategy offerings.

Rating ★★★☆☆

Price: £2.99/$4.99 **Developer:** Backflip Studios

Ragdoll Blaster 2 HD

A contender to Angry Birds' throne

There are a lot of similarities to be found between *Ragdoll Blaster 2* and *Angry Birds*. However, *Ragdoll Blaster 2 HD* differs in subtle ways. For one, the objective is simpler: you just have to hit the target with one of the ragdolls propelled from your high-powered cannon. But as with *Angry Birds*, how to do that up to you. While the difficulty of each level varies, so too does the solution, meaning each map represents a new challenge.

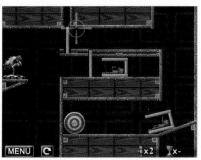

The only thing stopping *Ragdoll Blaster 2 HD* from aping *Angry Birds'* level of success is its visuals, which lack the charm and character that helped the latter's success.

■ It lacks Angry Birds' style, but the gameplay is still rock solid.

Overall Rating ★★★★★

Price: £9.99/$15.99 **Developer:** Electronic Arts

Need For Speed: Hot Pursuit for iPad

The law: if you can't beat 'em, join 'em…

Like its console counterpart, this iPad offering gives the player control over police missions in a series that has spent over a decade concentrating on how different a Ford Focus looks with and without neon lights. The result is a relatively truncated yet perfectly enjoyable racer, though one altogether more divorced from reality than even its rollercoaster of a relation.

Naturally, the technology jump has necessitated a trim or two. Gone is the world map, replaced with a threadbare array of

tubular tracks set within generic geographical climates Significantly altered, too, is much of the weaponry that made its full-price release equal parts *Police Camera Action!* and *Mario Kart*.

■ The console version is a great-looking game, and so's this.

Overall Rating ★★★★☆

Price: £2.39/$3.99 **Developer:** BBC Worldwide Ltd

The Mazes Of Time

Comic-book fun comes alive in this adventure

The story behind *The Mazes Of Time* is simple. The Doctor and Amy Pond answer a distress call to save the members of a family who have been warped off to different time zones that range from an Incan world to a sprawling Dalek ship.

It's a fairly simplistic story, but it does allow for a nice range of locations, even if they're aren't rendered to any great degree. But while it's not much to look at, the gameplay is

of a far better standard, with the Doctor and Amy having to work together. Initially, puzzles consist of switches that must be pressed and doorways that must be opened, but they do require more head-scratching later on.

■ The graphics aren't exactly pretty, but the gameplay's spot on.

Overall Rating ★★★★★

Price: £3.99/$6.99 **Developer:** Revolution Software

Broken Sword – The Smoking Mirror

Unravel the mysteries of the Mayans in this classic

While *The Smoking Mirror* has never been as good a game as the original, what Revolution has shown is that it's now the developer to beat when it comes to porting classic point-and-click adventures to iOS.

This isn't a director's cut like the first game, so you won't find any new puzzles or added scenarios, but it borrows that version's excellent transposition of mouse controls onto the touch screen, making moving, interacting, and managing your inventory a

snap. Also brought over are character portraits from comic-book artist Dave Gibbons (Watchmen), and a general cleaning up of the game's graphics, which largely remain detailed and beautiful.

■ We're inclined to agree with this fellow.

Overall Rating ★★★★★

Price: £1.19/$1.99 Developer: Navigation-Info

Forklift Guy

There are big bucks to be made running a forklift business… and a forklift game too, apparently. Shifting cargo from one vehicle to the next sounds like a chore, and it is. While the mechanics work well and the forklift follows the line you trace with your finger, the premise of *Forklift Guy* is no more thrilling than what we'd imagine a real dockyard career to be.

Rating ★★★★★

Price: £0.59/$0.99 Developer: Gp Imports Inc

iTraffic Light HD

Flight Control innovated when it first appeared, spurring the vehicle management genre into a new age of touch-screen addiction. As is always the case with success stories like this, hundreds of wannabes soon turned up, though rarely with that same level of quality. *iTraffic Light HD* is one such title, removing the interaction of directing vehicles yourself and limiting you to controlling the left and right stream of vehicles. The result is a game with poor visuals, lacklustre gameplay and none of the one-more-go appeal.

Rating ★★★★★

Price: £0.59/$0.99 Developer: Com2Us USA, Inc

Zombie Runway

Often the most basic ideas are the most impressive, and one of the reasons you won't be able to put *Zombie Runaway* down. Charging through the graveyard is simple; stay in one of three lanes to evade tombstones or leap traps. The risk-reward of the varied boosters – which increase speed and allow your tubby undead to barrel through stone – help those keen to keep an eye out for score-boosting opportunities, while unlockable bonuses add to the game's longevity. A simple and addictive title that keeps asking for just one more try.

Rating ★★★★★

Price: £1.19/$1.99 Developer: BluSped

X3000 HD

With nearly 30 years of genre heritage and thousands of shooter games in its wake, *X3000 HD* would have had to pull off a miracle to stand out from the crowd. Needless to say it doesn't. It's a typical *R-Type*-style game, involving one spaceship versus a horde of enemies spewing bullets, missiles and beams in the hope that one of them will destroy your ship.

Rating ★★★★★

Price: £0.59/$0.99 Developer: Bulkypix

Cardboard Castle HD

The iPad's screen makes *Cardboard Castle* a perfect partner to the device. Each scene asks that you help the knight travel from left to right, battling opponents, crossing chasms and prodding cows. Experimentation is the name of the game, though this is quickly undone when the majority of later puzzles need less cognitive thought and more trial-and-error.

Rating ★★★★★

Price: Free Developer: Appgeneration

Crazy Donuts

While we're not sure what makes these donuts crazy (apart from their bouncing), they do make for an entertaining puzzle game. The task is to place each of the contraptions around a level to reflect the donuts safely into the mouth of a monster. Unfortunately, not every donut bounces in the same way, which can be a nuisance in later levels.

Rating ★★★★★

Price: £1.19/$1.99 Developer: Darren Spencer

Shadow Run HD

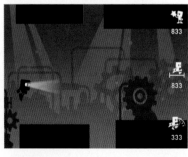

Ever since *Canabalt* ran onto the scene, there have been a handful of me-too titles. Now, we have *Shadow Run HD* bringing gravity defying into the tried-and-tested gameplay. In doing so, however, the skill and difficulty in timing your leaps between buildings has been stunted, especially when very few gaps provide much of a challenge at all.

Rating ★★★★★

Price: Free Developer: Emantras

Splosh

In this modern age, it seems children are more au fait with technology than we'll ever be, which is where interactive storybooks come in. Despite the few barriers to understanding, this app isn't intuitive to a child's use, unlike that touch-and-learn book in the corner. *Splosh* will entertain, but the confusing interface hinders what should be a simple title.

Rating ★★★★★

Price: £1.19/$1.99 **Developer:** Clickgamer Tech

Ink Ball HD

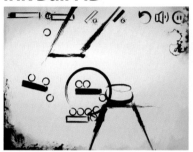

Sometimes, superficially generic iOS games are capable of surprising. After all, it appears that gamers are to be treated here to a *World Of Goo* clone. In actual fact, events prove quite different, if a little lacking in variety. The task is to guide a quota of bounding balls towards their destination pot, with only elastic and solid surfaces at your disposal.

Rating ★★★★☆

Price: £1.19/$1.99 **Developer:** Chocobaji Apps

Crazy Control HD 2

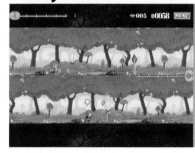

The cliché that often accompanies a release such as this would suggest a person's like or dislike of the hi-jinks contained within would vary with an ability to rub a stomach and pat a head at the same time. It doesn't take a lot to highlight how entertaining this isn't. Its action is arguably best observed in portrait, offering a more complete view of the route ahead.

Rating ★★☆☆☆

Price: £1.79/$2.99 **Developer:** Tower Studios

Speedball 2 Evolution

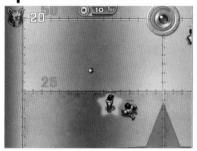

Speedball has always seemed the sports videogame for people who don't quite understand the real thing. With labyrinthine rules, brutal tackles and minimal subtlety, it's almost the perfect caricature. Built with more primitive controls in mind, it proves competent. Still, there's an immediacy of control this conversion lacks through both input methods.

Rating ★★★☆☆

Price: £1.19/$1.99 **Developer:** Ant Hive Games

The Line HD

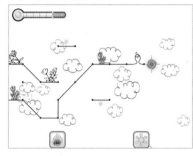

The Line HD takes advantage of the touch screen to deliver surprisingly intricate puzzle action. Unfortunately, controls that demand a slightly more deft touch stop an impressive concept from realising its full potential. Guiding a small figure around a line-drawn path, players must construct new point-to-point routes in order to avoid obstacles.

Rating ★★★☆☆

Price: £0.59/$0.99 **Developer:** Clickgamer Tech

Type Type Train

Type Type Train challenges players to tap various randomly generated words appearing on-screen via the sides of passing trains. Predictably, there's not a great deal of nuance to the gameplay beyond this one central concept. Bonuses are on offer for long, accurate runs, and there's naturally a slew of difficulty levels to test the very committed.

Rating ★★☆☆☆

Price: £2.99/$4.99 **Developer:** Qiao Jin

Codename Cobra: Desert Storm Deluxe HD

It's difficult not to be underwhelmed with *Codename Cobra*. Your interaction with the gunship is limited to movement, while your increasingly large arsenal fires automatically. Without much in the way of interesting enemy attack patterns to negotiate, it gives the whole thing the feel of a quick and cheap project thrown onto the App Store to see if anyone bites.

Rating ★★☆☆☆

Price: £2.99/$4.99 **Developer:** Kongzhong Corp

Zombie Crisis 3D 2: Hunter HD

It takes a lot for zombie games to stand out, and in that context mediocrity is enough to damn *Zombie Crisis 3D 2*. Shooting is automatic, leaving you to concentrate on manoeuvring, dodging and switching weapons, and on each level you must take out waves of the undead until you progress to the next level. The camera is zoomed in so far that tougher enemies get frustrating, appearing from nowhere and surrounding you without warning.

Rating ★★☆☆☆

Price: £1.79/$2.99 **Developer:** Prophetic Sky

Knights Vs Aliens

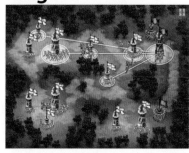

You're tasked with taking over towers for your faction, first by sending troops to pacify the locals, then by holding them against the onslaught of aliens. Bigger towers bring bigger armies, but you'll need more force to capture them, leading to fast-paced action as both sides go for the low-hanging fruit before clashing as they go for each other's bases.

Rating ★★★★☆

Price: £1.19/$1.99 **Developer:** id Software

Rage HD

In order to keep a tight grip on the technical side of things, Rage constitutes an on-rails shooter, offering players three levels to blast through with their weaponry. Visually it's obviously stunning, and the price tag is hardly prohibitive, making this glimpse of the future rather appealing. Visually stunning, and a tantalising snippet of the iPad's gaming capabilities.

Rating ★★★★☆

Price: £5.99/$10.99 **Developer:** FISHLABS

Galaxy On Fire 2

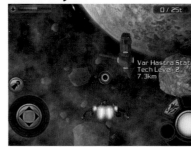

Galaxy On Fire 2 thrusts players into a world of space faring commodity trading packaged in role-playing wrapping. Technically the game shines, blending impressive visuals with decent voice acting. Sadly, fiddly controls and repetitive missions dulls the shine more than ten hours of meaningful gameplay would have offered. Broad, yet inescapably awkward.

Rating ★★★☆☆

Price: £1.79/$2.99 **Developer:** Revolutionary Concepts

Karate Champ XL

A blast from the past now, with one of the most influential fighters of yesteryear given a new lease on life thanks to this superb conversion. On-screen controls perfectly mimic the twin-stick set-up of the arcade original, and while it's not the most technical beat-'em-up, it's unquestionably the most faithful to its source material. It's an enjoyable jaunt into the past, and a lovingly taught history lesson in which fans would do well to stay awake. Wears its age with pride, and sings of a simpler past, all to great nostalgic effect.

Rating ★★★★☆

Price: £0.59/$0.99 **Developer:** Maverick Software

More Buffet!

The inclusion of some apps in the 'Games' category really does stretch the definition of the word. In *More Buffet!*, you choose the national cuisine of one of a handful of countries, fill a plate with your selection of delicacies, and then 'eat' it by tapping it to take bites out of the meal. Some of them, such as Mexico's taco, will let you do a bit of customisation and provide some interaction with the process, but you'll always end up with a virtual plate of food that you can pretend to eat. Seriously, that's it.

Rating ★☆☆☆☆

Price: £1.79/$2.99 **Developer:** Digital Legends

Bruce Lee Dragon Warrior HD

Considering how easy it is to bolt a famous name onto an app and make a quick buck, this one took us by surprise. Surprisingly sound mechanics mean the fighting itself is of a high standard, plus the characters, settings and presentation all evoke memories of the martial arts great in the way they should. It's as basic as 3D fighters come, but worth a bout or two.

Rating ★★★☆☆

Price: £0.59/$0.99 **Developer:** Chillingo Ltd

Sneezies HD

The aim of the game is simple: presented with a screen of floating Sneezies, you must strategically drop some sneezing powder into the pack to trigger a chain reaction of sneezes to burst them out of their bubbles. You have to pop a certain amount of bubbles to clear each of the 45 levels and the game is about luck as much as strategy – but it's jolly good fun.

Rating ★★★★☆

Price: £0.59/$0.99 **Developer:** Chillingo Ltd

Predators

We have to admit that, for a Rodriguez flick, the film was terrible, but mercifully the game is a full-throttle slash-'em-up of the highest order. Playing as the Predator, you must traverse jungle terrain hacking lumps out of weapon-toting humans while utilising your alien abilities (such as thermal vision) to stay one step ahead. Good old fashioned mindless fun.

Rating ★★★☆☆

Price: £2.99/$5.99 **Developer:** Chillingo Ltd

Minigore HD

As John Gore, you have to survive an endless onslaught of 'furries' – dark shaggy creatures with huge fangs – by filling them full of lead. The creatures attack from all angles and are likely to pounce out at you from the dark corners of the screen if you don't keep your wits about you. Like *The Hero HD*, this is also a blisteringly-crisp advert for HD gaming with plenty of charm.

Rating ★★★★☆

Price: £0.59/$0.99 **Developer:** Chillingo Ltd

The Hero HD

Your aim is to protect mankind from all manner of crime and terror, like raining missiles and raging fires. This app is a great showcase for how good games can look in HD, but it's more than a visual showcase. It's hugely addictive and features online leader boards that you will strive to get your name on. Kerpow! An amazingly-looking, genuinely compelling game.

Rating ★★★★★

Price: £1.19/$1.99 **Developer:** Sftwrfactory LLC

iPet Rock HD

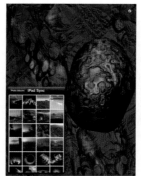

Sure, you could have a virtual pet that's based on a living creature, but isn't there more fun to be had with an inanimate object? The answer is no, unfortunately, and the fact that you have to pay for this 'game' is simply ridiculous. It's even stranger that there are several pet rock apps available to download, and if we're honest we really can't see the appeal. You have a rock which you can move, and you can change the background. That's literally it. Other than buying it for the amusement of owning a pet rock, Avoid at all costs.

Rating ★☆☆☆☆

Price: £0.59/$0.99 **Developer:** Pascal Inc

My Dog My Room

In *My Dog My Room HD*, you play with your pet in a variety of disproportionately sized 3D rooms, throwing a ball and doing what you would expect with a virtual pet. However, there's very little on offer, and the price doesn't really justify the few minutes enjoyment you'll get out of the game. After you've brushed and fed your puppy, you'll probably run out of things to do. One nice feature is that your dog can run around an image from your photo gallery, but it's a shame that there still isn't much to do once there.

Rating ★★★☆☆

Price: £2.99/$5.99 **Developer:** Chillingo Ltd

Master Of Alchemy

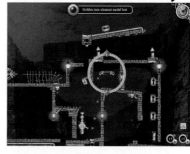

The aim of the game is to direct substances – solid or liquid – around the screen into their respective receptacles. The challenge comes in the form of obstacles that can only be by-passed by changing the properties of your substance – if it's a liquid it may need to become a solid to break through walls. It sounds complicated but it isn't and it's great fun.

Rating ★★★★★

Price: Free **Developer:** Jirbo Inc

Tap Reef HD

There're quite a few fish games available in the App Store, but *Tap Reef HD* was one of the few tailored specifically for the iPad that makes use of its larger screen. It's quite good fun looking after and breeding your fish inside the nicely rendered tank, but there isn't much to do without, you guessed it, spending real money to buy new things. Let this one sink.

Rating ★★☆☆☆

Price: £1.19/$1.99 **Developer:** 3Lynx LLC

Kimimon

Kimimon is so very nearly the virtual pet app we've been crying out for, but it falls just short of the mark. It's cute and very reminiscent of a tamagotchi, and there's plenty of environments and ways to accessorise your Kimimon, which is essentially just a blob of goo. You play games with your creature to progress, and while it does support in-app purchases, the in-built features are almost enough to keep you occupied without having to buy more. However, you will eventually tire of what's on offer as your Kimimon grows.

Rating ★★★★☆

Price: £2.99/$4.9 **Developer:** Gameloft

Brothers In Arms 2: Global Front HD

You'd think an FPS wouldn't work on the iPad, but *Brothers In Arms 2* is a surprise. It has its issues – it can't compare to using a controller, and some functions require an uncomfortable stretch up the screen – but it's playable and better than the fiddly iPhone version. A good demo of how this kind of game can work on the iPad, and well worth a look.

Rating ★★★☆☆

Price: £0.59/$0.99 **Developer:** Arthur Ham

Pet Playpen

It might sport some old, cheaply designed 2D graphics, but *Pet Playpen* is still a very good game. There's several different animals to choose from, with the little critter of your choice making demands in return for a reward such as what he wants for his next meal. No hidden purchases and plenty to do. Should be a benchmark for similar games.

Rating ★★★★☆

Price: £2.99/$4.99
Developer: Playrix

Royal Envoy HD (Full)

 In this strategy game you have to build up civilizations on nine islands across 63 levels. You build up your settlements and collect resources from the environment, as well as taking on a variety of challenges. It looks good and is mildly addictive. Recommended.

Overall Rating ★★★★☆

Price: £1.79/$2.99
Developer: Stuart Atkinson

Out Brake

 This impressive top-down racer boasts some fun visuals and intelligent track design across a variety of environments. Unfortunately it's let down by its controls, which are a little fiddly at times, but otherwise the concept is great.

Overall Rating ★★★☆☆

Price: Free
Developer: Big Fish Games, Inc

Flux Family Secrets – The Ripple Effect HD

 This game sees you solving puzzles in a point and click adventure with a humorous story and some great visuals. For a free game there's a decent amount of content, but we found some of the challenges a little easy.

Overall Rating ★★★☆☆

Price: £1.79/$2.99
Developer: Snappy Touch

Casey's Contraptions

 This game is very reminiscent of the board game Mouse Trap. In it, you build and activate 2D contraptions to achieve a certain goal. There's plenty of variety and you can even create your own contraptions. This app comes highly recommended.

Overall Rating ★★★★★

Price: £3.99/$6.99
Developer: Gameloft

StarFront: Collision HD

 This excellent real-time strategy game that clearly takes influence from the *Starcraft* series of games on PC has you building and managing a base and fighting opposing forces. Excellent gameplay.

Overall Rating ★★★★★

Price: £2.99/$4.99
Developer: GameHouse

Mortimer Beckett and the Secrets of Spooky Manor

 This point and click adventure has you searching a spooky manor for clues as you uncover the secret of his uncle's disappearance.

Overall Rating ★★★☆☆

Price: £3.99/$6.99
Developer: Days Of Wonder, Inc.

Ticket to Ride

 In *Ticket to Ride*, based on the popular board-game, you challenge AI bots or other humans to conque a variety of railroads across maps including the USA and Europe by use of trading cards. It's intuitive and different from anything else. We had a blast playing it.

Overall Rating ★★★★☆

Price: Free
Developer: Sony Pictures

Zookeeper

 Based on the summer flick of the same name, *Zookeeper* has a variety of game modes including a side-scrolling adventure and card matching. Ultimately the game is limited and not particularly satisfying to play, while the graphics are dodgy at times.

Overall Rating ★★☆☆☆

Price: £1.79/$2.99
Developer: Electronic Arts

Draw Jump HD

 In *Draw Jump HD* you draw lines under your character to fire him up in the air. The higher you go, the harder it gets to control him, and there's collectables and obstacles along the way as well. Good fun but eventually you'll probably get a bit bored.

Overall Rating ★★★☆☆

Price: £1.79/$2.99
Developer: Simogo

Bumpy Road

 We loved playing this adorable and artistic game. You use your fingers to manipulate the ground and direct your car as quickly as possible along randomised 2D levels. Unique and brilliant, we'd highly recommend this game to everyone.

Overall Rating ★★★★☆

Price: £3.99/$6.99
Developer: Telltale Inc

Back to the Future Ep 4 HD

 Relive the films complete with enchanting graphics and amusing but accurate voice-overs, some voiced by the original actors. Good fun, and fans of the films would be advised to pick up the first three episodes in the series as well.

Overall Rating ★★★★☆

Price: Free
Developer: Big Fish Games, Inc

The Serpent of Isis HD

 This enjoyable puzzle game sees you searching for clues to uncover the mystery of a missing valuable piece of art. The controls are simple and the story is good, if not great. Worth a try, although the full version costs more than this one, obviously.

Overall Rating ★★★★☆

Price: £1.79/$2.99
Developer: CGMatic Co., Ltd.

Grove Keeper - HD

 In *Grove Keeper* you have to defend your forts from waves of enemies with some intuitive touch screen controls. Packed with a ton of content, some cute graphics and a quirky story, this app is an enjoyable game for all ages. It is a little on the expensive side, though…

Overall Rating ★★★★☆

Price: Free
Developer: Z2Live, Inc

MetalStorm: Online™

 This basic (but free) air combat game sees you take to the skies as you battle against human and computer-controlled enemies. While the gameplay is simplistic, for a free download there's still plenty of fun to be had here, but you will have to pay for more content.

Overall Rating ★★★★☆

Price: £1.19/$1.99
Developer: Chillingo Ltd

Spoing HD

 This addictive game has you sling-shotting a critter across stylish (but occasionally bland) levels to reach a goal. It's easy to pick up but perhaps a little too difficult to master, which might turn some people off after a few goes – which would be a crying shame.

Overall Rating ★★★☆☆

Price: Free
Developer: Glu Games Inc.

Star Blitz

 This top-down space shooter is fun for a while, but once you discover that you have to buy dreaded hidden-purchases you won't have much to do unless you want to fork out. Still, the graphics and gameplay are both pretty enjoyable.

Overall Rating ★★☆☆☆

Price: £3.49/$5.99
Developer: Ankama

DOFUS: Battles HD

 Blending real-time strategy elements with tower-defense gameplay, you have to protect a dragon as wave after wave of enemies attacks you. It looks great and the gameplay is solid, while there's plenty of longevity to be had. Excellent fun.

Overall Rating ★★★★★

Price: Free
Developer: Kiloo

Frisbee® Forever

 In this game you flick a frisbee forward a steer it either via tilting or tapping the screen. It's an excellent free games with loads of levels that we had a huge amount of fun playing, and there are plenty of collectibles to keep you coming back for more.

Overall Rating ★★★★★

Price: £1.79/$2.99
Developer: Backflip Studios

Army of Darkness Defense HD

 In this game based on the cult classic *Evil Dead* trilogy you fight off wave after wave of attackers in a touch-based side-scrolling environment. We found the animation is fairly weak and the battles slightly tedious.

Overall Rating ★★★☆☆

Price: £2.99/$4.99
Developer: Playrix

4 Elements HD (Full)

 In this *Bejeweled*-esque puzzle game you match up coloured gems to complete the 2D levels. It's pretty addictive and the visual effects are nice, while it's also simple and easy to pick-up and play. Will definitely please puzzle fans.

Overall Rating ★★★★☆

Price: Free
Developer: Backflip Studios

Shape Shift HD

This simple puzzle game requires you to align tiles of same shape and/or colour, complete with explosions and colour for correct sequences. However, the graphical style is a bit plain, so it'll probably please puzzle enthusiasts only who won't be able to resist a new challenge.

Overall Rating ★★★★☆

Price: Free
Developer: Big Fish Games, Inc

Antique Road Trip: USA HD

This point and click adventure has you traversing the United States, unearthing various secrets and unravelling the story along the way. It's similar to other games by Big Fish Games who know how to make a decent adventure game.

Overall Rating ★★★★☆

Price: £0.59/$0.99
Developer: Chillingo Ltd

Let's Jump!

Another of the growing multitude of 'jump' games on the app store, this game again has you drawing lines under a cutesy character to propel him higher and higher. It's best feature is that you can go to head to head with a friend, but otherwise its fairly unoriginal.

Overall Rating ★★★☆☆

Price: Free
Developer: Volkswagen

GTI EDITION 35

In this driving game you race GTI cars around several different tracks in either time-trial or career mode. The graphics and controls work surprisingly well for a free app. It'll certainly keep you busy for a while.

Overall Rating ★★★★☆

Price: Free
Developer: Nitako

Popstar Physics (Save Toshi 2)

This bizarre 3D physics/puzzle game has you eradicated zombies by moving and manipulating the environment. The three-star score for each level (*Angry Birds*, anyone?) will have you coming back for more.

Overall Rating ★★★★☆

Price: Free
Developer: Skyworks

World Cup Table Tennis™ HD

In this 3D game you control your paddle with your finger as you face of against a variety of AI players in several modes. There's also multiplayer for head to head battles, but overall we found the controls a bit too unresponsive.

Overall Rating ★★★☆☆

Price: £1.79/$2.99
Developer: Electronic Arts

BATTLEFIELD: BAD COMPANY™ 2

This proved a hit on the home consoles so it is no surprise that a slightly scaled down version arrives on iPad. It looks great and is packed with challenging action, it's just that the control system lets it down.

Overall Rating ★★★★☆

Price: £0.59/$0.99
Developer: emobix Ltd

Magic puzzles: Castles

This jigsaw puzzle game has you reassembling various famous castles around the world in typical jigsaw style. You can adjust the number of pieces into which each castle is divided to alter the difficulty.

Overall Rating ★★★★☆

Price: £0.59/$0.99
Developer: ITIW

Inferno

In this retro top-down game you have to direct a craft around old-school 2D levels to put out fires. It's fun in short bursts and there's plenty of challenges and achievements to keep you going for a while, so give it a go if you long for the olden days of gaming.

Overall Rating ★★★★☆

Price: Free
Developer: ITIW

Reverse Jump

Reverse Jump is a mind-bogglingly challenging 2D side-scroller that you'll either find incredibly frustrating or an enjoyable challenge. Tilting your iPad right moves the monster left and vice versa, making for a unique and fun gameplay experience.

Overall Rating ★★★☆☆

Price: Free
Developer: NextGen Entertainment INC

Bubble Shooter – Flick Edition

In this puzzle game you move and shoot bubbles to match up colours and clear the screen as it slowly advances downwards. It's based on similar games but doesn't bring anything new to the table.

Overall Rating ★★☆☆☆

Price: £1.19/$1.99
Developer: DR Studios

Bug Wings

In this 3D game you fly your bug around and collect pieces of pollen before landing on various flowers and lily pads. While the touch controls are poor, the tilt functionality makes for an enjoyable experience that will mostly appeal to casual gamers.

Overall Rating ★★★☆☆

Price: Free
Developer: Backflip Studios

Strike Knight HD

In this bowling game (where a puck replaces the traditional ball) you flick the puck into the pins to score points, which is pretty much the entirety of the game. However, it's challenging to master and thus blindingly good fun. Worth trying out at the very least.

Overall Rating ★★★★☆

Price: £0.59/$0.99
Developer: Retro Dreamer

Velocispider

In this retro arcade shooter you battle enemies from above as they drop towards the bottom of the screen. The graphics have definitely got that old-school feel and the tilt controls work pretty well. With fast and furious action this should please most gamers.

Overall Rating ★★★★☆

Price: £0.59/$0.99
Developer: ASK Homework

Ball Towers HD

In *Ball Towers* you tilt and turn your iPad to keep the balls rolling on rail-like tracks, complete with attractive levels and some challenging gameplay to match. It looks great on the iPad 2 with some nifty tricks used, and there's plenty of levels to keep you occupied.

Overall Rating ★★★★☆

Price: £0.59/$0.99
Developer: Summit Applications Corporation

Anna's Dress Up II HD

In this 'game' you dress Anna up in a variety of environments with hundreds of different outfit combinations. There's not really much to do though other than try on a few different clothes, so we can't see this appealing to many kids.

Overall Rating ★★★☆☆

Price: £1.19/$1.99
Developer: Chillingo Ltd

Feed Me Oil HD

Procreate's incredibly advanced drawing tool lets you create some visually stunning images on your iPad. The minimalist interface lets you get on with drawing and there's a whole host of features on offer. Simply brilliant for casual or serious artists alike.

Overall Rating ★★★★☆

Price: Free
Developer: Mecca Bingo Ltd

Bin-Glo

This game is bingo with a twist. Instead of just waiting for the numbers, you have to pop your number within a time limit when it appears at the top of the screen. Fun for a few minutes but you probably won't have much desire to come back and break your high score.

Overall Rating ★★★☆☆

Price: £0.59/$0.99
Developer: Triniti Interactive Limited

Dino Cap 2 HD

On first glance this side-scrolling shoot-em-up looks like good fun, with an excellent graphical style and fun gameplay. However, you'll quickly discover you can't do much without making expensive in-game purchases, which is a shame as it has potential.

Overall Rating ★★☆☆☆

Price: £0.59/$0.99
Developer: Tap To Win

Zombie Pie

Zombie Pie sees you defending your home against hordes of oncoming zombies, with various methods of attack including throwing pies and blasting out redneck techno music. It's quirky and fun, offering a different approach to other 'wave attack' games.

Overall Rating ★★★★☆

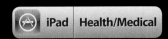
Health/Medical

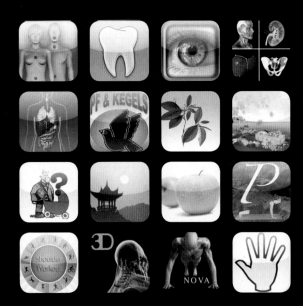

With an iPad and a bunch of apps you can start to phase out other, non-essential things in your life – like doctors. Who needs to sit in a stuffy surgery when you can learn all there is to know about your body and ailments from that thing in your hands? Get up to speed with the following apps…

Top Paid Apps	Top Free Apps
iMuscle – (NOVA Series) – iPad Edition ★★★★	3D4 Medical Images ★★★
Healthy Tips ★★★★	Vision Test ★★★★
Pilates For iPad ★★★	Cancer Signs & Symptoms ★★★★★

Staff pick of the section

3D Medical Animations ★★★★	Camping Recipes ★★★★

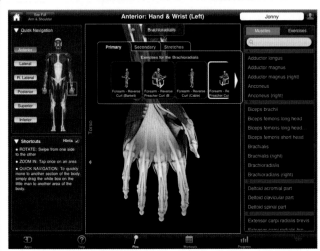

■ The app provides a detailed breakdown of each exercise and its potential benefits, making it easy to pick ones that are right for you.

Price: £2.99/$4.99 **Developer:** 3D4Medical.com

iMuscle – (NOVA Series) – iPad Edition

In-depth exercises for every bit of your body

 iMuscle is an exercise app that, through the use of a 3D rendered human body, allows you to choose which areas of your body you want to exercise and how. The amount of information and exercises on offer is excellent. You can pretty much pick any muscle in the body, and be given a range of exercises.

With each exercise comes an animation showing you what to do, and plenty of information on how to do it. To take it all one step further, you can track your progress and manage workouts, adding specific exercises to a particular workout you want to do, and see what effect it's having on your body. Our only problem is that the amount of information on offer can seem overwhelming at times, and those less in the know might be unsure of the benefits between two similar exercises. Recommended for fitness fanatics and phobes alike.

Rating ★★★★★

Price: Free **Developer:** 3D4 Medical

3D4 Medical Images
And you thought the human body was a thing of beauty…

If you're the kind of person who thinks the human body is a thing of beauty this app, from 3D4 Medical, may change your mind. Thanks to some impressive 3D technology your iPad is turned into a viewing device that gives you insight into all aspects of the human body – both the good and the bad.

Over 200 photographs are included and they show you many different parts of the human body in very different states. Many of the images certainly aren't for the squeamish – if you don't like the idea of viewing an adult penis in various states then don't download this app – but each and every photograph is amazingly detailed and beautifully rendered by 3D4 Medical's talented artists. Want to see greatly magnified strains of bacteria? Interested in learning how back pain is spread along the spine? Ever wondered what a female egg looks like when it's ready for fertilisation? Well thanks to this app you will and some of the imagery used is quite simply staggering.

They're frustratingly low on information, however. While the nicely presented menus explain what you're looking at and allow for photos to be shared via Twitter, email, Facebook or even used as wallpaper, it's a pity that the included descriptions are so short and don't give you some more useful information. Another rather disappointing aspect of the app is that while the images are brilliantly detailed, they're all static, so you can't manipulate them as you can with some of the other medical and encyclopaedia-styled apps that are available.

It dampens the overall experience somewhat, but it should also be noted that at the end of the day what's on offer is of a very high quality and it's all free to boot.

With that in mind, our advice is to set your device to portrait mode, select the included slideshow option and simply treat yourself to an amazing array of fantastic pictures as you're guided around the human body. Although many may just want to download and peruse the app casually before deleting it, was recommend keep this app tucked away in one of the more obscure folders on your Home screen to use as a reference tool in times of need. The depth of information it presents is, like we said, somewhat lacking in detail compared to other specialist apps, but the presentation and imagery more than makes up for this.

So while this app comes highly recommended because of its price and visual content, there's no denying that it could be improved greatly for future versions.

Rating ★★★★★

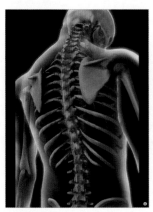
■ Some pictures illustrate ailments in the human body, but they are few and far between.

■ There are plenty of shots that show minuscule parts of the human body greatly magnified. They're fascinating to look at…

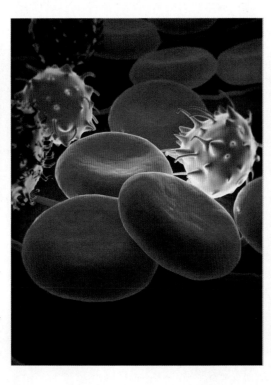

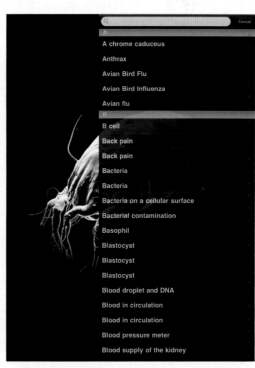

Price: Free   **Developer:** 3 Sided Cube Design Ltd

Vision Test

A free optician on your iPad

For years, people have been ignoring opticians' letters that tell the recipient they're due for an eye test. After all, what's the point in spending money on an eye test when you don't think that your eyes have changed since your last exam? Well now, thanks to 3 Sided Cube's Vision Test app, there's a free way to see if you need a new set of specs or not.

The app does this by testing for four things: visual acuity, astigmatism, duochrome and colour blindness. The visual acuity test is similar to the letter boards used in traditional opticians: you simply cover one eye, hold your iPad at arm's length, and identify which letter is being shown. These letters get progressively smaller, but never small enough to trouble anyone except those that should already know they need glasses.

The astigmatism test is a lot less familiar, and asks you to identify if any black lines are darker than the others,

Test	LEFT	RIGHT
Visual Acuity	100%	100%
Astigmatism	FAIL	FAIL
Duochrome	FAIL	FAIL
Colour Test	100%	100%

■ This is unfortunately about as detailed as the results get – at least you know if you've failed or not!

again with one eye. We're sure this is a legitimate test, but the app doesn't say how it's testing you. If you fail, you just get the option to find a local optician or watch a video on why you should have an eye test, which is the same after every test failure regardless of which test you have been unsuccessful at.

The duochrome test is found in many standard eye tests, and involves darkening lines, but this time set against coloured backgrounds. It's similar to the astigmatism one, and again there's not much information about how the app is assimilating the results.

The colour blindness test is where Vision Test really shines, however. Usually absent from a standard eye test, the colour test gives you four numbers to identify from different coloured backgrounds. These tests are far more effective than the previous ones, as they even tell you what people with colour deficiencies may see, as opposed to just failing you. Our only criticism is that there could have been more tests, especially as with a multiple choice setup some answers could be guessed.

Being free, the presentation is a bit sparse, and we were surprised when the optician finder didn't work, even though we had a working Wi-Fi connection. But Vision Test could be the app to get you to make a sight-saving trip to the opticians, and that makes it worth a download. It lacks information, but Vision Test offers worthwhile exams whose results could surprise you.

Rating ★★★★★

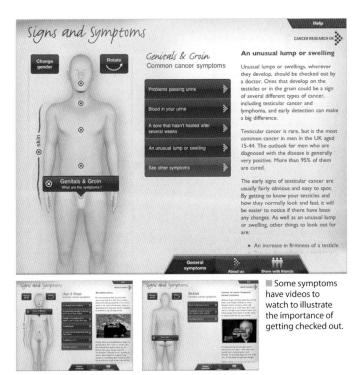

Some symptoms have videos to watch to illustrate the importance of getting checked out.

Price: Free **Developer:** Cancer Research UK

Cancer Signs And Symptoms for iPad

Catch the signs of cancer early

The Big 'C' is a concern for everybody, and when you consider that many of us will contract it at some point in our lives, it pays to be vigilant and take notice of the warning signs that your body throws out.

How do you distinguish what could be something very innocent from a more serious symptom, though? This free app from Cancer Research UK is very simple to use. Simply select your gender and tap on one of the red hotspots that you're concerned about on the illustrated human. If, for example, you click on the breast area, you're presented with a list of common cancer symptoms'. These categories are then explained in a little more detail, sometimes with video from sufferers and doctors with encouraging words.

What is good about this app is that it won't make you feel that every little lump, bump or cough could be a sign of a dreadful illness. Instead it holds your hand and encourages you to see a doctor without making you feel like you're wasting anyone's time. It doesn't cover every type of cancer, but just being aware of possible symptoms could save your life.

Rating ★★★★★

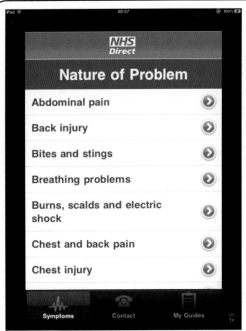

If your symptoms are bad or questionable, the NHS Direct team will call you back.

Price: Free **Developer:** NHS Direct

NHS Direct

An app that connects with medical professionals

This app was created so people who were concerned about someone's symptoms could call a professional to seek further advice if the situation didn't seem serious enough to call an ambulance. It mirrors the well-known service by letting you check symptoms via a series of questions.

At the end of the questions, if you've not got a satisfactory diagnosis, the app will link up to the Direct service and a nurse or doctor'll call you back. So that the best information is put forward to the call centre you'll be asked your postcode, whether you are the patient, your sex and your age. The next set of questions are then tailored to the party in question. Sometimes the outcome will be some advice that you can save to your favourites, other times you will be called back.

While we found this to be a great app, its speed does depend on your internet connection and is only for people living in England. So if you're really concerned about the ill party, don't wait to connect to the 'Collapse' symptom – call for an ambulance straight away.

Rating ★★★★★

Price: £1.79/$2.99 **Developer:** Karen Barton

Pelvic Floor And Kegel Exercises For iPad

The app all new mums should have

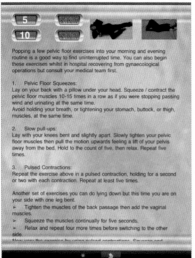

■ The rather lengthy menu of pelvic exercises.

■ Full descriptions of each exercise are included in the app.

You may wonder why it's important to exercise those muscles that you can't even see. However, pregnancy and childbirth especially can cause a woman's pelvic floor muscles to weaken. Over time this can lead to incontinence and an unfulfilling love life.

You'll start off by learning how to identify those all-important muscles and isolate them so that you can get to work getting them in shape, and there's even an introductory film telling you all about their role in the body.

Then you move on to the exercises. Some you will have to take time out to do, as they require floor work. Others can be done discreetly and as part of your everyday routine, even on your commute to work – no one need know you're working out. Further videos and timers that explain the exercises and ensure that you're performing them long enough give users a full program to work through. And while the icon does look like it's for some kind of martial arts app, it'll sit quite nicely on your iPad's desktop.

Rating ★★★★★

Price: £1.19/$1.99 **Developer:** Real Bodywork

Anatomy Quiz Pro

Test yourself on your body part names

The anatomy of our bodies is vastly complex, with miles of blood vessels, hundreds of muscles and myriad tendons. This quiz has been designed to test your knowledge of what lies beneath the skin.

Via a series of multiple-choice questions you'll discover how much you really know. Each question consists of just a part of the body, below which you're given four different beautifully rendered 3D images of various organs, muscles, joints and bones. Simply tap which one matches the word. If you're correct, you'll earn a big green tick.

You can choose from three topics: skeleton, muscles and organs. In each area you can create and tailor quizzes to the specific areas you'd like to work on. Each of the images can be enlarged so that you can get a closer look – to really test yourself you can turn on the timer option.

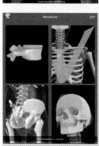

■ Beautifully rendered 3D images stand out on the iPad.

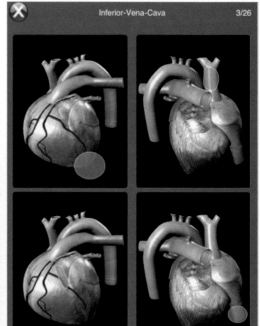

Rating ★★★☆☆

Price: Free **Developer:** Captivision Media Inc

3Dentist –
The Chairside Assistant

Discover what the dentist does

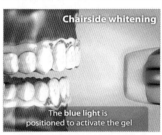
Chairside whitening

The **blue light** is positioned to activate the gel

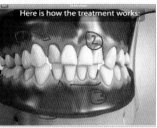
Here is how the treatment works:

Have you ever been to the dentist and been completely confused by the treatments on offer, or even by what the man in the white coat is going to do in your mouth? Then suggest that your dentist get this free app.

While it's designed for the practitioner to use as a tool to illustrate what will happen during a procedure, it could help dentophobics overcome their fears by seeing exactly what till happen. A drawing tool further helps with explanation.

■ The pen tool helps to illustrate procedures.

Overall Rating ★★★★☆

Price: Free **Developer:** Sybu Data

Digital Finger Tapping Test

Test your finger-bashing ability

This analytical tool was developed to help measure the motor speed of a person – those with a slow speed count could have neurological dysfunction or be at risk of some such condition. You simply open up the app, select which hand you're going to test, then place your palm flat on the iPad screen. When instructed, you tap your fingers, keeping your palm still, until the time has run out. While

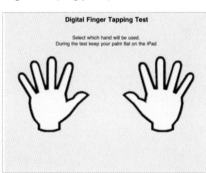
Digital Finger Tapping Test

Select which hand will be used.
During the test keep your palm flat on the iPad

this test was developed with illnesses in mind, no professional medical bodies have endorsed it. But even if you're not concerned about your health, it's a fun app that'll keep you and a friend amused.

■ You can choose the hand you want to test.

Overall Rating ★★★☆☆

Price: £34.99/$56.99 **Developer:** Potters Bar Eye Care Ltd

Vision Toolbox

A fabulous app for opticians and eye specialists

The Vision Toolbox aims to replace optician's charts and light boxes. With over 500 screens, the developer has re-created all the tests of the surgery with the simple slide-and-turn tech the iPad can offer. From near vision assessments such as the normal reading

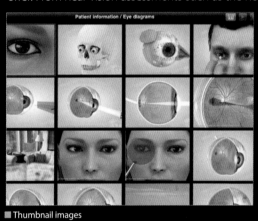
Patient information / Eye diagrams

distance and fixation targets to three-metre assessments like the single-letter charts and Children's visual acuity – there are many tests available.

■ Thumbnail images help you select the area to enter.

Overall Rating ★★★★★

Price: £8.99/$14.99 **Developer:** Theo Harisk

Human Anatomy
Structures

Find your way around the human body

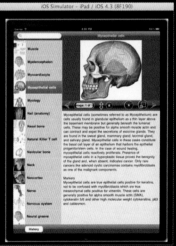

Whether you're studying human anatomy or are interested about what's happening in that body you inhabit, this could be the app for you. You can explore the regions of the brain, the bones of the skeleton and cell types. With a full search function from key word to related word you'll soon understand more about the body.

■ The text descriptions are easy to read.

Overall Rating ★★★★★

Price: £0.59/$0.99 **Developer:** Sagar Shah

Herbal Encyclopedia

Discover the plants for natural health benefits

Since the dawn of time, humans and animals have benefited from the medicinal qualities of plants. Historical texts and hieroglyphics have documented the procedure of turning petals, leaves and roots into tinctures and solutions to cure ailments. While some of these applications have been proven to have no health benefit, some plants are valuable. This app lists the plants that have a recognised medical use, and each entry has a photo, its common and scientific name and description of how it's used.

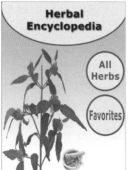

■ Detailed photos accompany the informative text.

Overall Rating ★★★☆☆

Price: £1.19/$1.99 **Developer:** Linda Burke

dad2b quiz

A frivolous and easy quiz for dads-to-be

This app is aimed at the first time dad who really doesn't have a clue what's going on. Presented with an air of fun, the quiz tests things such as the best time to plan your route to hospital, rather than giving you any solid and useful information. Far from being an educational app, this is more of a fun one. If you can't answer more than 80 per cent of the quiz questions you should be ashamed of yourself.

■ Some of the questions are far too easy.

Overall Rating ★★☆☆☆

Price: £1.19/$1.99 **Developer:** Dee Zee

Camping Recipes HD

Eat well in the great outdoors

The draw of sleeping under the stars in the great outdoors has taken a sudden rise in popularity over the past couple of years. Although you may trade some of life's luxuries, there's no need to scrimp on the culinary side of things. The recipes here, most American in origin, are created to be cooked on everything from a campfire to a campervan oven. You'll soon have all of the other campers green with envy.

■ You can share your favourite recipes via social networks.

Overall Rating ★★★★★

Price: £11.99/$19.99 **Developer:** Theo Harisk

3D Medical Animations HD – Vol 1

View the human body in animated videos

Static images and wordy descriptions are fine for some, but if you want a real understanding of how the human body works – from the various movements of joints to full animations of how the heart pumps the blood – check out this app. Biology and medical students especially will benefit from the 148 videos that are played at full screen size with voiceovers by experts.

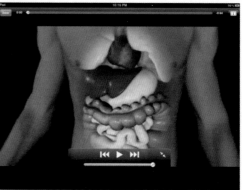

■ Some videos are best viewed before dinner.

Overall Rating ★★★★★

Price: £1.79/$2.99 **Developer:** fraga games Ltd

Ming's Memory

Release your stress with a matching ball game

At first glance this looks like it should be in the game category of the App Store. However, once you've been immersed in Ming's Memory's world for a while, you'll begin to notice that you feel more relaxed. The soothing tunes and subtle backgrounds almost

entice you into a meditative state, and you can feel the stresses from the day flow from your body.

Like all the best stress relievers, the premise is simple: match pairs of the floating yin/yang balls that are constantly moving. If you use it on the commute home from work we guarantee that you'll start your evening in a better frame of mind.

■ Calming backgrounds and sounds help to soothe.

Overall Rating ★★★★★

Price: £1.19/$1.99 **Developer:** ololac Interactive

eFitness Shoulder Workout

Learn more about the tops of your arms

The shoulder is an often-neglected part of the body. We tend to concentrate on having firm thighs, a flat stomach and eliminating those bingo wings; however, looking after your shoulders is,

according to this app, very important. And when you think about it, they do go through a lot each day, from lifting up the kids to carrying shopping. Here you can learn how to improve

the joint flexibility and tone the areas around them for added strength.

■ Workout routines are set for all levels.

Overall Rating ★★★★★

Price: £1.19/$1.99 **Developer:** Dee Zee

Healthy Tips For A Healthy Lifestyle

A healthy body means a healthy mind

Let's face it, we could all do with being a bit healthier. We know what we need to do to keep our bodies and minds healthy, but staying power is where we let ourselves down. However, this app will arm you with more information and some tips that can be incorporated into your life. Discover how to

increase your metabolism, how to eat good meals, and how a break from your desk each day will help keep your heart healthy.

■ Share your favourite tips via Facebook.

Overall Rating ★★★★★

Price: £2.99/$5.99 **Developer:** JX Mobile LLC

Pilates for iPad

Exercise techniques from an expert

Although the fitness and body toning technique of Pilates has been around since it was developed in Germany in 1880, it's only over the last decade that it has become popular. As it's one of the most popular

classes at gyms and village halls, getting into a class that suits your

timetable can be quite tricky. So this app which features exclusive movies that have been narrated and performed by a professional

instructor is perfect as you can practise the technique when every you have your iPad in a spot with a Wi-Fi connection.

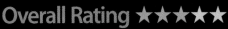

■ Follow the step-by-step instructions for each move.

Overall Rating ★★★★★

Price: £1.19/$1.99 **Developer:** Taconic System LLC

Blood Pressure Monitor – Family Pro for iPad

If you lead a stressful life coupled with a bad diet, you'll know that you're a prime candidate for high blood pressure. If you have your own blood pressure monitor and check yourself daily, enter the results into this app and it'll track your daily measurement, plotting the results on graphs so that you can see what causes spikes and dips.

Rating ★★★☆☆

Price: Free **Developer:** Puttenham Ltd

Be Confident in 7 Days with Tony Wrighton HD Lite

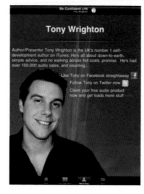

Using visual and audio technology, this seven-day confidence program will help you start to make the changes to you life to build a better you. Whether you're skeptical or not, give it a go, if anything the daily affirmations and confidence boosting statements made us feel slightly happier.

Rating ★★★☆☆

Price: Free **Developer:** Lloydspharmacy Ltd

Lloydspharmacy Diabetes Check-up

Diabetes is a disease that is becoming more prevalent in our population. Some of it is due to obesity but other factors such as age contribute too. This app calculates the possibility of you developing the disease via a series of questions. The result of your risk levels is given instantly, and if you're high risk it's reassuring to know that the come cases can be reversed. You're also given tips on how to maintain a healthy lifestyle and reduce the risks.

Rating ★★★★☆

Price: £0.59/$0.99 **Developer:** Prakrut Mehta

Pediatrics Glossary

Although essentially just little people, there is a huge gulf in the medical application given to youngsters than is given to adults. Pediatrics is a specialised discipline of medicine that comes with its own terminology and practises. Whether you're a med student just needing a quick heads up, or a hospital drama junkie, you'll find something interesting here.

Rating ★★★★☆

Price: £5.99/$11.99 **Developer:** Licitelco

Miniatlas Allergy

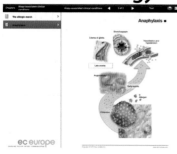

Whether pollens, foodstuffs or chemicals affect you, the effects of an allergy can be debilitating from itchy eyes, swollen tissue and, in extreme cases, death. This app aims to provide the sufferer and physician with detailed text descriptions and annotated illustrations that relate to the effects. A little text heavy in places, but an otherwise decent app.

Rating ★★★★☆

Price: £3.99/$7.99 **Developer:** Licitelco S.L.

Miniatlas Gastroenterology

Where does your food go after you've swallowed it? And what happens as it goes through the process of digestion? This app maps the human's entire intestinal system from how it prepares food for absorption, to the breakdown of waste matter into stools. This in-depth tool is packed full of annotated images and detailed explanations covering diseases, anatomy and pathology. It's great for medical students as well as practitioners.

Rating ★★★★★

Price: £0.59/$0.99 **Developer:** Cygnet Infotech

Opt Eyecheck for iPad

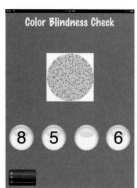

Using a range of typical ophthalmic tests such as the Snellen Chart (random letters in decreasing sizes), the Ishihara Colour Test and the Amsler Grid check, you can determine how good your eyesight is. The only danger is that you could diagnose yourself with a serious problem that doesn't exist, or miss something completely. While fun, you really should see an optical professional on a regular basis.

Rating ★★★☆☆

Price: Free **Developer:** David Tessitore

Back Pain Nerve Chart

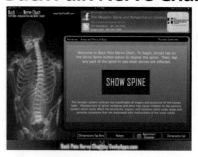

Through stunning graphics and informative text this app will help you to understand the structure of the spine and the nerves it controls. Although it's aimed at chiropractors, so that they can show the spinal structure to patients, along with an appointments diary, everyone can benefit from browsing this interesting free app.

Rating ★★★★☆

Meditation Karma

Price: Free Developer: The App Ranch Inc

Whether you need to escape the bustle of everyday life, calm down after a frantic day or just want to centre yourself and find inner peace, meditation will help you to focus on the finer things in life. *Meditation Karma* offers you tools to control your breathing and help you feel rejuvenated. This app comes packed with options to help you relax.

Rating ★★★☆☆

Anatomy & Fun Facts

Price: £1.19/$1.99 Developer: Brockle Tech Corp

We all like to store useless snippets of information in our head. Sometimes to break the ice at parties, sometimes to show off that you know the answer on a quiz show or even just to impress your friends. Here over 20,000 random facts and quotes covering the subject of the anatomy and sex from the mouths of famous people and books have been collected together. Open up the app on a boring commute, or tap in each day to learn a new fact. It's more fun that functional.

Rating ★★★☆☆

Diet Shakes – For fat burning & weight loss that builds lean muscle

Price: Free Developer: Our 3 Wishes

So all we need to lose weight is to drink a milkshake? Really? Pass the blender! Here's a collection of over 150 recipes that have been designed to target different health issues. Whether you want to lose weight, maintain your shape or build muscle, there are shakes here for you.

Rating ★★★★☆

Anatomy 3D: Organs

Price: £3.99/$7.99 Developer: Real Bodywork

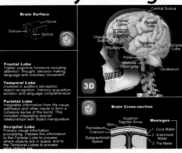

This is a beautifully presented app that is perfect for anyone who has a casual interest in the human body and its functions. There are 26 3D models of human organs, 24 audio lectures giving detailed descriptions of the functions and structures of the organ plus five videos showing an organ in action. Perhaps too vague for students but great for everyone else.

Rating ★★★★☆

Human Anatomy Dictionary for iPad

Price: £5.19/$11.99 Developer: Theo Harisk

Medical students and professionals can now forget heavy, dusty books that have crumbling spines and torn, stained pages. The iPad version of the *Human Anatomy Dictionary* is all you need to look up over 6,000 functions of the human body. If you're in a hurry the fantastic full text or header only search options will take you directly to the entry you want.

Rating ★★★★★

Find your way around the human genome.

Price: Free Developer: The Children's Hospital of Philadelphia

For those who want to take a look at more advanced medicine, this app gets to the root of the human genome. Viewing it is a pleasure as it is very intuitive and has an almost 'Google Maps' feel to the navigation system. Take a look at genome annotation tracks, zoom in, out and across a chromosome and even download the email information that is of interest. This app is very in-depth and great tool for studying medicine.

Rating ★★★★☆

Army First Aid

Price: £1.19/$1.99 Developer: Double Dog Studios

This app literally takes the US Army's guide to First Aid and puts it onto the iPad. These are the tips given to the soldiers for use in emergency situations on the ground, and the app is essentially just an eBook version. The guide offers clear advice with simple illustrations where needed and you can bookmark useful pages or skip through the chapters with relative ease. We presented and packed with advice, this is definitely a worthwhile app, it's just a little too expensive for what it is. Recommended, but it's not for everyone.

Rating ★★★☆☆

Period Pace

Price: Free Developer: Aesop LLC

Now you don't need to keep track of your period in your diary, then spend time counting through the weeks to see if you'll be on during your holiday. This app lets you input the details of your menstrual cycle, allowing you to record the date it begins along with other factors such as cramping and spotting. The in-built calendars will then plot dates for you.

Rating ★★★★☆

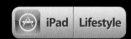
Lifestyle

Your iPad, your rules. There are so many apps available to fit into your lifestyle and even make the daily rigours of life, such as shopping, less stressful that you would be mad not to take a moment to browse through what's available. Here are just a few examples of what your iPad can do for you.

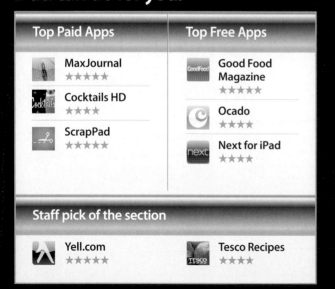

Top Paid Apps		Top Free Apps	
MaxJournal ★★★★★		Good Food Magazine ★★★★★	
Cocktails HD ★★★★		Ocado ★★★★	
ScrapPad ★★★★★		Next for iPad ★★★★	

Staff pick of the section

Yell.com ★★★★★		Tesco Recipes ★★★★

■ The app itself is free but this is essentially only a portal through which to view individual copies of the magazine, which you will need to pay money for.

Price: Free   **Developer:** BBC Worldwide Ltd

Good Food Magazine

How to bring a print magazine to iPad and do it well

 The BBC is renowned for its food programmes. Complementing the on-screen cookery masterclass is the brilliant *Good Food Magazine*. Within the pages, you'll find seasonal recipes, hints and tips from top cookery writers, fantastic features, dream kitchens, and all the latest must-have gadgets.

Now, the BBC has brought the *Good Food Magazine* to the iPad. Here, each issue displays all its glorious photography and mouth-watering recipes on a platform that does it justice.

So, what's to like? Firstly, the layout: it starts off like a conventional magazine, but touch the bottom of the screen, and you can view each spread as a thumbnail. Tap on one, and it springs up to full screen. If you're not sure what you want to cook, the filter on the contents spread will allow you to narrow recipes down into certain categories.

There's more to each page, though. We like the tools spread here; tap the image you want to read about, and the text relating to it appears to the side. Each recipe front image has a flip button that reveals the ingredients and cooking instructions. Tap the little 'i' icon, and a box will appear telling your more about a certain ingredient. It's just brilliant.

Rating ★★★★★

Price: Free   Developer: TouchShopping Inc

Amazon TouchShopping

Why swipe your card when a finger will do?

We're assuming that the developers of *TouchShopping* aren't big fans of the way Amazon appears on the iPad. The *TouchShopping* app is their answer, a custom-built user interface that does away with all the white space and numerous menus of the world's most popular online retailer, all in an effort to offer iPad owners a more intuitive and visually-enticing online retail experience. It's an idea we could see utilising a touch-screen interface and the extra screen real-estate missing from other mobile devices.

In practice however, *TouchShopping* represents a backwards step in terms of interfacing with Amazon, mainly due to the sluggish loading times, ugly design choices and superfluous features. The app groups products by the same categories as on Amazon – such as books, music, DVDs & Blu-rays – but the majority of the website's functionality is lost in translation.

Displayed simply on a rather familiar-looking grid, products can be browsed, clicked on for more details, dragged to a memo pad, or added to your basket, but product information is lacking, and things like wishlists, recommended items and account history haven't made the cut. The lack of the additional options that are present on the website is frustrating.

Trying to make the gateway to Amazon a little less like an

e-commerce site and more like a regular retail experience is undoubtedly a commendable enterprise, but bells and whistles aside, *TouchShopping* fails in its admittedly tricky remit. A misguided attempt to improve upon an interface which is already a hit with millions of customers worldwide. At last the developer is trying to innovate, but the results here are well wide of the mark in terms of what the consumers want.

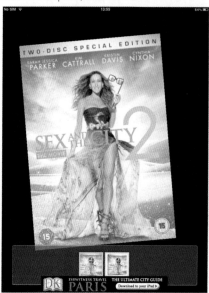

■ You can rotate or enlarge book or DVD covers and move them around at will.

Rating ★ ★ ☆ ☆ ☆

■ The search functionality is hampered by the way in which the results are displayed.

■ The app goes a little overboard with some of its menus, which end up taking up most of the screen…

Price: £1.79/$2.99 **Developer:** Omaxmedia

MaxJournal

This app lets you transform your iPad into an elegant daily journal

Diary apps tend to fall into two categories – there's the personal assistant style of app that organizes your appointments and schedules. Then there's the more relaxed type, based around the kind of journal in which some of us like to record the ins and outs of our day at its close, preferably with a nice hot drink and a curled-up pet snoozing somewhere nearby.

MaxJournal definitely falls into this second category, the design revolving around a virtual large-format journal of the type that can be found in expensive stationery shops. This instantly imbues it with an air of quality, oozing the sort of luxurious finger-appeal which makes it a pleasure to use.

The main interface consists of a large central page area with a dateline across the top which is also used for accessing the year and the month. Accompanying this is a set of small tabs down the left-hand side, each of which bears a date. When tapped, each tab brings up a whole page that corresponds to that day, ready to be filled with your thoughts and accounts of your exploits.

A cluster of buttons found on the upper right of the screen handles features such as: the comprehensive Export and Backup options, a search feature that can target specific words within your entries, the online help system and the font. Also handy is password protection setting where you can protect your thoughts from nosey family. Photos and tags can be added, scrapbook style, in a panel on the right of the screen, and a large 'Today' button rounds things off, allowing you to zip right to the current day's page with a single touch.

Tap a page and it zooms instantly to fill the iPad's screen, tap once more and up pops the keyboard ready to make an entry. There is a choice of 16 different fonts of variable size, old favourites such as Helvetica and Marker Felt Wide being joined by more esoteric choices like Journal and Kayleigh, which lend a more handwritten feel to jottings.

Other than changing the size and font however, there seem to be no other text style formatting options available, a shame as it would be nice to be able to use Bold and Italic styles for extra expressive entries. Overall, *MaxJournal* is one of the best of this type of app that we've seen and it should definitely be considered at the relatively low price.

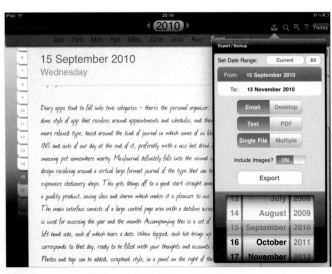

■ The main interface is uncluttered and efficient, getting you to your entries quickly.

Rating ★★★★★

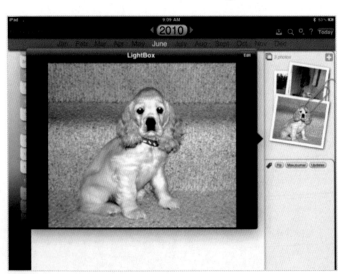

■ Excellent export and backup options include a variable date range.

■ Each entry in your journal can be accompanied by up to three photos…

You can add your best buys to a handy in-app favourites list.

With this app you can buy what you want online and wait for it to be delivered.

Price: Free **Developer:** Ocado Ltd

Ocado

Avoid the queues with this mobile supermarket

 Ocado is a UK-based online grocery retailer, which offers customers thousands of food and drink products – plus many other items – for delivery via its website and, more recently, this self-developed app. After registering at www.ocado.com (as well as checking your area is served), the app enables users to shop on the move, offering the full inventory available on the site. The smart decision to store the 22,000 offered products within the app – periodical catalogue updates actually add around another 100Mb to the app – rather than simply making it a portal to Ocado's site makes for a smooth browsing experience and enables you to drop products into your basket regardless of wireless connection.

Other features include the jotter, where you can write down and search for items, and the ability to add favourite products and browse your order history. There's also a shopping list section, but lists require creation on ocado.com, and can't yet be edited in the app itself. Internet shoppers will find the app intuitive enough, and the ability to shop on the move should attract newcomers.

Rating ★★★★☆

Hopefully you'll all have some high scoring months ahead.

The app allows you to access what is right and wrong in your life.

Price: £0.59/$0.99 **Developer:** Webdunia.com

Rate Your Life

The app to ensure you need never remember things again

 It's not often that when you review an app, you also get to review your life too; well, according to *Rate Your Life*, our lives are a mix of good and bad. If you, oddly, need an app to tell you this, Rate Your Life is a functional way to document your days.

The app lets you leave comments and notes about your experiences or feelings on each date, along with a rating from Excellent to Disaster. It then gives you verdicts and graphs about how your week, month and year have been. Using simple, touchscreen controls, you can scroll between graphs by swiping left or right, and touch the ratings at the top to make your decision. You can also set a password to keep out peeping eyes, but that's as far as the customisation goes. You wouldn't be chastised for thinking this journal-style app would be aimed at the teen market, but with its formal, functional backgrounds and graphs, this doesn't seem to be the audience it's targeting. For adults, then, there's nothing major to fault with this simple app, but it's visually unengaging and basic in its functions.

Rating ★★★☆☆

Price: £0.59/$0.99 **Developer:** El-Hitamy I&T

Tappy Memories

A time capsule you can always keep on you

Tappy Memories is a potentially clever little app that's let down by several annoying oversights. Upon entering the app, you'll be presented with a variety of questions, ranging from your most memorable trip as a child to where you spent your summer holidays. Once a question is selected, you can either type or record your answer – using your iPad's built-in microphone – and keep it safe for future generations to enjoy (and yes, we're positive Apple will have some compatible device in 30 years' time).

Presentation is admittedly simplistic, but the biggest issue is that you can't actually create new entries for different people, or record multiple answers for the same question. There's potential to make an excellent time capsule app that will store the thoughts and anecdotes of all your friends and family. Sadly, this isn't quite it.

■ There are a few great ideas in Tappy Memories, but they're spoiled by its limitations.

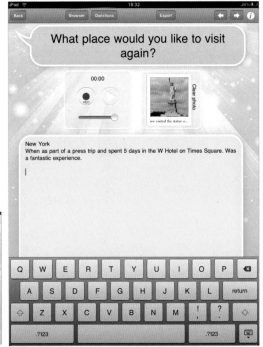

Rating ★★☆☆☆

Price: £2.99/$4.99 **Developer:** Pocket Cocktails

Cocktails HD

Tom Cruise will have nothing on you after you buy this app

■ There are many, many cocktails to choose from, all with step-by-step instructions.

■ You can now put a recipe to all those stupid cocktail names.

Don't know your Bloody Bulls from your Bloody Marys? Thought a Manhattan was somewhere in New York? Then this is the app for you, as it will turn you into a master cocktail expert quicker than you can say 'Tom Cruise'.

Cocktails HD at its most basic is a guide to making cocktails. And yet, thanks to fantastic presentation, easy-to-learn steps and stunning images, it becomes a completely unmissable app that any cocktail connoisseur will not want to ever be without.

Cocktails are split into eight distinct categories, ranging from Shooters to Martinis, and come with full instructions for making them, along with the required ingredients. If that's not enough there are also handy guides that explain everything from correctly shaking your chosen drinks to even how to correctly serve wine and beer. While there's nothing here that's not easily available on the internet, it's all put together with so much care and attention and the drinks look so mouth-watering that you'll always want to keep it handy in order to try out your latest tipple.

Rating ★★★★☆

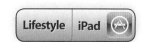

Price: £1.99/$2.99 **Developer:** Belinda Recio

In Your Dreams

Forget Inception, this is from which dreams are made

■ It's not as in-depth as a professional psychiatrist, but it's a damn sight cheaper.

■ You get a fair amount of dream-related content for the price.

Many a time, you'll doubtless have experienced an acquaintance's need to wax lyrical about last evening's festivities. Rather than some drunken tale of woe, we're focusing here on the contents of their dreams and the significance such bizarre imagery may hold for the rest of their working lives. While most of us lack the financial clout to employ a professional psychiatrist, this app provides a handy (and cheaper) alternative. Offering users the chance to keep organised dream diaries, as well as including many definitions of common themes, there's certainly potential value here.

Divided into a number of sections, the app offers swift and ergonomic access to even the most odd of apparitions. Besides its diary feature that enables users to enter their thoughts via a text-based interface, there's also a nifty search function and various quick-start guides. Though the information contained herein will doubtless prove useful for those of a more active night-time mind, the app's journal feature could have allowed for easier navigation.

Rating ★★★☆☆

Price: Free **Developer:** Next Retail Ltd

Next For iPad

Fashion in the palm of your hand

This neat little app from Next makes shopping an act of consummate ease, plundering the internet to retrieve details from the company's own catalogue, before displaying the results in an ergonomic manner. Upon loading the app, a query will be sent to the company's servers, bringing back details of various clothing items.

These can then be directly searched via various categories. Those who are short on time can then make a purchase straight from the app, or consult a set of directions via Google Maps, pointing out where exactly the nearest Next branch can be found, and of course where said item is sold. Naturally, the interface is a joy to navigate, though some images come oddly formatted, having clearly been placed in a particular folder labelled 'title screen', without much thought for where the screen furniture might be placed.

■ The entire Next catalogue is available, and you can make purchases straight from the app.

■ The map feature is handy, as it tells you where your nearest Next is.

Rating ★★★★☆

Price: Free **Developer:** Yell Ltd

Yell.com
Why shout for help when you can Yell?

Forget calling all those ridiculous premium rate numbers and just use this all-in-one, all-round awesome app when you need to find what you need to find. Want to locate the nearest supermarket? No problem. Fancy a pizza? Crack out the tomato sauce. Stuck in a new place with no way home? Find the nearest taxi firm with a touch of a screen and flick of a finger.

The Yell.com app presents you with a search bar or a list of areas such as restaurants, cinemas and hotels for you to choose from. Using your current location, it finds the nearest results for your request and presents you with either a list including the distance, address and phone number or a map view of where they all are. You can add the number straight to your contact book or to your favourites, share it on Facebook, Twitter or by email and even call direct from the app. The map can be presented in satellite view as well and it will also plot a route for you.

Yell.com was quick to load, and at no cost, it's a fantastic addition to your essential app line-up. It seems that, in our digital age, the old-fashioned Yellow Pages directories can now be relegated to doorstops, as this has all the info on local businesses you need.

Rating ★★★★★

Price: £2.39/$3.99 **Developer:** Aloompa

Tabletopics HD
How exactly can conversations be more interactive?

Tabletopics – originally a card game to be played with friends – seeks to make conversations 'better' and 'more interactive'. Now it's been ported over to the iPad, bringing the card game from the dining room to the coffee table.

With the initial purchase, you'll have two packs – Starter Set and Happy Hour – each with a collection of 60 themed questions, intended to provoke interesting, entertaining and/or enlightening answers for you and your friends. There are no rules, and there is no failure; simply one question after another. How you decide to handle these questions is up to you. Each pack can be played in two ways: either by picking a card from the top, or choosing from six overturned cards. Alongside this is the option to hide unwanted questions so they won't appear, or mark favourites from the collection, including saving the most memorable responses.

Tabletopics HD does its job just fine. But the price isn't worth what is essentially a handful of questions. However, it is a great idea for those who like a good get-together.

Rating ★★★★★

Drag businesses into your route to plan a shopping trip, night out, whatever!

All the information you need, at your fingertips

■ The app contains all of the information on local businesses that you could ever need.

■ Handy maps show you exactly where you need to go.

■ This app is a good ice-breaker for get-togethers…

■ Each pack comes with a stack of 60 questions.

Price: £2.99/$4.99 **Developer:** Album tart LLC

ScrapPad

Due the sheer scale of this app, we're glad that it's for iPad use only. A massive chunk of memory gets you an app that's easy to use, as well as 12 themed kits that are packed with loads of elements (950 in total), so you'll never make the same page twice. The controls are so simple a child could use it – perfect for keeping them entertained on long car journeys.

Rating ★★★★★

Price: £2.99/$4.99 **Developer:** Invent Software

ScrapApp

This app offers you simple controls and intuitive options that will have you creating scrapbook pages in no time. The advance photo editing that allows you to crop and zoom, add borders and create effects such as black and white is a welcome idea, while the precise colour palette ensures your scrapbook has that professional touch.

Rating ★★★★★

Price: £0.59/$0.99 **Developer:** Boram Kim

Interior Bible HD

When faced with a blank canvas of a room, knowing where to start and how to execute a specific style can be somewhat daunting. The *Interior Bible HD* is an iPad-only app packed full of stunning images that will give you inspiration for any room in the house; there's even a section for the garden. So if you're not sure whether a certain colour scheme will work for you, check out how it's been done in one of the virtual show houses. The only downside is that there's no indication of where to purchase some of the show-stopping pieces.

Rating ★★★☆☆

Price: Free **Developer:** ACP Magazines

Shop Til You Drop

Shop Til You Drop, an Australian women's magazine, is now available for iPad, but will struggle to win over new readers without so much as a taste of the publication in this free app. Owners are expected to take a punt on each issue to the tune of £2.99/$4.99 via an in-app purchase, rather than pay up front for the app and get the latest issue free. It seems like something of a backwards step as many apps of this nature give you a taster to see if you wish to try before you buy, but this particular publication is obviously confident that it is something special.

Rating ★★☆☆☆

Best Of French Cuisine

Price: £1.19/$1.99 **Developer:** Sucré Salé

If you've ever wanted to try your hand at French cuisine then you'll find this app incredibly beneficial. There are 101 recipes covering starters, main dishes and desserts and they all come with easy to follow instructions and mouth-watering pictures. You can add the ingredients of whatever you fancy making to a shopping list and there's a glossary to explain the terminology.

Rating ★★★☆☆

Cookineo: Recipes

Price: Free **Developer:** Dornolib

More French cooking, but this one really benefits from being on the iPad. While it only features 25 recipes, an additional 75 are available for just £1.19 and the presentation is superb. Sliders can be used to adjust for the number of people you're cooking for (which adjusts ingredient amounts) while huge pictures show each step. It's even possible to share recipes on Facebook. Although there isn't much choice, the additional asking price is a small cost to pay for such a beautifully presented app. While there aren't many recipes, the presentation is very good.

Rating ★★★★☆

Price: Free **Developer:** Tesco Plc

Tesco Recipes

If you loathe trawling around your local supermarket, then *Tesco Recipes* is about to save you a lot of hassle. There are two ways of utilising this app, either by purchasing food through the Shop section, or by browsing the thousands of recipes, instantly adding ingredients into your basket. It's an easy-to-use app that can cut your 'big shop' time in half.

Rating ★★★★☆

Price: Free **Developer:** Architectural Digest

AD Amazing Kitchens

Architectural Digest brings us inspiration for kitchen design. Scroll through designs with a swipe of a finger, and click on the 'i' button to gain extra information. There are 50 kitchens displayed, as well as products to browse. The app also uses your current location to point you in the direction of your closest dealer. Great for providing kitchen inspiration.

Rating ★★★☆☆

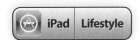

Price: Free **Developer:** QR Code City

Scan

QR codes are messages hidden within a cryptic image that only a specific QR program can read. There's plenty of readers available to download, but none are as simple or basic as *Scan*. It loads instantly, and scanning a QR code takes a matter of seconds, revealing the hidden message or URL on a plain white screen. It's a nice, simple app but lacking features. With the appeal of QR codes, we suspect, limited, there isn't a great deal of enjoyment to derive from this app beyond the initial novelty factor. A cool toy for your iPad 2, though…

Rating ★★★☆☆

Price: £2.99/$4.99 **Developer:** Publications Int

iCookbook

There are plenty of recipe apps in the App Store, but most of them are lacking in something. *iCookbook* may be a little more expensive, but it offers a hell of a lot for your cash. It features 2,000 recipes that are easy to make and suitable for a variety of tastes. It has voice command so you don't have to touch the iPad while cooking, a notes option, a 'spin' section that picks out recipes depending on your criteria, shopping lists, timers and more. This is brand-supported, which may deter some, but this really is the complete food package.

Rating ★★★★☆

Price: £0.59/$0.99 **Developer:** Chase The Moose

The Total Network

THE NETWORK

Safari on iPad helps out users a lot by being able to open up multiple pages, but it can be a bit of a pain to have to switch back and forth between them. *The Total Network*, however, allows you to view three pages on the screen at the exact same time. Now you can be checking Twitter, Facebook and doing a Google search, for example, all at once.

Rating ★★★☆☆

Price: Free **Developer:** Rakugaki Inc

Enjoy Japanese Origami

This app is designed to coach you through this pasttime using step-by-step moving images. You can set the app to autoplay, or manually move through each section. You get six free examples, with more available through in-app purchases, and it also connects you to Twitter and Facebook posts about Origami. There's even an option to Tweet a photo.

Rating ★★★☆☆

Price: £5.99/$9.99 **Developer:** L Li

Creativity Brainwave

Claiming to increase your creativity within minutes, *Creativity Brainwave* includes two professionally designed isochronic sessions – with a further two available to purchase in-app – made up of soothing tones and hypnotic patterns to help increase relaxation and relieve thought pattern blockages. It also offers a number of useful tips on how to relieve stress and is well-presented. The only possible downside is the price. But if you fork out then the app will immediately make you feel better about doing so.

Rating ★★★☆☆

Price: £0.59/$0.99 **Developer:** Jordan Eccles

iBrain Choosinator

This app is one that you and your friends will enjoy messing around on for a few minutes, but otherwise you'll quickly lose interest, and the bland text-based style certainly doesn't help. Basically, you can assign rankings to people (either the in-built celebrity names or your own additions) based on how well you think they'd perform in a particular category, such as in a 'Zombie Apocalypse'. You can create your own categories but, after a few minutes, will you really want to? It's not terrible by any means, but chances are that you'll get bored very quickly.

Rating ★★☆☆☆

Price: Free **Developer:** Amazon Eurasia Holdings Sarl

Windowshop

Brought to your iPad by Amazon, *Windowshop* offers an alternative way to browse and shop the virtual shelves of the world's biggest online retailer. Amazon's massive range of product categories, from books and DVDs to electronics, clothing, home improvement and more are placed within easy reach beneath your fingertips.

Rating ★★★★☆

Price: Free **Developer:** Cooliris Inc

Discover

Taking a fresh approach to exploring the extensive and ever-growing Wikipedia database, the *Discover* app presents Wikipedia articles in the format of a digital glossy magazine. Enter your search keywords, and relevant articles will be displayed in an eye-catching and easy-to-read style, or simply shake the iPad in order to generate a new cover. It's a novel approach to repurposing the somewhat sterile content of Wikipedia and well worth checking out if you are partial to a bit of impromptu fact-finding.

Rating ★★★★☆

Price: Free **Developer:** Nikolaj Schumacher
ShopShop Shopping List

A simple shopping list app that helps to take the hassle out of the weekly trip to the supermarket. Add a description and number of wanted items and tick them off as you go around the shop. You can have multiple lists for different shops and change the font size to accommodate larger or smaller lists. Its simplicity is its real strength.

Rating ★★★★☆

Price: Free **Developer:** Luke Campbell
Calculator XL

The large screen interface clearly put Apple off simply porting the iPhone calculator across to the iPad. Fear not, however, as *Calculator XL* fills the gap nicely. Use it in either landscape or portrait mode and it will do all of your complex calculations with ease. Obviously there are loads of apps like this available but this works well and costs nothing.

Rating ★★★★☆

Price: £0.59/$0.99 **Developer:** Peter Breitling
Clinometer

Some of the best iPad apps utilise its built-in technology for maximum effect. *Clinometer* is one such app: it makes the most of the built-in accelerometer to give you an angle finder – turning your iPad into a high-tech spirit level. It's probably utterly useless for the vast majority of people, but it shows off one of the best features of the iPad.

Rating ★★★★☆

Price: Free **Developer:** Joakim Anderson
Timer for Cooking

There's already a simple countdown timer on the iPad, but if you prefer the look of an old analogue timer for your culinary exploits then *Timer for Cooking* should suit you. As well as a traditional countdown timer animation, it features a selection of other styles to make sure that your cooking is never overdone. It's also free, which helps things greatly.

Rating ★★★★☆

Price: Free **Developer:** Truphone
Truphone for iPad

Now you can make phone calls from your iPad with Truphone. Simply sign up for an account and add some credit and you'll be calling any number you want directly from the iPad. Calls from Truphone to Truphone users are free, too. You can use a standard iPhone headset to make the experience even better. This just adds another function to your bit o' kit.

Rating ★★★☆☆

Price: Free **Developer:** Ender Labs
EventBoard

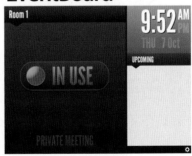

An automatically managed room-scheduling display that uses the free Google calendar tools. Simply log into your account and all events are listed in *EventBoard* already. To create rooms, make a new calendar and make it public or keep it private. It's a really great alternative to expensive meeting room scheduling and management software and it is incredible easy to use.

Rating ★★★☆☆

Price: Free **Developer:** Santiago Lema
Battery Free HD

The battery meter on the iPad is a fairly simple affair and it can be difficult to work out what exactly 67% means. *Battery Free HD* shows you the time remaining on your iPad, but also lets you know how many hours and minutes that equates to. It shows music playback, video playback and browsing time left, as well as total standby time remaining.

Rating ★★★★☆

Price: £2.99/$4.99 **Developer:** Garret Murray
Ego for iPad

Are you obsessed by your Twitter follower count or how many hits your website is getting? *Ego for iPad* will let you know instantaneously what the numbers that matter to you are. If you have Google Analytics set up, it can also pull in the information stored there for an even more detailed analysis of your popularity. Handy for those with an eye on the traffic.

Rating ★★★☆☆

Price: £1.79/$2.99
Developer: MERI Media

POST Gravity

POST Gravity is a selection of videos and information presented on the iPad in a visually attractive and impressive style. Included are short films, such as one shot on the International Space Station, for your perusal. Not bad overall.

Overall Rating ★★★☆☆

Price: Free
Developer: Rolls-Royce Motor Cars Limited

Rolls-Royce Phantom

This app gives you some neat interior and exterior views of the Rolls-Royce Phantom. If you're a fan of Rolls-Royce or just cars in general then give it a download and have a browse around the luscious vehicle. You can even create your own custom cars to store and share.

Overall Rating ★★★☆☆

Price: £0.59/$0.99
Developer: mob4.com

Recipe Pro for iPad

Recipe Pro brings a large selection of recipes to the iPad, each voted on by the users. While the number of recipes on offer was impressive, the whole thing was just a little too average to really stand out from the crowd. There's better out there.

Overall Rating ★★★☆☆

Price: £0.59/$0.99
Developer: Perception System

Chinese Food PRO

A decent array of Chinese recipes are on offer here, with instructions on how to make each meal. The best feature is the ability to add your own and rate or comment on other peoples' creations. It's not quite the Facebook of Chinese food, but it's almost there.

Overall Rating ★★★★☆

Price: £1.79/$2.99
Developer: Castle Builders (IL)

Kung Fu Panda 2 Cookbook

This is a fun idea for an app, especially for kids. It features a ton of child-friendly recipes complete with clips and animations from the popular *Kung Fu Panda* movies. With the addition of a read-out-loud function, this is great.

Overall Rating ★★★★☆

Price: Free
Developer: Condé Nast Digital Britain

British Vogue

If you're a fan of *Vogue* magazine and have more than a passing interest in the world of fashion and the latest trends, then you might want to check this virtual magazine out. Some attractive presentation and detailed information make it a worthy download.

Overall Rating ★★★☆☆

Price: £0.59/$0.99
Developer: Panorama Concepts

Magic Screen Montage – DIY App Skins Home Screen

If you want a selection of images to use as backgrounds on your iPad then try this. It comes with an impressive array images at a price.

Overall Rating ★★★☆☆

Price: Free
Developer: PressPlane Inc.

Zapd

With *Zapd* you can easily make basic websites in minutes. The app lets you add photos, text and other features, in addition to providing some fairly in-depth but simple editing tools. Although sceptical at first we were soon very impressed.

Overall Rating ★★★★☆

Price: £0.59/$0.99
Developer: Genesan Kim

Stay Awake!

This is certainly a unique app. Basically, it sends you notifications at certain times to 'stimulate' you and keep you awake. It might work for some people, although it didn't for us. If you're that desperate to stay awake then maybe, just maybe, give it a try.

Overall Rating ★★☆☆☆

Price: £4.99/$7.99
Developer: Time Home Entertainment Inc

Southern Living Big Book of BBQ itunes

Based on a book known as the Big Book of BBQ from Southern Living magazine, this app features a variety of BBQ tips, recipes and suggestions for casual and experienced cooks. You can also play useful audio phrases.

Overall Rating ★★★★☆

Price: £3.99/$6.99
Developer: HuddleTech

Jamie Magazine by Jamie Oliver

This app is for those casual and hardened cooks who can't get enough of all things Jamie Oliver. Included is an impressive array of recipes from Jamie and other chefs, with detailed instructions for each.

Overall Rating ★★★★☆

Price: £1.79/$2.99
Developer: Jingaz

Stress Buster HD – Exercises and Techniques

This app provides you with a variety of facts and information to help beat stress and ultimately become more relaxed. It works well too.

Overall Rating ★★★★☆

Price: £0.59/$0.99
Developer: Matt Facer

Cookit – cooking meal timer

If you are cooking a large meal with a variety of ingredients that will be ready at different times then this is a great app. You can set individual cooking times for each thing, and a pop-up notification let's you know when it's ready.

Overall Rating ★★★☆☆

Price: £1.19/$1.99
Developer: Bright Light Apps

Spanish Phrases for English Travellers

If you're thinking of trying to learn Spanish then you might want to give this a try, although there's much better apps out there. You're presented with translated phrases in a bland and boring style, with no tutorials or tips.

Overall Rating ★★☆☆☆

Price: £0.59/$0.99
Developer: Dirk Bost

My Scrap Life

My Scrap Life is a fun and interesting way to make a scrap book with no hidden charges and a ton of features packed in. It's brightly coloured and there's loads of ways to design each page of your scrap book. Very impressive and cheap at the price.

Overall Rating ★★★★☆

Price: Free
Developer: Condé Nast Digital Britain

WIRED Magazine

The popular *WIRED* magazine makes its way to the iPad. It's free for print subscribers, and the app includes additional interactivity not on offer with the printed magazine. It's well put together and easy to read. An excellent all round package and a good showcase for your iPad.

Overall Rating ★★★★☆

Price: £1.79/$2.99
Developer: Halcyon Creations LC

Metropolis!

In *Metropolis!* You're presented with some stunning imagery of various cities from around the world. The quality of some of the pictures is breathtaking, and while you can probably find similar photos elsewhere for free, it's a nice collection to have on your iPad.

Overall Rating ★★★☆☆

Price: £0.59/$0.99
Developer: Callaway Digital Arts, Inc

Martha Stewart Cocktails

This app provides detailed instruction on how to make a variety of Martha's best cocktails, including how-to videos. Unfortunately, there's only 20 cocktail recipes on offer with the app, and if you want more you have to pay extra.

Overall Rating ★★★☆☆

Price: £1.19/$1.99
Developer: Kurt Schuster

QuoteMail

Don't. Buy. This. App. Seriously. This is, quite frankly, a terrible idea an app. *QuoteMail* gives you the opportunity to read inspirational messages and share them with others. In reality it's all utter tosh. We couldn't recommend this to anyone, especially at this price.

Overall Rating ★☆☆☆☆

Price: Free
Developer: Padopolic Inc.

Catalog Spree

If you're the sort of person that loves store catalogues then you'll love this app. Featuring the latest issues from many stores (although not that many well known ones), you can scroll through and shop from the catalogues with ease. Not too shabby.

Overall Rating ★★★☆☆

Price: £1.19/$1.99
Developer: JI Software Company

My Daily Journal

If you're the sort of person that keeps a regular journal and you want a nice, easy and simple way to record your thoughts then consider picking up *My Daily Journal*. Simple editing tools and a variety of features – including adding photos – make this worthwhile.

Overall Rating ★★★★☆

Price: £1.19/$1.99
Developer: Ultiapp, LLC

Ultimate Groupon

If you use Groupon a lot this app is the perfect way to sort and manage through the various offers. It shows you where and when offers are valid with detailed information on each one. It's handy and useful, so if you like your offers then you'll get a lot of use out of this.

Overall Rating ★★★★☆

Price: Free
Developer: Montblanc International

Montblanc – The Art of Writing Exhibition

This app showcases a variety of writing instruments on display at The Art of Writing Exhibition, an exhibition of historical writing equipment. If that sounds your sort of thing then you might get a kick out of this visually attractive app.

Overall Rating ★★★★☆

Price: Free
Developer: Hearst Communications, Inc.

Esquire iPad Edition

If you're a fan of Esquire magazine but not already a subscriber you might want to check out this digital magazine. While it's not free for print subscribers, there's enough here to make shelling out on the digital version worthwhile.

Overall Rating ★★★☆☆

Price: Free
Developer: ModiFace

Ultimate Beauty

Ultimate Beauty is a surprisingly in-depth and extensive modelling tool for photographers to play around with, supplying a variety of features to edit photos and make them look top-notch. It works very well and it's easy to use.

Overall Rating ★★★★☆

Price: Free
Developer: AMZN Mobile LLCv

Amazon Mobile

Frequent Amazon users will no doubt find this app very useful. Quickly and easily browse through the Amazon store and make purchases on your iPad. While it's missing some of the search functionality from the full website, it's still fairly decent (and free).

Overall Rating ★★★☆☆

Price: £0.59/$0.99
Developer: Apalon

Pimp Your Screen – Wallpapers

Yes, we know, another app offering wallpapers for your iPad. However, we especially liked this one because the designs on offer were unique and original, compared to the bland images you see elsewhere. Not bad at all.

Overall Rating ★★★☆☆

Price: Free
Developer: MERI Media

POST Pavilion

This app is part of an art piece for the 54th Venice Biennale. It features work from a variety of artists as part of a 'Commercial Break' theme, but overall the app is lacking any interesting interactivity or capabilities. Bland and boring –one for the hardcore gallery-goer only.

Overall Rating ★★☆☆☆

Price: £1.19/$1.99
Developer: Callaway Digital Arts, Inc.

Whole Living Smoothies

If you're health conscious about your treats then it's worth picking this up. While it doesn't contain useful nutritional information there's an array of tasty and varied healthy smoothies to keep you satisfied.

Overall Rating ★★★★★

Price: Free
Developer: David Gulbrandsen

iSmoothie HD Free

If you're looking for a few quick smoothie recipes then this app is pretty decent. Unfortunately, some of the recipes are lacking enough information and are thus somewhat difficult to decipher, so you might want to test this free app before checking out the full version.

Overall Rating ★★★☆☆

Price: Free   Developer: Martha Stewart Living Omnimedia, Inc.

Martha Stewart Living Magazine for iPad

This digital edition of Martha Stewart Living is well presented with some nice imagery but isn't particularly exciting, unfortunately.

Overall Rating ★★☆☆☆

Price: Free
Developer: MyClickapps.com LLC

VoteItNow! - Your Friends Have Voted

In *VoteItNow!* you can thumbs up or down specific products and see what people think about a particular product. It's a cool idea but it'll need a few more users to really be worthwhile, because at the moment it's all a bit limited.

Overall Rating ★★★★☆

Price: £0.59/$0.99
Developer: Rocking iApps

Egg Recipes – All In One

For those egg-enthusiasts, here's a collection of some tasty and varied egg recipes. While some of the things on offer are good, the lack of videos and a bland presentation style make this all seem a little underwhelming.

Overall Rating ★★☆☆☆

Price: £0.59/$0.99
Developer: 138App.com

The Flowers Bible

In theory this is a good idea for plant enthusiasts, with information and images supplied for a variety of different types of plants. Unfortunately the information on offer is limited and poorly presented. This could really do with an overhaul.

Overall Rating ★★☆☆☆

Price: £1.19/$1.99
Developer: Garrett Langley

Etsy for iPad

Etsy is basically the home-made version of eBay, with people selling products they've made themselves. While you can browse through said products in this app, there's no option to put items up for sale, a feature that is sorely lacking.

Overall Rating ★★☆☆☆

Price: Free
Developer: Tweakersoft

AroundMe

This app is an excellent one for finding services and points of interest around your current location or somewhere you are going to visit. With plenty of content and directions to each attraction, this app is a must-own for all iPad users curious to explore their surrounds.

Overall Rating ★★★★☆

Price: £1.19/$1.99
Developer: hindig Digital Constructions Inc.

Remembary Connected Diary

This app is yet another way to record your daily thoughts, but it does one over its competitors by allowing you to import Facebook and Twitter statuses, which is a great feature. No option to upload photos is a drawback.

Overall Rating ★★★☆☆

Price: Free
Developer: Tim Barber Inc.

Thrillist for iPad

Thrillist is a fun and interactive way to plan a trip if you're visiting a new city. It's packed with content and things to do, complete with videos and images. While it only supports a few US and UK cities at the moment, we're sure more will be added in the future.

Overall Rating ★★★☆☆

Price: £2.39/$3.99
Developer: Tri Active Media Ltd

AirForces Monthly Magazine

This digital magazine brings you the latest and greatest news from the world of military aviation. Unfortunately this digital edition is just a reprint of the print addition, with no exciting digital extras added to spice things up.

Overall Rating ★★★☆☆

Price: £1.79/$2.99
Developer: Zeeplox

Wallpaper Remix for iPad – DIY Home Screen and App Skins

The good thing about this wallpaper app is that you can combine some different original ideas to get the perfect background.

Overall Rating ★★★☆☆

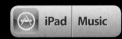

Music

Seeing as the iPad is a technological evolution of the iPod, it's only natural that it serves as a music tool on a multitude of different levels. Aside from simply playing music, the iPad is also an accomplished music-making device, as you will soon discover.

Top Paid Apps	Top Free Apps
OMGuitar Advanced Synth Guitar ★★★★★	**Shazam for iPad** ★★★★★
djay ★★★★	**Beatwave** ★★★★
TabToolKit ★★★★★	**iBend Midi** ★★★★

Staff pick of the section

KORG iMS-20 ★★★★	**Bloom HD** ★★★★★

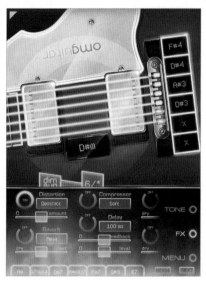

■ The device is designed to be played flat on your lap as opposed to held like a conventional guitar.

■ The interface is stunning to behold and the app is packed with options.

Price: £6.99/$11.99   **Developer:** Ilya Plavunov

OMGuitar Advanced Synth Guitar

We finger the hottest new musical instrument app

One of many synthesisers available in the App Store, *OMGuitar* is slightly different to the rest in that it is designed to retain the crucial human element that can fill music with feeling. The strings on the virtual guitar are sensitive to so many different types of interaction, not just tapping and strumming, but also note bending and muting. Importantly, the app can also distinguish the speed and rhythm with which you strum the strings, allowing you to attach your own personality onto the performance.

As it stands, *OMGuitar* is the best guitar synthesizer on the App Store. But who is it designed for? It's certainly a fun novelty if approached as a distracting digital toy, but the high price almost pushes the app out of the range of most dabblers. As a serious musical synthesizer program, the price is a bargain and we've heard from many musicians who agree and have regularly used the app for composing and even recording.

Rating ★★★★★

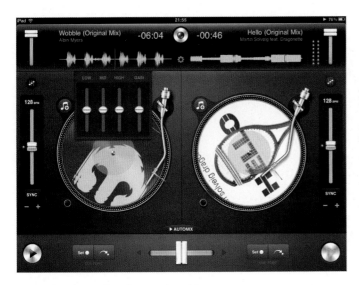

Price: £2.99/$4.99 **Developer:** algoriddim

djay

Is this music-mixing app Grandmaster Flash or flash in the pan?

 Could the iPad be the next DJ turntable? With algoriddim's *djay* app, it's certainly an authentic-looking alternative. Its striking turntable/cross-fader interface reacts convincingly to touch input, but is it enough to substitute the unmistakable feel of working with 12" vinyl records? Perhaps not, but the cost and convenience of an iPad-based DJ set-up certainly has its advantages.

Getting started is a breeze; simply open the app, and select a non-DRM track from your iTunes library. *djay* will calculate its tempo (or BPM – Beats Per Minute), draw a waveform of the track, and apply any available artwork to the record on the turntable. From choosing a track till it's ready to play, the whole process takes about 15 seconds.

The interface is reasonably intuitive, and within ten minutes of use it's possible for an experienced DJ to sound like they're performing on traditional DJ equipment. Novice DJs are also catered for within the app, with BPM sync tools that assist with mixing. Annoyingly, the BPM calculations can occasionally go awry, and we could find no way of manually correcting it.

Whatever your skill level, *djay* also includes some fun and easy-to-learn scratching tricks that could otherwise take years to perfect on traditional DJ equipment.

Sadly, the Automix function doesn't always automatically 'beat-match' your tunes. Results seem to vary from one record to the next, making it possibly more suited for background music purposes. AirPlay support is included, but our attempts

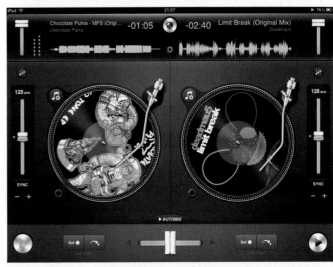

■ Getting started is a breeze, simply open the app and select a track from your iTunes library. You can then experiment and get accustomed to the set-up.

to wirelessly broadcast music created a latency that made beat-mixing records incredibly difficult.

You can also record your masterpieces within the app and have it saved in AIFF format. Recordings can be exported via iTunes, or played back within the app itself.

Arguably, *djay* may lack the prestige of owning a proper turntable set-up, but it remains an accessible option for any wannabe DJ. Alternatively, experienced scratch DJs, or those accustomed to feature-packed 'CD Turntables' may find *djay* slightly lacking in advanced tools. Ultimately, it is best suited for enjoying at home, or for adding some excitement to a party. Intuitive, accessible and fun, *djay* is a solid turntable app.

Rating

Price: £5.99/$9.99 **Developer:** Reactable Systems

Reactable Mobile

Getting to grips with the coolest synthesiser on iPad

Best described as a bizarre, futuristic synthesiser, the Reactable is a circular table, backlit with a deep blue light, to be used in a darkened room. The table itself is a touch-sensitive computer display that reacts to objects, called tangibles, that are placed on the screen, moved around and rotated. This creates different sorts of music depending on the type of tangibles that are placed on the table, their spatial relationship to one another and the way in which they are manipulated.

It's a very cool, almost sci-fi idea, and one that has been used by a number of high-profile performers including Björk. Sadly, at a price of around £8,500, the Reactable is far out of the reach of your average bedroom DJ, which is where the *Reactable Mobile* app comes in…

At a mere £5.99, Reactable Mobile is much more affordable than its rather expensive tabletop counterpart, and it does a pretty good impression of it too. Just like the original, it allows you to place various synthesiser functions onto the surface and play around with them to create your own music in real time. The large iPad screen also works really well with it. When laid down flat on a table or other surface, we felt like we were getting a fair approximation of the original technology, especially with the room to use both hands freely.

There's a truly mind-boggling array of options at your fingertips with *Reactable Mobile* – loop players, oscillators, wave shapers, sequencers and all number of other things we don't really understand but are sure will be most welcome with the musically inclined, especially as the software allows you to incorporate your own samples into the mix.

As amateurs with a distinct lack of any kind of electronic or acoustic musical talent, we had a lot of fun when simply experimenting with Reactable's 'tangibles' and were surprised by the music we were able to create, suggesting that those who know what they're doing will be able to produce absolutely exceptional results.

Just about the only fault we encountered was that the software struggled to keep up when we overloaded it with too many tangibles at once, but that may not be such big a deal. After all, how many bands do you see use more than a handful of instruments at once? *Reactable Mobile* is an overwhelmingly complex music app that's sure to strike the right note with those who 'get it'.

Rating ★★★★☆

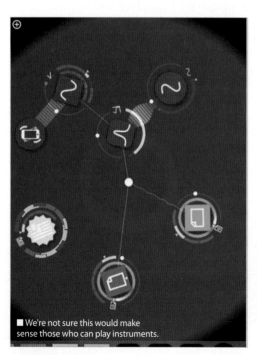

■ We're not sure this would make sense those who can play instruments.

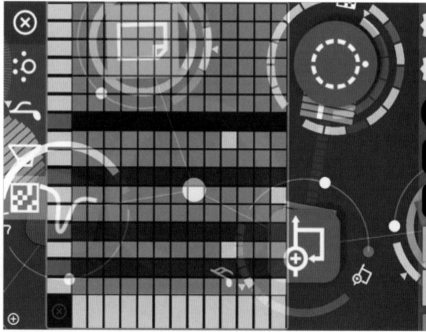

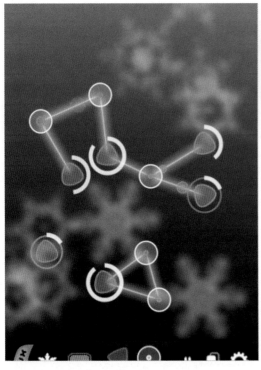

■ Ambient tunes are what Aura's about, so don't be expecting any insane solos.

■ Trial and error is to be expected, even for those who know what they're doing.

Price: £1.19/$1.99 **Developer:** Hige Promotions

Aura 2: Flux

Make sweet, ambient music on your iPad

Fans of ambience should certainly check out Hige Promotions' new app, as it enables you to create your own chilled-out tunes. Upon loading you'll be presented with a fairly simple menu that allows you to set the tone of your music and create Generator and Reactor Nodes, which power your songs.

Nodes are simply dragged onto the screen and will make a sound upon pulsing. Generator Nodes are the main source of your tunes, while Reactor Nodes create additional noises when they are placed next to Generators. Tapping on a Node will allow you to do everything from set the sound a Node produces to determining how quickly it will actually pulse.

It's an intriguing system that enables you to make surprisingly complex tunes, but the downside is that it takes a fair amount of trial and error before you work out what everything does. Add in the opportunity to create different background ambience and the ability to save your compositions and the end result is a very clever app.

Rating ★★★☆☆

■ A simple 4-channel mixer helps you take control of your tracks.

Price: Free **Developer:** David Fumberger

Beatwave

A visually engaging grid-based sequencer

Embracing the concept of the Tenori-on electronic instrument, *Beatwave* revolves around a bar passing repeatedly across a grid of notes. You simply tap a note anywhere on the grid to activate it and the bar plays it as it crosses the screen. Endless patterns of rhythm and tone can be created and the notes are tuned to a particular scale, so that even the most random sequences are easy on the ear.

Three sounds are provided initially, with new ones available as in-app purchases. Unusually deep for a free app (with no ads in evidence either), up to four pattern layers can be created and played simultaneously, but it's when you invoke the clever grid morpher tool to splice two layers together that things start to get really interesting. You can leave this thing running as the patterns constantly entwine and evolve, then when you hit upon a good one, simply pause and save it as a new layer – as long as you haven't fallen into a deep hypnotic state by then!

This is really fascinating stuff and well worth downloading.

Rating ★★★★☆

Price: Free **Developer:** Amidio

Loopj Interactive DJ Station

Become a mixing marvel with this fantastic free app

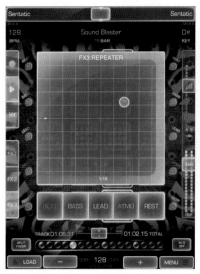

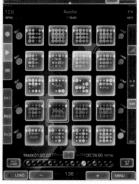

■ You are presented with 20 pads that require different techniques to create various effects.

■ Two tracks can be played at the same time and the decks are always properly synced.

LoopJ Interactive DJ Station is an interesting combination of a loop player and DJ device, but can be somewhat confusing for the uninitiated. Instead of being presented with dials or sliders, here you are given 20 pads that require different techniques to create effects. Press and hold to preview the sound, tap to queue it, double-tap for an immediate start or stop, drag up or down to control the volume of a loop, drag left for a HP filter, right for HP and so on. It's complicated, but natural once you get the hang of it.

The cool thing is that two tracks can play at the same time, and the decks are always properly synced via a timestretch algorithm based on the BPM value you set at the bottom of the screen. You can crossfade to change the balance between tracks, and there are effects that you can add by moving the circle to the appropriate position on a graph.

This app is better suited for more experienced dance DJs and musicians, but there is a lot of fun and experimentation to be had for those less used to mixing.

Rating ★★★★☆

Price: £2.39/$3.99 **Developer:** Opal Limited

Bloom HD

Create relaxing ambient tunes on your iPad

There are a lot of ambient music apps out there for your iDevices, many purporting to offer, in whatever way they can, a relaxing background soundtrack to relax or fall asleep to. What they don't offer you, though, is what the original *Bloom* and now its HD brother do – the ability to compose your own tracks for you to pass out to. Thanks to the sheer usability of the app, this is made possible even if you have absolutely no musical talent whatsoever. Created by renowned ambient musicians Brian Eno and Peter Chilvers, *Bloom HD* is an aural and optical treat that some will claim brings together audio and visual art for all to enjoy. We don't necessarily disagree with that claim, but we do instead want to concentrate on the fact that *Bloom HD* is surprisingly good to simply experiment with. Hypnotic, captivating and fun.

■ You simply tap anywhere on the screen to created different, looped notes.

Rating ★★★★☆

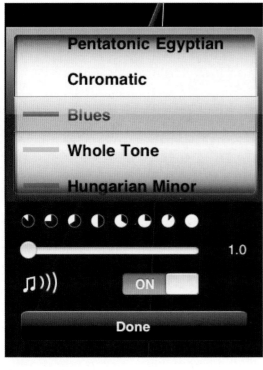

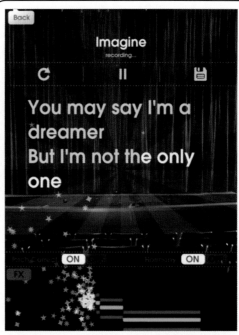

■ Wherever you touch the screen a harp string will appear…

■ There are options to change the tone, but the music it creates isn't great.

■ Singing with this app is easy and enjoyable, what's more, it makes you sound great.

Price: £0.59/$0.99 **Developer:** Scott Snibbe

Bubble Harp

We get our fingers on this clever music app, but is it worth the hype?

There's something about touch-screen devices that makes them rather suitable for interactive musical toys, and you'll certainly find many great examples of these in the App Store. Sadly, *Bubble Harp* is not among the greatest.

The idea is simple; perhaps even too simple. Wherever you touch the screen, a harp string will appear. Slide your finger along, and more will spring forth in a sort of spider web or indeed, bubble-like pattern. These patterns then form the basis for a tune that the harp plays, indicated by a single note moving around the web in accordance with the movements of your finger.

We certainly had a lot of fun creating the webs, it can be fascinating to see the patterns they organically grow into as you play with the screen. But we're sad to say that there was nothing rewarding about the actual music that was created. With only one note playing at a time, the device never really approaches anything you could realistically call a 'tune', and the music soon becomes monotonous and annoying as a result.

Rating ★★☆☆☆

Price: £0.59/$0.99 **Developer:** Smule, Inc

Glee Karaoke

Sing like the stars

This won't be for everyone, but Gleeks – fans of TV series *Glee* – will love the opportunity to sing along with their favourite songs from the show. Like *Glee*, the app is bright and colourful and is beautifully presented.

Plug in your iPad's headphones with their built-in microphone, hit Sing and you're ready to go. Choose a song from the list and the lyrics will scroll across the screen, while bars along the bottom will tell you which notes to hit. For the out of tune, pitch correction and harmonies make you sound like a real star and the more adventurous can try a capella or sing along to their favourite iTunes songs. Superb community features mean you can listen, rate, comment on and compete with fellow users and share your songs via social networking sites such as Facebook and Twitter.

Despite all these positives, with only one tutorial song included and extra songs costing 59p each, this could turn out to be a very expensive app instead. So, although it's a lovely-looking app with some great features, the potential costs are a major downside and could hamper the long-term enjoyment you'll get from this singing sensation.

Rating ★★★☆☆

Masterdaelion

Price: £12.49/$20.99 **Developer:** Nicola Rohrseitz

If you are a keen musician and often use sheet music, you'll be aware of the irritating necessity of having to flick through the pages during play. Luckily, if you own both an iPad and iPhone there is a solution. This app uses the iPad to show the music, and then the iPhone as a sensor to trigger a page turn. It works well, just don't move about too much.

Rating ★★★★☆

Soundprism Pro

Price: £9.49/$15.99 **Developer:** Audanika GmbH

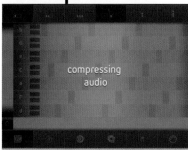

Take music creation, the ability to compose wonderful melodies – and record and export said melodies – and put them together in a simple-to-use package. Throw in further midi-functionality that only those versed in the ways of composition will understand, and you'll have some understanding as to why we recommend this.

Rating ★★★★☆

SoundGrid

Price: £1.79/$2.99 **Developer:** mifki

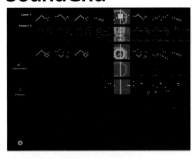

For those wanting to tinker with music creation without being bogged down by techno jargon, *SoundGrid* could be just the thing. Utilising a sound board split into layers, you simply add whatever instruments and effects you want to flesh out your sound, and can construct a semi-professionally-sounding composition in a matter of minutes.

Rating ★★★★☆

TabToolKit

Price: £5.99/$9.99 **Developer:** Agile Partners

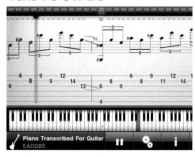

If you've ever considered learning to play guitar or keyboard but haven't the time to sit down at a desk, *Tab Toolkit* is the solution to your problem. A utility for learning guitar tab and keyboard finger positions while accompanied through your favourite tracks step-by-step, this fantastic piece of software exemplifies how integral a role apps can play in learning music.

Rating ★★★★★

Shazam for iPad

Price: Free **Developer:** Shazam Entertainment

After Google Maps, facebook and Twitter, *Shazam* should sit in pride of place on any Apple device. Though this fresh iPad version of the ubiquitous music detection software allows users to peruse lists of songs currently being tagged by other program users and listen to 30-second previews of desired songs in-app, it's most valuable use is to quell that aching sense of discomfort caused by hearing a song and not knowing what it is. Reliable in most outdoor situations, this is simply essential.

Rating ★★★★★

Seline HD Music Instrument

Price: £4.99/$9.99 **Developer:** Ilya Plavunov

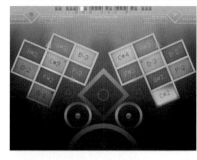

This may be an impressive music creator, but like so many others it's let down by its presentation. There are a number of ways that you can manipulate tunes, but there are no instructions at all, putting the entire process down to trial and error. It's a real shame that *Seline HD* falls at this simple hurdle.

Rating ★★☆☆☆

Drums!

Price: £0.59/$0.99 **Developer:** Ben O'Dwyer

While *Drums!* was great fun on the iPhone, it really shines on Apple's iPad. The larger area makes playing the drums an absolute breeze and even with 11 different drums and cymbals to hammer it never gets too cluttered. Amazingly responsive – it's easy to do fills and fast drum rolls – and beautifully presented, *Drums!* is a great time waster.

Rating ★★★★☆

Metallic Spheres

Price: £0.59/$0.99 **Developer:** Sony BMG

Metallic Spheres is a smart music generator that features input from The Orb and David Gilmour. As with many similar apps you simply drag or tap your fingers on the screen to create new music patterns. Unfortunately, despite the calibre of the artists involved, this is a simplistic offering with few particle effects and uninteresting samples. There's also a complete inability to manipulate chosen music, which makes it feel rather basic. It's not a complete disaster by any means, but we were hoping for a lot more.

Rating ★★☆☆☆

Price: £0.59/$0.99 **Developer:** Talent Media LLC

BEP360

Presented in full 3D 360 degree-o-vision, this app comprises a special edition video of the band's last single The Time (Dirty Bit) – in which you can pan around a bumping warehouse party as if you were actually there – plus an addictive *Tetris*-style game, a photo session (that allows you to take pictures of the band), a Twitter link, and an augmented reality section that makes full use of the iPad 2's camera. If you're into the Peas then this is a great app that could well be just 'The Beginning'.

Rating ★★★★★

Price: £1.19/$1.99 **Developer:** Turon Tech

Synthbot

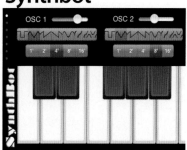

This app is feature-packed with ways to tweak pretty much any aspect of your synth. There's in-depth modulation, pitch, frequency and oscillation controls, and you can really fine-tune it to get the exact sound you require while the app opens quickly and saves your previous settings. An octave keyboard lets you tap out your tunes, but it lacks a save feature.

Rating ★★★★☆

Price: £1.79/$2.99 **Developer:** SmileyApps

Piano Tutor

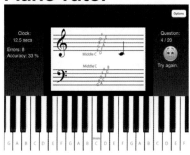

Getting to grips with the piano on the iPad seems like the most natural thing to do with the touch screen offering a high level of interaction. The *Piano Tutor* app starts with just two initial options: to play, or see the key map. The latter is useful in viewing at a glance which notes correlate to which key, but press play and you can begin.

Rating ★★★★☆

Price: £0.59/$0.99 **Developer:** Obie Leff

Beatbox!

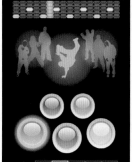

The *Beatbox!* app is problematic in the sense that it appears to somehow be stuck in a logical hole. On the surface, it appears to be a serviceable small title determinedly following in the mould of *Guitar Hero*, only with a series of whoops and popping noises taking the place of actual notes. But each of its five levels fails to actually score players based on how they perform, leaving satisfaction on matching a series of, well, noises to beat dependant purely on personal rhythmic taste. As it lacks the capacity to simulate or entertain, give this a miss.

Rating ★★☆☆☆

Price: £9.49/$15.99 **Developer:** KORG, Inc

KORG iMS-20

Lovers of Korg's iconic Seventies' MS20 monosynth will be amazed at this excellent software recreation. Not only does everything look and sound totally original, with all controls faithfully reproduced for the iPad's touchscreen format, it even employs a system of virtual yellow patch cables that work to connect the internal components. A great sound-maker.

Rating ★★★★☆

Price: £0.59/$0.99 **Developer:** Roger Bruder

iBanjo

If you've ever dreamed of being a penniless, *iBanjo*'s your ticket to an instant hoedown. Depicting a 12-fret banjo, this allows users to play any of its notes with a simple tap on the fret board, with no strumming required. Obviously enough, picking each individual tone out on an iPhone proves a exercise in pinpoint accuracy. On iPad though the experience is much more accommodating, and, though unable to be handled in anything like standard fashion, offers a low risk entry point to quite a fiddly instrument.

Rating ★★★★☆

Price: £2.99/$4.99 **Developer:** O-Music Ltd

O-Generator Acoustic

O-Generator Acoustic uses a looping system of wheels, each one having spots for instrumental samples to be placed – speed it up, slow it down, loop it; it's music making 101. Those overwhelmed by what is initially presented to them can use the handy tutorials that are provided. These are some of the best parts of *O-Generator*.

Rating ★★☆☆☆

Price: £2.99/$4.99 **Developer:** Random House Group

Jay-Z Decoded

The memoirs of one of the world's most popular rappers allows users more interaction with song lyrics – 'decoding' them to find out what was written and why – along with the videos and songs themselves. It's no doubt interesting to see how the mind of a millionaire musician works, and *Decoded* is a great fan service. The pricing is all over the place, though.

Rating ★★☆☆☆

Price: ££2.99/$4.99
Developer: Cipher Prime Studios

Pulse: Volume One

In this rhythm based music game you have to tap along to the beat in a *Guitar Hero*-esque style. The futuristic design is very nice to look at, while the gameplay is simple but addictive. Worth checking out if you're a music fan or are just into music games.

Overall Rating ★★★★☆

Price: £1.19/$1.99
Developer: Rambax

Piano Sharp HD

This virtual piano lets you learn and play the piano in addition to recording your own songs. Impressively, you can also import your own midi songs that the app will translate into a piano-friendly format. This is a feature packed and fun to use app.

Overall Rating ★★★★☆

Price: Free
Developer: Amy Faulkner

The Acoustic Guitar Tuner HD

This guitar tuner does pretty much exactly what you'd expect; tune your guitar strings to a standard, Drop D or ½ step down setting. Works averagely and could do with some additional tuning options, but for a free app it's decent.

Overall Rating ★★★☆☆

Price: £0.59/$0.99
Developer: Chris Martone

dubbox HD

In *dubbox HD* you can use several different effects to create a dubstep song, including drum loops and wobble effects. You can use the iPad's accelerometer to perform most of the functions, but the app is fairly light and not very good looking.

Overall Rating ★★★☆☆

Price: Free
Developer: Wallander Instruments

WI Orchestra™

In *WI Orchestra™* you can put together orchestral music instrument by instrument. The depth of editing is decent, but there's only a few instruments included for free. The rest you have to pay to download, which can get quite pricey. But otherwise this is well worth a look.

Overall Rating ★★★☆☆

Price: £0.59/$0.99
Developer: BidBox LLC

Bass Guitar Trainer

With *Bass Guitar Trainer* you can learn a variety of guitar chords and playing methods through a variety of lessons, modes and mini-games. A good, cheap, tool for those looking to improve their guitar skills and relatively easy to use.

Overall Rating ★★★☆☆

Price: £0.59/$0.99
Developer: BRUNKT

BRUNKT BEATZ Dubstep HD

If you want a selection of stock images to use as backgrounds on your iPad then this app might be for you. It comes with an impressive array of HD images built into the app, but in all honesty you might find similar stuff for free elsewhere.

Overall Rating ★★★☆☆

Price: £4.99/$7.99
Developer: Musicroom.com

Adele Piano Songbook

If you're an Adele fan you'll love this app, which provides sheet piano music for some of her most popular songs. Our only gripe is that is can be a little hard to read sheet music on the iPad, but otherwise this is a good app.

Overall Rating ★★★★☆

Price: Free
Developer: The Live Shot

Darbuka Doumbeck Classic

Finally, you're dream of playing a Darbuka Doumbeck drum has come true. This app lets you play a variety of different sounds made by a Darbuka player. With no-doubt limited appeal and a bland presentation, it's not great.

Overall Rating ★★☆☆☆

Price: £1.79/$2.99
Developer: YUJI HASEBE

HarpSS

Whether you know how to play the harp or not, *HarpSS* is worthy of a download, letting you use your iPad to strum along a 46-string harp. However, there's no tutorials included, so if you don't know how to play then you might get a bit bored.

Overall Rating ★★★☆☆

Price: £0.59/$0.99
Developer: William Kautter

Diner Jukebox

Diner Jukebox let's you view your music library in the style of an old-school jukebox. It's a neat and original little app, complete with 'virtual quarters', and while there's not much else to do other than play music it gets this done pretty well.

Overall Rating ★★★☆☆

Price: £0.59/$0.99
Developer: Utku Uzmen

Voix Vocoder

This synthesiser turns your speech or singing into synthesised music. You alter the pitch with a limited virtual piano and then record and share your created songs, but it's a little clunky to use. Hopefully a future update will improve upon this decent idea.

Overall Rating ★★☆☆☆

Price: Free
Developer: NOTION Music, Inc.

Progression Free

If you play guitar then we highly recommend you download this free app. With it you can create an edit guitar tabs of any song you want, and the editing tool is easy and quick to use. It's also feature packed with editing options, making it a must-download for guitarists.

Overall Rating ★★★★★

Price: Free
Developer: Miriam Duran

PianoBand Free

Unlike other virtual pianos, *PianoBand* let's you play along with a video-tutor or with other instruments to recreate the experience of playing in a band. It's fairly good fun and easy to use, so if you want a piano-app with a difference then pick it up.

Overall Rating ★★★★☆

Price: £1.19/$1.99
Developer: Khoa Tran Anh

ATK Player

This video player lets you play a wide variety of video formats from iTunes on your iPad. However, it's bland and poorly presented, and we had a few problems with video conversion in the first place. Not brilliant, and needs an overhaul if it is to attract any fans.

Overall Rating ★★☆☆☆

Price: £1.19/$1.99
Developer: Howcast

Guitar Lessons from Howcast

In this app you're given an impressive array of guitar lessons in the form of instructional videos, with detailed information given on how to play guitar, whether you're a beginner or slightly more experienced.

Overall Rating ★★★★☆

Price: £1.79/$2.99
Developer: U-Apps

TT Progress HD

This App takes you 'behind the scenes' of Take That's new album, called 'Progress, including photography and information from the album tour itself. Somewhat limited in content, and an app that's definitely for die-hard Take That fans only.

Overall Rating ★★☆☆☆

Price: £2.99/$4.99
Developer: MagicAnywhere

Classical Music II: Master's Collection Vol 2

Fans of classical music will definitely get a kick out of this app, with 100 songs presented in excellent audio quality for your listening pleasure.

Overall Rating ★★★★★

Price: Free
Developer: Musicnotes

Musicnotes Sheet Music Viewer for iPad

For people with a musicnotes.com account this is a must-have app. You can keep all your iPad-compatible sheet music together in one place.

Overall Rating ★★★★☆

Price: Free
Developer: Varrion Ltd

Beatdock

This app has a variety of royalty-free music that you can listen to on your iPad. That's pretty much all there is to it. There's a decent array of songs, from Dance to Latin, but you can't see song information and the app overall is pretty shaky. Poor.

Overall Rating ★☆☆☆☆

Price: £2.99/$4.99
Developer: Texas Parallel Imaging, LLC.

iPianoMate

 This is an excellent and original idea for an app that works pretty well. Basically, it records and visualises anything you play on the piano, and shows you which keys you pressed and for how long. However, it can only really record one-handed tunes.

Overall Rating ★★★★☆

Price: £0.59/$0.99
Developer: Reza Pekan

ElectricGuitar HD

 This app provides you a virtual electric guitar to play on, as you might have guessed. However, it's incredibly basic and there's very few features on offer other than zooming into and out of the guitar. Not really worth it – and certainly not fit to lick *GarageBand*'s boots!

Overall Rating ★★☆☆☆

Price: £0.59/$0.99
Developer: tkumars.com

ChaosticKit HD

 This app is an interesting and fun way to make music. You're basically given a blank canvas onto which you place sounds and noises from a variety of instruments and link them together. It's pretty good fun and certainly a bit of a time-waster if you have minutes to kill.

Overall Rating ★★★★☆

Price: £0.59/$0.99
Developer: Rumi Humphrey

Slewpi

 In this app you create synthesised loops of music by 'painting' them on screen. It's fun and easy to use but the loops are limited and short. Good in short bursts but it won't hold your attention for too long and there are far better apps out there.

Overall Rating ★★★☆☆

Price: Free
Developer: Marcus Scherer

Congas

 Everyone likes congas, right? Sure! Tap along to your favourite conga songs with this app, but don't expect much else. Apart from the tapping there's very little to do, so unless you absolutely love congas then you'll probably quickly get bored.

Overall Rating ★★☆☆☆

Price: £8.99/$14.99
Developer: C.L. Barnhouse Company

A.P.S. MusicMaster Pro

 This pricey app is definitely one for serious musicians only. You can view and edit music in PDF format, and there's a whole host of features and functions you can apply to each piece of music. If you know what you're doing then this app is great.

Overall Rating ★★★★☆

Price: Free
Developer: Rouet Production

iBend Midi

 iBend Midi lets you add a pitch bend joystick for midi instruments and keyboards. It supports a wide range of channels and connecting it up is relatively simple. If you need a midi controller then you can't go wrong with this. A wonderful free download.

Overall Rating ★★★★☆

Price: £2.99/$4.99
Developer: Tsukurimichi

Nail That Note

 If you've ever wanted to check how close to pitch-perfect your ears are then this app might be for you. Play and attempt to recognise a variety of notes, chords, intervals, scales and arpeggios on guitar and piano. Pricey but fairly decent.

Overall Rating ★★★☆☆

Price: £2.99/$4.99
Developer: Avid®

Avid Scorch

 If you use the Sibelius music program then this app could be for you. It lets you view sheet music on your iPad and perform some minor editing tweaks. However, there's other apps on the market that do a better job. Overall, not too great just yet.

Overall Rating ★★☆☆☆

Price: £1.19/$1.99
Developer: Mad Calf Apps

Pedal Steel

 If you prefer steel guitars over regular ones then you might want to check this out. The app lets you play and mess around on a steel guitar, but it's not presented very well and it all seems a bit hap-hazard. Still, not terrible, but probably one for the enthusiasts.

Overall Rating ★★☆☆☆

Price: £0.59/$0.99
Developer: Quick Fingers

Step Seq

 In *Step Seq* you tap out a song on a variety of squares that the app then plays back to you, with eight different tones on offer and some additional FX. It's quite fun but probably only good for messing around on now and again and impressing your mates with.

Overall Rating ★★★☆☆

Price: Free
Developer: Matthew Gao

MusicWall HD

 This cool and visually appealing app provides a wall of music for you to listen to, with songs randomly taken from the internet. Tapping one of the many images on screen plays the track with a video, and the app also supports Airplay. Pretty neat.

Overall Rating ★★★★☆

Price: £1.19/$1.99
Developer: Kevin Andrews Industries

Karaoke Tone: Finding Your Note + Tips

 Are you one of the millions who suffers from being terrible at Karaoke? Well, unfortunately this app probably won't help.

Overall Rating ★★☆☆☆

Price: £0.59/$0.99
Developer: Reza Pekan

Piano HD™

 If you're looking for a fun, feature-rich and extensive virtual piano then… you might want to look elsewhere. While *Piano HD™* is simple to use and colourful there's just not enough on offer to make it a worthwhile purchase, even if it is relatively cheap.

Overall Rating ★★☆☆☆

Price: £1.19/$1.99
Developer: Scott Snibbe Studio, Inc.

OscilloScoop

 This funky little app lets you create electronic dance music by touching and dragging spinning and fluctuating visualisations. A cool idea but ultimately limited in application. It's fun for a while but there's really not much to it, especially for the price you're paying.

Overall Rating ★★★☆☆

Price: Free
Developer: Play Music Publishing

How2Play

 This app comes with a whole host of methods and techniques for playing the guitar. It'll teach you some more complex musical manoeuvres, with videos and detailed information provided for each one. A decent app all round.

Overall Rating ★★★☆☆

Price: Free
Developer: Inspike s.r.l.

iMusician PJS: Everybody Play!

 This app lets you create your own songs using piano and guitar chords. It's a little complex to use and not entirely clear what you're supposed to be doing at times, but once you get to grips with it then it's not too bad.

Overall Rating ★★★☆☆

Price: £5.99/$9.99
Developer: 955 Dreams

On the way to Woodstock

 If you have even the smallest interest in the Woodstock music festival then you might want to consider downloading this. The app provides extensive information, photography and interactivity from the event.

Overall Rating ★★★★☆

Price: Free
Developer: Batsu

easyGuitar HD

 This app lets you play an acoustic guitar on your iPad, but it's currently very limited. Apart from moving up and down the fret there's little to do, and the app seems somewhat broken. It's definitely in need of a major update to even become average.

Overall Rating ★☆☆☆☆

Price: £0.59/$0.99
Developer: Reza Pekan

Drums™

 This extensive drumming app is quite good fun if you just want to mess around on various drums and percussion instruments. It's more a toy than a proper virtual drum-kit though, and with very few features there's not a lot here to keep you interested.

Overall Rating ★★★☆☆

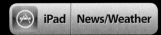
News/ Weather

Gone are the days when you have to actually sit down to watch the news on the TV, and then sit through an entire bulletin just to catch the weather forecast. Armed with an iPad you can get up-to-the-minute reports when you need them plus instant weather updates.

Top Paid Apps		Top Free Apps	
Read It Later Pro ★★★★		The Daily ★★★	
InstaPaper Pro ★★★★		Weather 4D ★★★	
Engadget for iPad ★★★★★		Flipboard ★★★★	

Staff pick of the section

Evening Standard ★★★★	News360 ★★★★

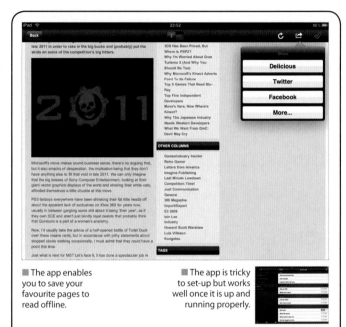

■ The app enables you to save your favourite pages to read offline.

■ The app is tricky to set-up but works well once it is up and running properly.

Price: £2.99/$4.99   Developer: idea Shower

Read It Later Pro

Save your favourite web pages to read offline later

 Get past *Read It Later Pro*'s fiddly front end and you'll discover a truly excellent way of reading everything on your iPad. Unfortunately, the app is fiddly to actually install onto your browser, despite an accompanying tutorial video and Q&A that's available.

Once everything is set up you simply browse a web page, select 'Read It Later' in your bookmark and it's instantly saved for later use. You can synch everything with your computer so that pages can be read on your device at a later time.

Read It Later Pro also features a very good free version, so a number of improvements have been included – ranging from the ability to read full screen, sharing pages with a number of different social apps and One Touch Rotation locking – to ensure it is worth the additional asking price. One annoyance we did encounter however is that the excellent Digest feature – which automatically organises all your items into relevant folders – isn't actually included and costs an additional £2.99. Even with this hidden cost, and the troublesome setup, *Read It Later Pro*'s number of options make it unmissable.

Rating ★★★★☆

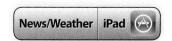

Price: £2.99/$4.99   Developer: Marco Arment

Instapaper Pro

Save what you're reading and catch up later

Instapaper Pro is an incredibly handy app that enables you to save whatever you're currently viewing so that you can read it at a later date.

Once you've registered the app – something which Read It Later Pro also requires you to do – you'll gain access to plenty of useful features that make using this app an absolute breeze. Due to the way apps are set up, you'll need to make a few physical adjustments in order to add Instapaper to Safari, but the instructions are straightforward and a lot easier to use than Read It Later Pro's. It's also compatible with Tumblr and Twitter, which is very handy indeed.

After everything is set up, it's simply a case of looking through your favourite sites and choosing what you want to read. Simply select a page, go to your bookmarks, hit 'Instapaper: Read Later' and it will immediately save your page. Anything you select is instantly saved to folders in the Instapaper app, ready for you to view when you actually have the time.

It should be worth noting that the saved pages are very basic – getting rid of most of the available pictures and ads that were on the previous version – but you're left with just the text which is nice and easy to read and something that Apple is incorporating into Safari as standard with the forthcoming iOS 5 update, due this Autumn. If reading is an issue you can change the font and size and even switch between light and dark text. You can even enable a tilt mode to scroll through articles if you're too lazy to do it yourself.

While the free version of Instapaper is more than adequate for most of your daily needs, there's no denying that the additional features included in Instapaper Pro are worth it.

Extremely easy to set up and very user-friendly, Instapaper Pro is an excellent app that ensures that you'll always find to time to look at everything you need to, regardless of whether or not you currently have access to Wi-Fi. We're not sure how the developer will evolve the app so that it is still appealing to the masses and useful after Apple's aforementioned software update, but for now it is undoubtedly the best app of its kind.

With some very useful features, Instapaper Pro is the perfect way of reading the web in your own time, minus all of the clutter and adverts that you usually have to navigate your way through to read the bare bones of the pages and stories that interest you. Download it now and you'll be surprised how quickly it becomes integrated into your daily web-page-reading routine.

Rating ★★★★★

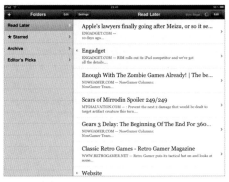

■ You can save pages to read later, minus all of the pictures and clutter.

■ The app is integrated into Safari and is accessible from the 'Bookmarks' button.

Price: $0.99 (per week)/$39.99   **Developer:** News DP Holdings, Inc

The Daily

Murdoch is first out of the blocks with an iPad-exclusive newspaper

The iPad sometimes seems like a solution looking for a problem. This, the world's first iPad-only newspaper, perhaps best exemplifies this mindset. This isn't to say that *The Daily* is in any way problematic, it's just because it's inaccessible to so many vast tracts of the app-using public that its existence has to be questioned from the outset.

It's not even as if the paper particularly makes much use of the iPad's unique features. Re-orienting the screen often fudges the display, filling it with blank spaces to the point where portrait view is the only real option, and its use of interactive features is scant when compared to other apps.

Still, what's here – and interactive – makes fairly novel use of some of the journalistic possibilities that a portable device has to offer. Interactive features include informative diagrams with touchable elements to reveal extra material, polls on news topics linked to *The Daily*'s servers in order to reassure yourself that everybody else also believes in freedom of speech for controversial bloggers (or a similar issue of the day), as well as the usual embedded video material. It's a nice little touch that *The Daily*'s own news team puts these video reports together, and again adds to the paper's unique feeling of being an absolutely self-contained news source.

Again though, it's difficult to judge if the digital platform is the best place to be fed such a singular angle of news. With so many services out there, aggregating news from services you can pick yourself and consolidate with ease from the palm of your hand (and for free), *The Daily*'s approach feels much like it has been placed on an uncomfortable middle ground between embracing the future while simultaneously holding readers firmly back in the physical media age.

The newspaper's editorial stance isn't even blessed with a particularly individual voice, choosing to hedge its bets with a rather disproportionately tiny output of news and predominantly apolitical opinion writing, while then launching with gusto into a much safer 'Gossip' section, with arts, games and sports reporting.

All in all, it's a brave experiment in making an iPad-exclusive news source, but *The Daily* will have to prove that its uniqueness runs beyond simply existing in order to hold a readership. In fairness it's still early days, but right now it feels like a jack of all trades; and the master of none. *The Daily* explodes onto the tablet market with a solid, if not perfect, foundation on which to build.

Rating ★★★★★

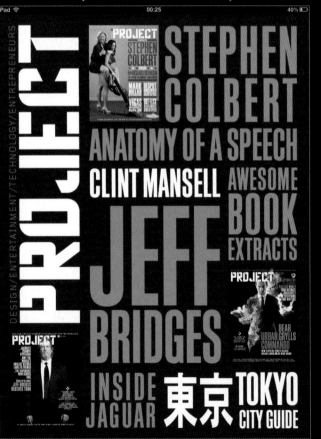

■ Unfortunately for an app of this type, there isn't as much interactivity as we would've liked; many similar apps have nailed this aspect.

■ The iPad's screen works great for newspapers, and *The Daily*'s News and Gossip sections make the most of it.

Price: £3.49/$5.99 Developer: Olivier Bouyssou

Weather 4D

Adding a whole new dimension to meteorology

Weather 4D equips you with a decent amount of global weather knowledge at whatever time you care to check it. The app itself is easy to use – simply choose your region, and it'll download the relevant information. Once this has been selected, you can go into the Orbit mode to spin the globe, although unfortunately it'll only display the weather and temperatures in the region that you've picked, which, as a result, renders this a fun but fruitless exercise.

You can zoom into the towns and cities when you've selected your area of choice, and in the process take a closer look at the weather in that region. Pressing 'Play' will fast-forward the clock in order for you to see how the conditions will develop during the rest of the week. Meanwhile, the Time mode means that you can speed up or rewind time at the touch of a button (or a drag of your finger across the screen), allowing you to check out the week's forecast.

While we have no real complaints about the usability of the app itself – the menus are clear and the Globe function is easy to get to grips with – we do have a bit of an issue with the price. At over three pounds, its recommended retail price seems pretty steep; especially when you consider that much of this information could be obtained from many other apps for free. Although you don't get a spinnable globe with those, mind.

While there's no doubt it's useful, and the spinnable globe works well, it's nevertheless a pricey app.

Rating ★★★☆☆

■ Weather 4D contains weather reports all over the world, as this screenshot from North Germany shows – handy for all markets.

■ As with most weather apps, the further you zoom out, the more general the icons become – but they're usually accurate.

Price: Free **Developer:** Flipboard, Inc

Flipboard

This is social networking, but not as you know it

Flipboard is essentially an organiser – you enter in your favourite blogs and social network sites and it'll display this mass of information in a magazine-style format. This is more than just a long list of bullet-pointed updates or hilarious quotes from friends and family, however – *Flipboard* blends your Twitter and Facebook feeds into one, well-designed publication for you to browse while you're on the go or at home.

Like the look of a pull-quote in one of the articles? Click on it to read more. All those articles that you could never be bothered to read on your phone's tiny screen? Peruse them at your leisure. The excellent page layout and creative use of white space means that you're never overwhelmed. *Flipboard* enables you to digest each morsel as you read it, or – if you'd prefer it – use your fingers to skip past. If you would like to add a new section to your Flipboard, simply click 'add a new section' from your home screen and you'll be presented with a search dialog box. It's simple and intuitive.

Rating ★★★★☆

■ The app organises all of your social network feeds into one magazine-style book to flick through at your leisure.

■ It certainly brings a fresh new perspective to how you catch up and share your news.

Price: Free **Developer:** Newsweek

Newsweek

Get your fill of comment and current affairs here

More and more publications are easing themselves into the seat of digital distribution and *Newsweek* is no exception – this weekly current affairs magazine is now available on your iPad. While the app itself is free and comes with a complimentary Obama edition, you'll have to pay $2.99 for each issue thereafter. It has its perks, though: early access on each new issue, for one plus a full back-issue collection so that you can store as many as you like.

As expected, *Newsweek* is relatively easy to use and, thankfully, there were no page-flicking delays to speak of – then again, its simple design means there's really not much to struggle with here. The app is by no means inadequate, it's merely functional – the text is presented clearly, with the ability to zoom in and out when required. The ad strips along the bottom aren't particularly intrusive, and you can purchase additional issues of *Newsweek* at the click of a button.

Judging by *Newsweek*'s companion website, we did expect a little more in the way of creativity and functionality in its design, so it's disappointing in that respect. However, if you're looking to save paper and a bit of money then *Newsweek* could be the app for you. What you see is what you get – a digital edition of a highly successful US publication.

Rating ★★☆☆☆

■ The app works well on iPad – it's clearly defined and very easy to navigate.

The look and feel of the app is quite sterile but it definitely serves its purpose.

The app includes two different font sizes to ensure that it is easy to read…

Price: Free   **Developer:** Evening Standard

Evening Standard for iPad

All the latest news in an easy-to-read format

If you live in London or the South West area then you'll find this app to be highly informative. While the iPhone version is rather cluttered, it truly shines on the larger iPad thanks to good design and layout and very easy-to-read text. There are five separate categories to choose from: News, Business, Sports, Showbiz, and Life and Style, as well as the option to look at any previous stories that you have saved. Video is also included, although we were unable to view anything as the pad stated it wasn't enabled for HTML5 delivery.

When held in landscape mode all the latest stories are displayed down the far left side of the screen, and it's a relatively simple task to scroll through for older stories. Topics of interest can be mailed or linked to Twitter and Facebook and there are two different font sizes for easier reading. While there are ads on every page, they aren't too intrusive and it's difficult to complain when you're getting regular information for absolutely nothing. It is fairly sterile in its look and design, but as a quick, easy to use news source it's still highly useful.

Rating ★★★★★

Price: Free   **Developer:** AOL

Engadget for iPad

Essential technology news

Upon loading the app you can tap into four channels: Engadget, iMobile, Engadget HD and alt.Engadget, and are served up a rich feast of regularly updated news stories, plus photo galleries and video feeds. The screen is efficiently presented with scrollable stories across a top bar, and news previews in the main window that you can tap on to be taken through to the full story and accompanying links. What's more, a handy side-tab allows you to post comments on any of the stories, and a side-column on the front page displays the most-commented stories, so you can instantly jump to what everyone's talking about.

The app is completed by launch pads along the bottom of the screen that take you to photo and video galleries, saved stories, hot topics and news archives. But the real icing on the cake is the 'Podcasts' tab that lets you listen to Engadget's latest audio feeds within the app itself.

Whether you have an enthusiastic interest in technology or simply want to gaze at how a great news app should be done, Engadget is a must-download app that is a joy to behold. One of the best news apps available for the iPad that deserves to be digested.

Rating ★★★★★

A timeline is regularly updated with all the latest happenings…

The app draws content from a rich list of sites so that you always stay informed.

Price: Free Developer: Intelligenti Ltd

Swipe – News for iOS

A new electronic serving of iOS news

A new, weekly digital e-zine from the people behind the iPhone Secrets Tips and Tricks series, Swipe promises to focus on all things iDevice and iOS-related, and judging by the free first issue, things are off to a promising start. The content is well-written and soundly researched, the presentation is impeccable despite the slightly sluggish page turns, the design ticks all the right boxes and there's a satisfactory mix of news, features, tutorials and reviews.

The main drawback is how short the issue is – at only 34 small pages, all in fairly large print, chances are that you'll be left wanting more for your money when the next issue comes out. However, nowhere in the app or on the developer page does it mention how much each subsequent issue is going to cost, which is surely the issue of most immediate concern to most potential readers.

Rating ★★★★★

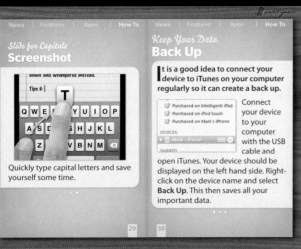

■ Helpful tips and tutorials abound.

■ Informative mini-reviews look great.

Price: Free Developer: News360

News360 for iPad

Innovative and attractive news aggregator for your iPad

News aggregator apps are pretty common these days, so it takes something fairly radical to make us sit up and take notice. *News360* has all the usual features of an app of this type, uniting news feeds from a wide variety of sources into a viewer with a snappy and visually appealing front end that features video support and tabs for switching to more coverage of the same story by alternative sources. What stands out, though, is the 360 view – at the tap of a button, the display changes to a horizontally swipeable, 3D multi-layered panorama of photos pertaining to current world stories, flowing past the screen as if you were in the centre of a spinning cylinder of news images from across the globe. Tapping on any photo brings up the story in the regular interface, making it an unusual and refreshing way to browse the news. You can also focus on local news, and there is a useful support forum at the developer's website.

Royal Wedding Album

■ Relive the day with high-res photos…

■ Enjoy shots of the couple together.

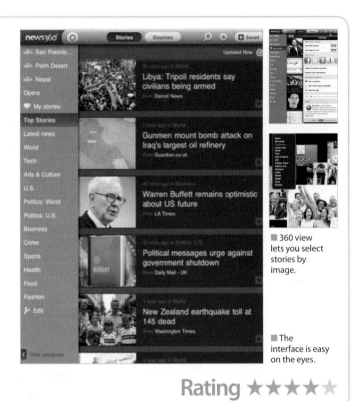

■ 360 view lets you select stories by image.

■ The interface is easy on the eyes.

Rating ★★★★☆

Price: £2.99/$4.99 **Developer:** Just Mobile

Relive the wedding of the year with this digital souvenir

The wedding of Prince William and Catherine Middleton in April was the sort of event capable of uniting a country with a unique sense of pride and wellbeing. Patriotic iPad users can now look back on the day with fondness courtesy of this app from the Press Association, a comprehensive reminder containing a total of 349 photographs, split over four categories. Of these, though, only 83 are of the actual wedding day itself; 164 are of Prince William from when he was born up to the present, 64 are of Kate Middleton, and 38 are of the couple together.

Overall, it's a pleasant enough collection of photographs, but the package is marred a little by some amateurish presentation niggles. The text commentary boxes that accompany each shot aren't always the right size, either obscuring the shot or making it necessary to scroll the text to read the end of it, and the images themselves sometimes get stuck in mid swipe. Somehow the design of the interface feels unfinished, which lets the whole thing down a bit.

Rating ★★★☆☆

Price: Free **Developer:** National Geographic Society

National Geographic Magazine

Digital version of a publishing institution comes to iOS

National Geographic Magazine has made a name for itself as one of the most prestigious periodicals you can buy. Like most digital versions of print magazines, the fact that this app is free is slightly misleading in that it is purely an empty vessel for displaying purchased content. Each digital issue costs £3.49, although there is a free sampler issue available for download, allowing you to get the measure of things with a few taster articles. The magazine's content is exactly the kind of stuff the iPad was built to display, and the colourful and spectacular images contained within really leap off the screen. The sample feature on the Inca civilisation and the unearthing of Machu Picchu featured exactly the blend of fascinating subject matter and breathtaking photography that the magazine is known for.

Rating ★★★★★

■ Design and layout quality is as you'd expect.

■ Photographs are vibrant, colourful and relevant.

Price: £1.79/$2.99 Developer: Jilion

Aelios Weather

Weather with a wow factor – meet Aelios Weather

■ Use the viewing lens to explore the world.

■ Definitely one of the prettier weather apps.

It's not often that we encounter an app whose innate beauty provokes a sharp intake of breath, but *Aeolis Weather* definitely falls into that category. It really is quite stunning, the interface boasting a level of craftsmanship and ingenuity that's seldom seen. On a basic level, it provides the current outlook and a seven-day forecast for anywhere in the world, much like any other weather app, but that's where the similarities end.

Aelios's unique selling point is the finely crafted virtual Swiss-watch-slash-magnifying-glass device which is used to browse locations. As each spot on the world map falls under its lens, a little silver hoop shoots out to lock onto the most populated area, and a tap at the top of the screen sends gorgeously rendered little weather pictograms shooting out around the device's outer edge. Rotating the lavishly rendered knurled outer ring switches from 24-hour to seven-day view, or you can just use the one-touch geo-location feature to view your local weather. Outstanding in every possible way.

Rating ★★★★★

Price: £5.99/$9.99 Developer: Ned Kubica

Weather™

All-round weather performance – but at a price

 Some weather apps show the current temperature as an icon badge. Others offer a four day forecast as well as current conditions. Some offer real-time radar maps, satellite maps or space weather, but very few apps offer all of these things. *Weather™*'s developer seems to have gone all out to cram as many meteorological features into his app as he could think of, and the result is a pretty comprehensive set of forecasting tools. Whether it's worth shelling out six quid for is open to question, but it's obvious that a lot of effort has been made. The icon badge temperature display works well, and the app's main interface has a pleasantly airy feel. Sadly, the radar maps pertain only to the US, which makes the app less appealing to Europeans, but as an exercise in how much can be squeezed into a weather app, this is right up there.

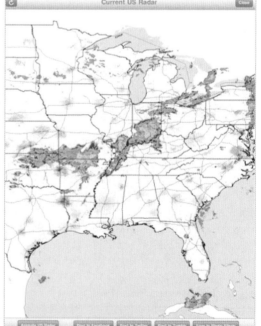

■ The main screen is clear and easy to read.

Rating ★★★★☆

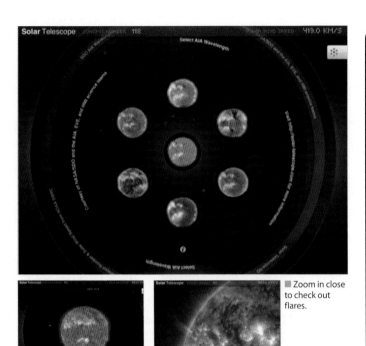

▪ Zoom in close to check out flares.

Price: £1.19/$1.99 **Developer:** egrafic

Solar Telescope HD

Monitor solar activity on your iPad screen

"Don't look at the sun, you'll hurt your eyes!" If this sentence is still fresh in your memory from childhood, then egrafic's *Solar Telescope HD* will provoke a small smile of satisfaction. It allows you to view regularly updated, high-resolution images of the sun in seven different AIA wavelengths (or 'colours' as we call them here on Earth) taken by NASA's dedicated sungazing SDO (Solar Dynamics Observatory) spacecraft.

The shots are very impressive, revealing the apparently benign yellow ball in our sky to be what appears to be a raging, angry fiery giant. The app's interface is brilliantly sci-fi, actually making you feel like you're using a real telescope, and the navigation is intuitive, allowing you to zoom in close and pan around the images by double-tapping and finger-scrolling. Plenty of information is provided, with the date and time that each image was taken, the sunspot number in the frame and the real-time solar wind speed. Fascinating stuff for sungazers, with zero peeper damage incurred.

Rating ★★★★☆

▪ The minimal design is very easy on the eye

▪ Choose one of 12 different themes…

Price: £1.19/$1.99 **Developer:** Bigsool

Weather Station World

Transform your iPad into a global weather station

If you've ever lusted after one of those digital weather centres that you used to see in the Innovations catalogue, now's your chance. *Weather Station World* turns your iPad into a £500 version of that very device. The app's clear, uncluttered layout and minimalistic design really does look fabulous on the crisp iPad display, particularly in the dark, and it displays a wealth of weather-related information, including the time and date, current temperature and barometric pressure, five-day forecast, humidity, wind speed and direction, dewpoint, probability of rain and sunrise and sunset times. A selection of 12 different colour schemes are available too, so you should have no problem finding one that suits your mood. You can easily set a new location by dropping a pin onto a global Google map, which can then be saved to a favourites list for easy retrieval later on. A great-looking app that's great to use.

Rating ★★★★★

Price: Free Developer: Media Applications

BBC News

The left panel offers the most recent news coverage from across the world, the UK and sport, with hidden tabs for more niche content. Meanwhile, the right pane displays the current news story, as well as the option to flick through stories in the same category. Live news is also here, and while its picture quality is poorer than Sky News, there are no adverts.

Rating ★★★★★

Price: Free Developer: The New York Times Company

NY Times For iPad

Compared to the rest of the apps on this page, NYTimes for iPad limits the content you can view at a single glance. While the majority link to the rest of their coverage, NYTimes offers only a glimpse, and hides the rest behind locked menus for a four-weekly subscription fee. Features such as image and video galleries alleviate the cost.

Rating ★★★★☆

Price: Free Developer: Alphonso Labs

Pulse News Reader

Pulse News Reader takes a series of RSS feeds and keeps them live all in one place. With neat icons and an easy-to-use interface, this is perfect for those that want to keep track of their favourite sites. It's easy to add and remove whichever RSS feeds you like, although it does require a bit of messing with sub-menus to manage. It can all get a bit cluttered…

Rating ★★★☆☆

Price: Free Developer: BSkyB

Sky News for iPad

Sky News is a refreshing app for consumers. While the majority of news apps try to mimic a newspaper, Sky News opts for its own unique and slick approach to providing its content. The latest stories are laid out in a timeline, and can be selected in the swipe of a finger. Doing so offers a video of the story with related content around the edges of the video.

Rating ★★★★★

Price: Free Developer: Pixelmags

HowItWorks

HowItWorks' content is delivered via the Pixelmags method, allowing users to flick through in sequential order or select pages via the in-app dock. Though simple, this interface maintains a degree of familiarity with its source pastime, ensuring users don't find themselves having to quit the app in confusion. A great read that is well worth subscribing to.

Rating ★★★★☆

Price: Free Developer: The Telegraph

The Telegraph for iPad

The Telegraph is the closest thing to having a newspaper on the iPad. By using a strictly professional layout, you'll see clearly the most important news of the day, with additional tabs available at the top of the screen. With only a single image per page, The Telegraph could do with more visually to draw the reader in to each story, but the same could be said of the paper too.

Rating ★★★☆☆

Price: Free Developer: Zinio

Zinio Magazine

Selling the likes of Rolling Stone, The Economist and thousands more, there's a wealth of back issues as well as the current ones; you can even read popular articles for free. With fantastic resolution and intelligent zoom, it's almost as good as holding a printed copy in your hand. The ultimate newsagent that lives on your iPad.

Rating ★★★☆☆

Price: Free Developer: Newport Television, LLC

WXXA – Fox23 News on the Go

Having the news wherever you go has been one of the most common uses for iDevices. This app connects to Fox23's news stream, covering local and state broadcasts as well as national and global news. The easy-to-navigate menus make finding information specific to your needs easy. If WXXA is your news source of choice, then get this app.

Rating ★★★★★

Price: Free Developer: Media Convergence Group Inc

Newsy

Newsy presents the best of the days news in video form selected from many sources The quality is good, although scrolling through the previews is fiddly. Videos can be viewed online or downloaded for watching offline later. The news is mainly focused towards US audiences, which makes the app less useful for people in other countries.

Rating ★★★★☆

Price: Free Developer: Newspaper Direct Inc

Press Reader

Get access to over 1,500 newspapers from around the world! You pay per download and the paper appears exactly like the hard copy. Pinch to zoom in and the text is highly readable. It's not an economical way to read your regular daily, perhaps, but good for occasional looks, especially at foreign papers or at the home papers when you are abroad. If you read a specific paper every day you'll probably be better off getting a subscription to their digital edition, should they actually have one.

Rating ★★★★☆

Price: Free Developer: Fwix

Local News by Fwix

Feeds you news local to your location from registered sources. It works reasonably well but the amount of news depends on where you are. You need to register to use the app. Oddly, we found we could then post our own news stories and they went live immediately – bit of a security problem there! As this is a free app its worth a look simply because it can be tailored to your specific use. We do, however, think that the news upload system will be taken advantage of and possibly abused by those looking to cause mischief.

Rating ★★★☆☆

Price: £0.59/$0.99 Developer: Vladimir Borisov

News Browser

We think that this must get the prize for the ugliest icon and interface in the App Store! We also struggle to see its point. The Lego-like coloured dots at the top of the page take you to various news sites, but there is no way of customising what sites are listed – what you see is what you get. It is little more than a web browser with some links embedded at the top.

Rating ★☆☆☆☆

Price: £5.99/$9.99 Developer: Newsgator Technologies Inc

NetNewsWire

Often considered the daddy of RSS readers for desktops and the iPhone, here is its incarnation for the iPad. If you've not seen or heard of it before, it's essentially a conventional Google Reader supported app and, as such, does virtually what most other similar apps do. And there in lies the rub – it doesn't do any more than the others, nor does it do it better.

Rating ★★☆☆☆

Price: Free Developer: Fluent Mobile

Fluent News Reader

Consolidates news feeds from various sources but you can only select from those which are listed within the app – it's not an RSS reader – and many of the sites are US-centric. We struggle to see why you would choose this over a more flexible RSS reader that allows you full control of where you get your news from. Either that, or just go to a single news site. If you can't get near a connection, we do like the fact that that you can still access the news.

Rating ★★☆☆☆

Price: £2.99/$4.99 Developer: Gdiplus

Blogshelf

A good-looking RSS reader that displays your feeds in the form of 'books' on a shelf similar to that of *iBooks*. It's fine if you only subscribe to a small number of feeds; if you have many, it's hard to see at a glance which have been updated. The lack of syncing is disappointing, especially if you already subscribe to feeds with, say, Google Reader. The price may also put a few people off as for the money, you can get much better, more productive readers that are easier to use and read.

Rating ★★★☆☆

Price: Free Developer: ABC Digital

ABC News

This US news app has the coolest looking interface: a globe that you can turn in any direction to reveal a selection of stories. Click on a story and you go to more conventional pages to read articles or view videos. As neat as the spinning globe looks, it's not actually that great for browsing content. It's a case of looks over functionality. But it is free!

Rating ★★★☆☆

Price: Free **Developer:** Alligator Digital Magazines Inc.

Alligator Magazine

Interesting and well-designed digital magazine concerned with the future of digital publishing, including interviews with industry experts and features on the tablet PC market. This first issue is free, and updates are promised every three months.

Overall Rating ★★★★☆

Price: Free
Developer: Livestation

Libya TV

A groundbreaking app that allows you to watch Libya's first independent satellite TV channel, broadcast in Arabic 24 hours a day since March 2011. Described by its founder as 'a voice for free Libya' on your iPad, the app is a remarkable achievement.

Overall Rating ★★★★☆

Price: Free
Developer: NASA

NASA Television

Watch NASA events unfold live or select from a list of recent uploads with this brilliant app from NASA. Includes mesmerising footage of the space shuttle Endeavour docked at the International Space Station, and updates from Mission Control in Houston.

Overall Rating ★★★★★

Price: Free
Developer: IOP Publishing

Physics World

Stylish and accomplished digital version of the world's leading physics magazine, *Physics World*. The app may be free, but access to issues of the magazine is only granted if you're a member of the Institute of Physics, which costs $25 a year.

Overall Rating ★★☆☆☆

Price: £1.79/$2.99
Developer: Joindup

Readable

This auto-scrolling web page reader makes innovative use of the iPad 2's front camera to detect when you're looking at the screen, pausing the scrolling should you look away. Nine scroll speed settings allow for a totally hands-free reading experience.

Overall Rating ★★★★☆

Price: Free
Developer: FOX News Digital

FOX News for iPad

Competent news app from America's FOX News Channel, including video reports, live ticker feed, radio reports, news alert notifications and 'Happening Now' section. Plastered with oil company adverts though, and not much use if you live outside the US.

Overall Rating ★★★☆☆

Price: £2.99/$4.99
Developer: DaiZW

Mage Reader

A social news feed reader, *Mage Reader* allows you to browse the news, photos and videos that your friends are sharing on Twitter. It's a little overpriced, but it's easy to use, supports offline reading and performs its allotted task well enough.

Overall Rating ★★★☆☆

Price: £1.19/$1.99
Developer: Chillingo Ltd.

News Heat Map

The iPad version of the newsheatmap.com website, a world map made of colour-coded dots indicating which countries are in the news. A horizontal ticker of current internet trending topics runs beneath, adding up to an interesting new way to browse the news.

Overall Rating ★★★★☆

Price: £1.79/$2.99
Developer: Top Pick

Police Scanner Radio Pro

Unlike most police scanner apps, this one also lets you listen to news and music broadcasts, for a total of over 40,000 radio stations. Built-in recording functions, alarm clock and sleep timer make it a bit of a jack of all trades.

Overall Rating ★★★☆☆

Price: £1.19/$1.99
Developer: Ola Balola LLC

The Final Hours of Portal 2

This interactive, multimedia 'appumentary' by journalist Geoff Keighley, filmed over 3 years, lifts the lid on the production process behind Valve's *Portal 2* videogame. A fascinating glimpse into the gaming industry.

Overall Rating ★★★★★

Price: Free
Developer: Darkness Production

iGuides

At first glance, *iGuides* appears to be a free app that aggregates news stories concerning all things Apple and iOS. And so it is, but even though the iTunes page states both English and Russian localisations, the entire app is in Russian. Fail.

Overall Rating ★☆☆☆☆

Price: Free
Developer: Mediafed

Mediafed News Reader

An RSS feed reader in the simple tradition, with a no fuss interface that's pleasant to use. Sadly, we found it preloaded with a bewildering array of Spanish, Italian, French and Russian feeds at launch, that we couldn't find a way to delete.

Overall Rating ★★★☆☆

Price: Free
Developer: mjclabs

Newsbits for iPad

Newsbits

Aggregating news from several sources into one place is a popular task for iPad apps. *Newsbits* handles the job with more aplomb than you'd expect from a free app, presenting news stories and relevant photos in a series of nicely presented 4x4 grids.

Overall Rating ★★★☆☆

Price: Free
Developer: Orange Vallee

RadioMee iPad

Cleverly designed radio station, podcast player and alarm clock app aimed at the French, Belgian and Swiss markets. Pick a decade, then rotate your iPad to landscape orientation to transform it into a vintage radio from that decade. Nice touch.

Overall Rating ★★★★☆

Price: Free
Developer: Ripe Apps Inc

Weblicious

Interesting and experimental web browser that lets you configure and customise your own personal layout of multiple web pages from multiple sites, giving you the freedom to have as much or as little content on the iPad's screen at any one time.

Overall Rating ★★★☆☆

Price: £1.19/$1.99
Developer: ORION Microsystems

iQuakeMini

With earthquakes seemingly striking with increasing regularity, this handy app monitors seismic activity by using US Geological Society data to display earthquakes on a colour-coded map according to size, severity, location, and date and time they occurred.

Overall Rating ★★★☆☆

Price: Free **Developer:** Moneyweb Internet Publishing Ltd

Mineweb for iPad

The world's premier mining and mining investment news website on your iPad, *Mineweb* really is a mine of information, and the fact that it's free is an added bonus. A nicely put-together, attractive and informative app for those in the mining trade.

Overall Rating ★★★★☆

Price: £2.39/$3.99
Developer: Navanit Arakeri

Palimpsest

Palimpsest presents you with a personalised selection of articles from magazines such as *The New Yorker, Vanity Fair* and others, based on how you voted for previous articles. Text-optimised viewing, an offline mode and *Instapaper* integration add to its appeal.

Overall Rating ★★★★☆

Price: Free
Developer: Park Media

RadioTodayUK

RT

Potentially useful resource aimed at people working and interested in the UK radio industry. Sadly, in our tests the majority of the links provided resulted in 'File Not Found' errors, although the content was eventually accessible via the archive links.

Overall Rating ★★☆☆☆

Price: Free
Developer: Diligent Media Inc

YouExtra for iPad

YouExtra claims to connect communities with the local news and information they care about. However, the app is supplied with zero instructions on how to use it, and is so badly implemented as to be completely unfathomable in our tests. One to avoid.

Overall Rating ★☆☆☆☆

Price: £1.19/$1.99
Developer: al.com

Day of Devastation

Jaw-dropping appumentary detailing the devastation left behind by the raft of tornadoes that hit the US state of Alabama on 27 April 2011, claiming 238 lives. Eyewitness reports and footage from before, during and after make compelling viewing.

Overall Rating ★★★★★

Price: Free
Developer: Mach Software Design

Hurricane Track for iOS

Hurricane Track allows you to track hurricane activity over the Atlantic with a selection of eight radar types overlaid on a static map. The animation runs a little fast for easy interpretation, but the images are clear and the app is ad free.

Overall Rating ★★★☆☆

Price: £0.59/$0.99
Developer: Code Stork LLC

Heat Warning

Heat Warning displays the current outdoor heat index based on your location's temperature and humidity levels. You can view a map image of apparent temperature, but only in the US, and an internet connection is needed to display the heat index.

Overall Rating ★★☆☆☆

Price: £1.19/$1.99 **Developer:** Utah State University Space Weather Center

SpaceWx for iPad

Developed as an educational project by the Utah State University, *SpaceWx* is a quite visually spectacular near real-time display of space weather, revealing how events such as solar flares affect the near-Earth space environment. Fascinating stuff.

Overall Rating ★★★★☆

Price: Free
Developer: fm

Wea Pro HD for iPad

Simple four-day forecast app that treads the familiar path of presenting weather data against a scenic backdrop reflecting the conditions. If the socking great banner ad annoys, you can upgrade to an ad-free version for just 59p.

Overall Rating ★★★★☆

Price: £1.79/$2.99
Developer: Lifeware Solutions

Deluxe Moon HD

Moon phase apps tend to look nice, and this one is a stunner. Featuring a gorgeous moon-phase calendar complete with zodiac signs, countdown timers for moonrise and moonset, and even gardening advice, this is both beautiful to look at and a joy to use.

Overall Rating ★★★★★

Price: Free **Developer:** Weather Decision Technologies

iMapWeather Lite

iMapWeather Lite boasts an attractive interface, but is a little unstable, crashing out a number of times in our tests. The radar display also failed to find any evidence of the cloud we could see above our heads. A stylish package hobbled by poor performance.

Overall Rating ★★★☆☆

Price: £2.99/$4.99 **Developer:** Ron Herrman

Marine WeatherFax Viewer HD

This app distributes the latest marine radiofax high seas weather maps straight to your iPad, from the Point Reyes, Kodiak, Boston, Honolulu and New Orleans broadcast stations. Needless to say, this makes it no use if you're not a US-bound seafarer.

Overall Rating ★★☆☆☆

Price: Free
Developer: William Alexander

SunJam

Eschewing postcode-based location search tools, *SunJam* allows you to pan a map around to find the location you need weather information for. This is fine as long as you know where it is on a map, but sometimes entering a postcode is just easier.

Overall Rating ★★★☆☆

Price: £0.59/$0.99
Developer: Presselite

Weather Motion HD

Possibly the most soothing and beautiful way to check the weather, *Weather Motion* displays the current outlook against a restful HD video backdrop representing the prevailing conditions. Pure atmospheric eye candy.

Overall Rating ★★★★☆

Price: £0.59/$0.99 **Developer:** Paul Cotarlea

Earthquake Survival Kit

This is a well-executed and comprehensive suite of 11 mini apps that could help out in the event of an earthquake. Includes an earthquake detection alarm, visual, acoustic and positional SOS, torch, battery life indicator, whistle and safety and first aid tips.

Overall Rating ★★★★☆

Price: £0.59/$0.99
Developer: Chun-Hsin Chen

iWeatherClock

Date, time and local weather information with a four-day forecast are overlaid as a transparent layer over an attractive scenic backdrop pertaining to the current weather conditions. An added alarm clock function makes for an attractive app to wake up to.

Overall Rating ★★★★☆

Price: £0.59/$0.99
Developer: WiDev

Meteo Widget HD

If you prefer a little Gallic flair to your weather, you could do a lot worse than *Meteo Widget HD*. With 3-day forecasts updated every 30 minutes, this is a nicely presented app that can display weather for anywhere in the world, not just France.

Overall Rating ★★★☆☆

Price: £2.39/$3.99
Developer: Justin Time

Tornado Spy HD

Tornado Spy enables users to upload sightings of tornados to its database, which are then displayed on an interactive map. User-submitted reports can often preempt official reports, so the app can serve as a useful early warning system for other users.

Overall Rating ★★★☆☆

Price: £0.59/$0.99
Developer: South American Travel Guides

Weather Paper

Simplicity seems to be the ethos behind Weather Paper, with time, date and current outlook displayed with minimum fanfare in the corner of an image based loosely on the conditions. 100,000 locations are featured globally with images updated daily.

Overall Rating ★★★☆☆

Price: £0.59/$0.99
Developer: Haptic Apps LLC

Easy Weather HD

A weather app that talks to you – how cool is that? Okay, the choice of three synthetic voices used to announce the outlook are a bit flat and wobbly, but the graphics have enough of a satisfying comic-book chic to compensate, delivering a summary with a smile.

Overall Rating ★★★★☆

Price: Free
Developer: BTypeMan Software

RadiationMapViewer

Aimed at monitoring the situation in the area around the Fukushima nuclear plant in Japan, this app displays current radiation levels at 66 locations on a map of Japan. Above-normal radiation levels are marked by a red pin, normal levels are green.

Overall Rating ★★★★☆

Price: £0.59/$0.99
Developer: Andrea Tondo

SatWeather

SatWeather is a real-time satellite weather image viewer for the UK, US and Europe. Configure your country, number of frames and required animation speed, then watch a fullscreen progression of cloud activity for your region over the past 16 hours.

Overall Rating ★★★★☆

Price: Free
Developer: diMobile

UV Position

A simple app that displays the current day's UV index at your location on a gaudy yellow screen. If you ask for a seven-day forecast, a hidden 59p charge is demanded. So much for the "Enjoy, *UV Position* is free!" quote on the developer page. Sneaky…

Overall Rating ★★☆☆☆

Price: £1.79/$2.99
Developer: Paul Armstrong

Weather View

Weather View's minimal interface replicates a virtual window, through which the current weather conditions are displayed as if you were looking through it up at the virtual sky, complete with accurate positioning for the sun depending on the time of day.

Overall Rating ★★★★☆

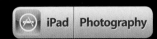

Photography

Although you can only take photos on an iPad 2, there are loads of apps available to help you enhance your images and make your pictures look amazing. From retro effect filters to colour enhancers, the photography category on the Appe Store is a buzzing hive of activity. Here are some highlights.

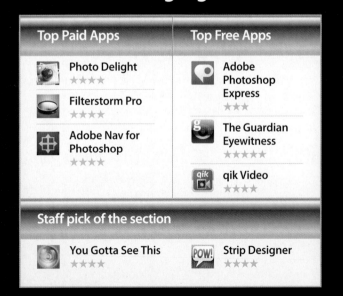

Top Paid Apps	Top Free Apps
Photo Delight ★★★★	Adobe Photoshop Express ★★★
Filterstorm Pro ★★★★	The Guardian Eyewitness ★★★★★
Adobe Nav for Photoshop ★★★★	qik Video ★★★★

Staff pick of the section

You Gotta See This ★★★★	Strip Designer ★★★★

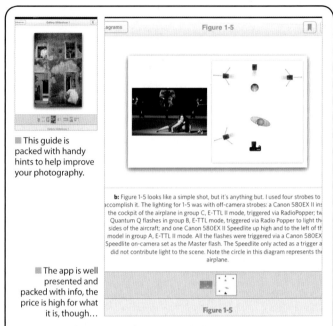

■ This guide is packed with handy hints to help improve your photography.

b: Figure 1-5 looks like a simple shot, but it's anything but. I used four strobes to accomplish it. The lighting for 1-5 was with off-camera strobes: a Canon 580EX II ins the cockpit of the airplane in group C, E-TTL II mode, triggered via RadioPopper; tw Quantum Q flashes in group B, E-TTL mode, triggered via Radio Popper to light the sides of the aircraft; and one Canon 580EX II Speedlite up high and to the left of th model in group A, E-TTL II mode. All the flashes were triggered via a Canon 580EX Speedlite on-camera set as the Master flash. The Speedlite only acted as a trigger a did not contribute light to the scene. Note the circle in this diagram represents the airplane.

■ The app is well presented and packed with info, the price is high for what it is, though…

Figure 1-5

Price: £8.99/$14.99   **Developer:** Standard Nine

Light, Camera, Capture

How to cram an entire book into your iPad

 Photography books can cost a fortune, so it's pleasing to find an app that not only delivers plenty of essential information for budding photographers, but also tools to back it up. While *Lights, Camera, Capture!* seems rather expensive, you're actually getting quite a lot of information for your money. In addition to eight large and informative chapters to wade through, there are also eight appendices (one of which features lot of handy links to useful websites), gallery slideshows, an in-depth look at exploring lighting and plenty of videos.

Based on the popular book by Bob Davis, *Lights, Camera, Capture!* offers an interesting look at creating superb imagery with minimal lighting equipment. The chapters include Understanding Light, Getting the Basics Right, Getting the Most From Your Lighting Kit and Travelling Light. Each and every one is extremely well written and insightful.

Rating ★★★★★

In the opening interface there are some cool tips and tricks to help you get started.

You can upload pictures to the Photoshop website where others can view them.

You can add borders to your photographs to add a nice finishing touch to frame the moment perfectly.

Price: Free **Developer:** Adobe

Adobe Photoshop Express

Professional photo editing from an industry powerhouse

Adobe is one of the premiere photography software companies and now it has brought its industry standard Photoshop application to the iPad. This version doesn't even come close to the original in terms of features but what it does provide are some stripped down functions in an incredibly slick and easy to use application.

As only iPad 2 has a camera, you will have to sync some pictures you've already taken in order use that app on an iPad 1. When it loads you have to select a picture to edit and from there you can do a number of cool things to enhance what you and your camera have already achieved.

The most basic functions are things like cropping and adding borders and on a more professional level you can adjust brightness, saturation and contrast. You can also add preset effects in a very simple way too. You can save your creations back to your picture library or upload them to Photoshop online (but this requires a membership). If we're totally honest there are far more advanced image editing apps on the store, though we doubt any

are as polished as Adobe's offering. The app is so easy to use that you can fumble your way into expertly enhancing your pictures without trying too hard.

There are lots of in-app purchases that you can invest in as well. These include the Adobe Camera Pack, the option to reduce noise (this smooths out flaws to quickly improve your photos), a selt timer for devices that come with a built-in camera and 'Auto Review', which instantly allows you to assess your pictures within the app and delete them if you feel that no amount of Photoshop trickery can do them justice.

Updates are released regularly too, the most regular of which includes full Retina Display support and multi-tasking, so you can do even more on the move. If you have used the desktop Photoshop app, however, then this will fall far short of your initial expectations. An extremely well made app if a little limited in some departments, this isn't a replacement for the desktop app.

Rating ★★★☆☆

Price: £1.19/$1.99 **Developer:** Global Delight Technologies

Photo Delight

Hand paint some colour into your pics with this cool app

Although there are a number of apps with similar functions available within the App Store, *Photo Delight* nevertheless manages to score highly thanks to its ease of use, smart tools and great options. The reasons for this success are plentifold. Firstly, its got some pretty smart styling, making the picture you load to edit look like it's on an easel. Down the side of the interface are the tools and options. The set up works in both landscape and portrait so you can adjust it according to the kind of picture you are editing. When you load a file from your library, you will find that it has been turned black and white, giving you the option of finger-painting the colour back into the picture. On top of that simple system are a couple of other cool features that will enhance the treatment you can give your composition. The first is the mask tool, which can be used to more easily view the area you are going to colourise. You also have the option of using different sized brushes for more detailed work, and you can choose between a soft or hard brush to reveal colour in a more subtle or obvious way. With some practice, you can create some truly stunning pictures. This is a great, easy way to sex-up your photos and the results are very rewarding. A very simple but effective app for those of a creative disposition.

Rating ★★★★☆

■ You can transform your photos into fabulous works of art with this easy-to-use app…

■ The app works in portrait or landscape orientation and any images you're proud of can be instantly circulated on the various social networking sites.

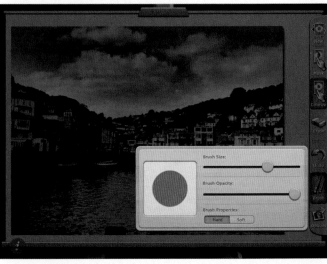

■ With a simple set of tools at your disposal you can mask certain areas of your picture and apply colour to other parts to lift it.

Price: £8.99/$14.99 **Developer:** Tai Shimizu

Filterstorm Pro

Edit your photos on the go with this feature-rich app

Photo editing apps are always a great addition to your iPad, especially now that the iPad 2 is sporting a pair of cameras to help you shoot on the go. *Filterstorm Pro* attempts to offer everything available in a desktop editing suite, with a huge range of options at your fingertips. The app is an evolution of the original *Filterstorm* and as such it takes all of the original app's photo editing capabilities and expands and enhances them as well as bolting on its own ready made photo library. Using *Filterstorm Pro's* photo library lets you store multiple versions of the same image, manage IPTC information and export destinations for images. You can send images to your iPad's photo library, FTP them, email them or use other applications such as Flickr and Dropbox. There is much to see and do with this app.

The app allows you to edit the physical attributes of your photo in seemingly limitless ways. You can crop, scale, rotate and flip, add borders and text, and edit the background colour. The options are all pretty self-explanatory and simple to use, although we quickly found that playing around with certain settings would add borders or zoom out of the image. Luckily, there is also a History tab that shows previews of your photo at every step, so if you do inadvertently make a mistake, it's simple to go back and change it.

You can also add filters to photos, and each has a selection of options, meaning that no two of your photos needs to look the same. However, some of the features are a little complex, and there is no obvious Undo button, which can be a little frustrating, but there are a number of online tutorials available that the *Filterstorm Pro* provides links to from within the app.

The sharing options are somewhat limited, with no Facebook support, and you can't take photos within the app, but hopefully these are issues that can be sorted out with future updates. Version 1.2 adds a noise filter, the option to split the preview (show the original image and the altered image) and the ability to show mask as a coloured overlay, amongst other things, so it's only a matter of time before this gets significantly better. *Filterstorm Pro* may have limited sharing options, but still a great purchase, with a huge range of photo-editing tools on your iPad.

There is an extensive array of options included to help you enhance your photographs.

Rating ★★★★★

The beauty of the app is its ease of use. It may be designed with photojournalists in mind but anyone can pick it up and get great results in a matter of minutes.

The app is receiving regular updates, so it's only a matter of time before you can take your own photos within the actual app itself.

Price: £1.19/$1.99 **Developer:** Adobe

Adobe Nav for Photoshop

Hook up your iPad and computer for a Photoshop cruise

Looking for ways to simplify your Photoshop workflow? With a wireless network, your iPad becomes a remote control with which to manage open documents.

Nav's toolbar enables you to select your 16 most-used tools, and switch them from the iPad. You can also zoom in and out, change screen modes or swap foreground and background colours. It's potentially brilliant, but every Photoshop user will have their personal extras wishlist, probably including hidden tools.

Where *Nav* really comes into its own is with its file management system. Here you can view thumbnails of up to 200 documents and switch them with ease. You can open documents and close others. Double tap any thumbnail to see that file's data. All open Photoshop documents are cached on the iPad, so you can disconnect and share your work away from your computer.

Rating ★★★★★

■ The on-screen keyboard encourages even more customisability.

Price: Free **Developer:** Guardian News & Media

The Guardian Eyewitness

Striking images from around the world

An ideal showcase for the iPad's high-definition display, *The Guardian Eyewitness* represents a perfect example of a great idea that has been beautifully executed. A repository of some of the most beautiful and thought-provoking photography from around the globe, a new image is added every day from the *Guardian*'s digital archive, with the bonus of explanatory captions and pro tips giving an insight into how each photo was taken.

The app also provides free access to the latest 100 photos taken in the series, with the option to download more images via the Wi-Fi connection.

Additionally, there is a video presented by the *Guardian*'s head of photography, Roger Tooth, in which he discusses the creative motivation behind the app, especially relating it to the newspaper's commitment to photojournalism. Fans of photography and striking images will love this, and there is plenty to enjoy. Brilliant.

Rating ★★★★★

■ The *Guardian* is well know for capturing the best images.

Adobe Eazel

Price: £2.99/$4.99   **Developer:** Adobe

Adobe has designs for your iPad. We take a look at the blueprints

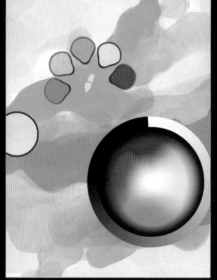

At the top of many mobile artists' wishlists is a fully featured mobile Photoshop, but with the launch of its latest apps, Adobe is inviting us to look in a different direction.

Enter *Eazel*, *Lava* and *Nav*; showcase apps intended to be of as much interest to developers as they will be to photographers, artists and designers. *Eazel* introduces a completely new way of working on a touchscreen, possibly more akin to playing a musical instrument than painting with a brush.

As the name suggests, it has been conceived as a mobile tool with which to make field sketches that are transferred wirelessly into Photoshop for refining and completion. It beautifully replicates the fluid quality of watercolour paintings, but this may present a challenge for users; that of learning to master a challenging medium, combined with adapting to a new way of interacting with a touchscreen. However, it is certainly worth taking time out for a bit of playful experimentation, as once you're comfortable with it, *Eazel*'s creative possibilities shine through.

■ You can achieve some fairly arty designs in *Eazel*.

■ It's possibly the least intuitive of the three Adobe apps reviewed here, but it contains the most creative possibilities.

Rating ★★★★★

Adobe Color Lava

Price: £1.79/$2.99   **Developer:** Adobe

Transform your iPad into a virtual colour-mixing palette

Remember how as a kid you loved to paint? With Lava, you use your fingertips to mix colours on the iPad, creating custom swatches and collections that can be transferred and used in Photoshop CS5.

Mix colours from scratch on a white ground, or import a photo from the camera roll to select and blend colours within it. Lava's materials behave realistically, and it's fun to swish a finger in the water well and smudge colours together. Also realistically, there's no undo, so remember to clean your finger in water before dabbing it on the palette, or you could accidentally remix a colour and possibly lose a perfect shade forever.

Useful developments would be extendable themes and the ability to select the mixing ground colour, but otherwise it's hard to imagine how else Lava might be improved upon. A useful and addictive addition to your creative toolkit, but doesn't have enough for it to be worthwhile for print designers.

■ As you'd expect, the colours look great on the iPad screen.

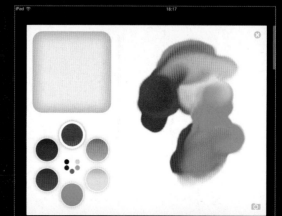

■ The color mixing is easily the best part of *Lava*.

Price: Free **Developer:** Qik Inc

Qik Video Connect Plus

A great streaming video app

We'll admit that at first we were a bit sceptical of yet another video recording app, but *Qik* won us over. You can record and edit videos, and then upload them to Facebook, Twitter and YouTube, or send a link via SMS and email for others to view. Where it really excels, though, is allowing you to stream video live on the web for any of your friends to see. It's a great idea and, while it was a bit jittery at times, it worked pretty well.

■ The sharing aspect of QikVideo is nothing short of amazing.

Overall Rating ★★★★★

Price: £2.39/$3.99 **Developer:** Adtec System Co Ltd

Floating Photo

Ever wanted to see you shots on water?

There are many photo apps available, but *Floating Photo*'s selling point is that it displays images as if they were on water. With a flick of the finger, you can send your photo around the screen. You can also pinch to enlarge, and use two fingers to rotate it. There are colour options such as greyscale, as well as the ability to download from Flickr.

While it's a unique idea, the limited features mean it doesn't give you much more than the built-in Photos app. There are also plenty of free apps out there that will tweak the colours, and more.

■ For a rather lofty price, there's not that much content.

Overall Rating ★★★★★

Price: £1.79/$2.99 **Developer:** Jens Egeblad

Strip Designer

Turn your boring photos into amazing comics

This app enables you to transform relatively ordinary photos from your albums into dynamic comic strips. With over 100 different layouts to choose from, you simply import your photos into pre-designed strips and then add speech bubbles, caption boxes and eye-catching stickers to tell a story. It's a great way to present and share your pictures with other people as the app also supports Facebook,

Flickr and Twitpic. It's straightforward to use and pretty addictive when you start to see the results – plus the kids love it. An easy-to-use app that can make even the most mundane snaps come alive.

■ Funny captions can add flavour the to the most drab photos.

Overall Rating ★★★★☆

Price: £1.19/$1.99 **Developer:** Boinx

You Gotta See This!

A neat photo-editing montage app

You Gotta See This! is a way of sending photo montages to your friends to give them a taste of the experience you're enjoying. There's a choice of six different themes to put these incredible photos on, including lightboxes and magic lights, and you can upload the results to your Twitter feed including a caption. A very clever photo manipulation program that really shows off the power of apps.

■ You can get the most out of this app if you have an iPhone 4.

Overall Rating ★★★★☆

Color Burst HD

Price: £0.59/$0.99 **Developer:** Smart Solutions

Following in the footsteps of the very popular *Color Splash* app, *Color Burst* is another app that converts your images to grayscale and then enables you to paint the colour back into specific areas with a fingertip. Burst differs by allowing you to change the hue colour or remove it altogether, and also by not being as good.

Rating ★★☆☆☆

iRemoveRedEyes

Price: Free **Developer:** Third World Apps LLC

Red-eye removal is one of the standard tools in a digital editor's toolkit, so you would think that finding a free app dedicated to that task would be something of a bonus. In reality though, although the app is easy to use, once you've placed and resized your targeting circles over the desired part of the eye and hit the 'remove' button, all you're rewarded with is a blocky black rectangle covering the iris. Okay if you're photographing the zombie apocalypse, but no good for regular party snapshots.

Rating ★☆☆☆☆

Photo Exchange

Price: Free **Developer:** MySpace.com

Photo Exchange offers an easy solution to the problem of swapping photos between iDevices. It's not immediately clear that you have to install the app on both devices, but once that's done, connecting is a breeze either over Wi-Fi or Bluetooth, then you flick the photos you want to transfer up off the top of the screen and marvel as they appear on the other device. Drawbacks include having to save each received photo manually, and the awkward scattered pile interface, but overall a very useful, free app.

Rating ★★★☆☆

I Can Animate

Price: £1.79/$2.99 **Developer:** Kudlian Software

I Can Animate simplifies stop-motion animation, allowing anyone to create stop-motion movies on their iPad 2. Either camera can be used to capture frames, while exposure, white balance and focus can be adjusted for each frame. The app display features onion skinning, making it easy to gauge the movement required for the next frame.

Rating ★★★★★

Skrappy

Price: £2.39/$3.99 **Developer:** Riada International Pty

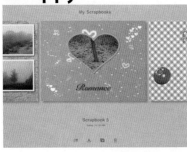

If you enjoy scrapbooking, this one's for you. *Skrappy* lets you combine attractive built-in themes with your own music, videos, audio notes, weblinks, text and images to produce stunning virtual scrapbooks complete with slick animated page turns. This app is packed with useful functions and features, such as easy one-touch web clipping.

Rating ★★★★★

Shuttersnitch

Price: £9.49/$15.99 **Developer:** 2nd Nature

Shuttersnitch enables instant wireless transfer of your photos as you take them, directly from an Eye-Fi or otherwise wirelessly-equipped camera. A few seconds after you take the shot, it appears on the iPad's screen, where *Shuttersnitch* analyses the photo's shutter speed, ISO, aperture, focal length and light level and alerts you if any one of those parameters differs from the rules you've set up. It may be relatively pricey, but the features it provides in a studio environment are more than worth it.

Rating ★★★★★

Wedding Photographer's Toolkit

Price: £5.99/$9.99 **Developer:** Sync ISD, LLC

The *Wedding Photographer's Toolkit* is a collection of tips, tricks and other useful resources such as blank contract forms and pose guides, all designed to help you produce better shots for your clients. Some of the content is web-based, so the app requires an internet connection to work properly, and a lot of the information is quite basic.

Rating ★★★☆☆

Viewbook Portfolio

Price: Free **Developer:** Viewbook

Viewbook Portfolio acts as a mobile portal for your Viewbook.com account, allowing you to show off your work in a stunning, swipeable interface featuring thumbnail grids and slideshows with a clean, modern look. You can sign up for a Viewbook.com account within the app and get a 30-day trial period for free.

Rating ★★★★☆

Price: £1.79/$2.99
Developer: Horizon Software i.t

007 Camera HD

 This simple photography app superimposes a fake *iBooks* page over the camera viewfinder. You swipe up and down to adjust transparency and tap to take a shot. The fake screen looks nothing like *iBooks* though, so don't try using it in an Apple Store.

Overall Rating ★★☆☆☆

Price: £0.59/$0.99
Developer: Jaimeson Bilodeau

Color Pro for iPad

 A useful tool for graphic and web designers, *Color Pro* lets you convert quickly and easily between RGB, hex codes, float values and HTML colour names. Four separate adjacent workspaces allow for easy comparison of selected sampled colours.

Overall Rating ★★★☆☆

Price: £2.99/$4.99
Developer: conceptual films Inc.

FOTO with Struan

 The *FOTO* app explores how professional photographers approach their craft, by following fashion photographer Struan on a shoot. There are also comprehensive video tutorials and an interactive forum aimed at showing you how to take better pictures.

Overall Rating ★★★★☆

Price: £0.59/$0.99
Developer: G.P.Imports Inc

iPerfect Camera

 Photo editing app offering a comprehensive selection of tools and filters, including the all-important crop tool that a lot of apps seem to miss out. The blue neon interface might not be to everyone's taste, but the large controls make it easy to use.

Overall Rating ★★★☆☆

Price: £1.79/$2.99
Developer: i-App Creation Co Ltd

Remote Shutter Pro

 Install this on two of your iDevices, connect via Bluetooth, then use one as a remote shutter release. The resulting image is saved to both devices. Great for iPad 1 owners, brilliant for group photos.

Overall Rating ★★★★★

Price: £0.59/$0.99
Developer: Occipital

360 Panorama

 Take 360 panoramic images with your iPad 2. You stand still and move around in a circle, pausing momentarily to let the app take a picture. It then uses software to stitch the images together into one long panorama of the scene around you. Clever stuff!

Overall Rating ★★★★☆

Price: £0.59/$0.99
Developer: Chang Cheng Lung

Colorful Gray

 Colorful Gray starts by transforming a colour photo into a monochrome one, then allowing you to paint the colour back in an element at a time. While this concept isn't particularly original, the app's ten-colour mosaic effect feature is a new one on us.

Overall Rating ★★★☆☆

Price: Free
Developer: Moobila

FotoEditor

 A basic set of eight free photo editing tools for your iPad, including Greyscale, Gamma Correction, RGB Balance, Sepia, Mirror, 180 Rotate, Negative, Brightness and Contrast. No zoom function or crop tool, but easy Facebook and Twitter sharing.

Overall Rating ★★★☆☆

Price: £2.99/$4.99
Developer: Carrafix

Photo Boost HD

 Photo Boost HD packages four image editing effects into one app. You get stretch, colorize, focus and 'twirl and bump' modes. The focus mode in particular is great for creating depth of field effects, as you tap the area you want to remain in focus.

Overall Rating ★★★★☆

Price: £1.79/$2.99
Developer: Penny Road, Inc

Retouch Photo Editor

 An effective image editing toolkit, *Retouch Photo Editor* blends preset filters for instant photo enhancement with a set of 16 editable controls for parameters such as hue, saturation, shadows, highlights and white balance.

Overall Rating ★★★★☆

Price: £0.59/$0.99
Developer: Escalation Studios LLC

Achiev.es

 Achiev.es lets you caption photos of your achievements with unique icons and placards, then share them with friends or upload them to the achiev.es website for the world to see. Photos are taken within the app, which supports all iDevices with a camera.

Overall Rating ★★★★☆

Price: £0.59/$0.99
Developer: Red Hot Bits

Doubleshot Photo

 Clever little app that lets you merge two photos together into one 'Doubleshot', using a supplied selection of 28 different layouts. Images can be taken within the app or imported from your Camera Roll or other device, and the app is AirPrint compatible.

Overall Rating ★★★★☆

Price: £0.59/$0.99
Developer: Kit Da Studio

Fotometer Pro

 Fotometer Pro is a beautifully designed light meter that covers a wide range of values to cater for most photographic scenarios. It supports incident and reflective measurement modes , ISO settings from 25 to 6400 and aperture values between 0.95 and 1000.

Overall Rating ★★★★☆

Price: £1.79/$2.99
Developer: EnSight Media

Photo+Folder HD for iPad

 The iPad still lacks any kind of photo management app, leaving a pile of unsorted images in your Photo Roll. *Photo+Folder* fills that void, providing a colourful folder system for your images that's both attractive and functional.

Overall Rating ★★★★★

Price: £5.99/$9.99
Developer: Perry Trotter

The Wedding Photographer

 Tutorials, tips and tricks of the trade for wedding photographers from Perry Trotter. Packed full of useful advice from capture, through editing to final production, this is a great resource for aspiring snappers in any genre.

Overall Rating ★★★★★

Price: £1.79/$2.99
Developer: Feel Great Games

AR Album

 Offering innovative and elegant ways to browse your GPS-tagged photos using augmented reality, *AR Album* has three main viewing modes (Map Overview, AR View and Fullscreen View) to really enhance the way you view your images on your device.

Overall Rating ★★★★☆

Price: £9.99/$16.99
Developer: MACK

Figures & Fictions

 Figures & Fictions is a complete multimedia catalogue for the exhibition of the same name currently running at the V&A Museum in London, showing the work of 17 South African photographers. Haunting? Yes. Captivating? Yes. Overpriced? Perhaps.

Overall Rating ★★☆☆☆

Price: £0.59/$0.99
Developer: Tim Schroeder

Image Resizer

 A simple app to resize images, resulting in smaller file sizes that can then be emailed more easily. Sadly, there's no obvious way to preserve the aspect ratio, so you have to calculate the appropriate dimensions yourself, which rather defeats the object.

Overall Rating ★☆☆☆☆

Price: £2.39/$3.99
Developer: Franck Duez

PhotoTeam Worldwide

 A great resource for photographers who might need to crew a shoot local talent at a moment's notice, *PhotoTeam* is a directory of model and photography agents, make-up and hair stylists and gear rental outlets.

Overall Rating ★★★★☆

Price: £1.79/$2.99
Developer: Studio Namu

uAlbum HD

 Stylish and functional photo management app designed to replace your iPad's Photo Roll and let you do more with your photos. You can reorder and rename multiple albums and create animated slideshows, but the current version lacks support for video files.

Overall Rating ★★★★☆

Price: £1.19/$1.99
Developer: Greg Fodor

Cartoon Booth

Cartoon Booth uses the iPad 2's cameras to superimpose cartoon eyes, noses and mouths onto subjects' faces. The clever part is that it does it before you take the picture, the cartoon elements tracking the subjects features with surprising, hilarious accuracy.

Overall Rating ★★★★☆

Price: £1.79/$2.99
Developer: Tapone Technology Inc

Fotoboard for iPad

A stylish image transfer and management utility, *Fotoboard* features a WiFi sharing function with a permanent URL, and provides an easy way to get photos from your iPad to your desktop computer.

Overall Rating ★★★★☆

Price: Free
Developer: Sander Grout

Photo Rage

You can now deface photos on your iPad without making a mess thanks to *Photo Rage*. Although the app is well executed, some instructions wouldn't go amiss, and if you want to share your destructive endeavours with the world, you have to pay to upgrade.

Overall Rating ★★★☆☆

Price: £0.59/$0.99
Developer: Black Frog Industries LLC

Pimple Eraser

This spot-healing tool is nicely implemented, with a virtual magnifying glass to aid your zit-targeting reticules and a single tap comparison toggle to compare your edited image with the original. Results are halfway decent, but not totally transparent.

Overall Rating ★★★☆☆

Price: £0.59/$0.99
Developer: Chang Cheng Lung

Reminiscent Brush

Reminiscent Brush aims to recreate a vintage feel for your shots, which it does quite successfully using a combination of colour tints and filters, together with a distinctive mosaic effect. You can choose to adjust the whole image, or just a specific area.

Overall Rating ★★★☆☆

Price: Free
Developer: misskiwi

ClassicBooth Free

ClassicBooth recreates the PhotoMe booth experience, but embellishes it with a choice of layouts and colour tints. You can't zoom or separate the resulting images, but you can email them or save them to your Photo Roll. A 59p ad-free version is available.

Overall Rating ★★★☆☆

Price: £1.19/$1.99
Developer: NextRoot

Instamap

Instamap is an app dedicated to viewing Instagram photos on the iPad. You can group photos to be viewed via location or tags, and browse photos either in a grid view or on a map. Feeds are live, so you can view and comment on photos as they are added.

Overall Rating ★★★★☆

Price: Free
Developer: Six Voices LLC

Photo to Toon HD Lite

This app attempts to turn photos into cartoons, but the effect just makes everything look terrible. Aside from that, a massive watermark plonked right in the middle of the frame makes the whole exercise pointless. One to avoid.

Overall Rating ★☆☆☆☆

Price: Free
Developer: Dimlight Software LLC

Pixeroid

Pixeroid is a fun way to turn your photos into generative art. Start with a normal image, select from an array of art objects to use and watch as the app builds your Pixeroid from thousands of elements, eventually forming the original image. Very cool.

Overall Rating ★★★★☆

Price: Free
Developer: Dimlight Software LLC

Slika eCards

Attractive suite of 25 virtual greetings card templates to which you can add your own photos and then email to friends. The card designs aren't that flexible, and only ten of them feature text, but they do adjust to landscape mode when the iPad is rotated.

Overall Rating ★★★☆☆

Price: £1.19/$1.99
Developer: ArchSquare

Collagraphy HD

Collagraphy creates editable collage effects, making a photo appear as if it's made up of several smaller photos scattered in a pile. The results are pleasant, although we couldn't find a way to get it to use multiple photos, which would be even better.

Overall Rating ★★★☆☆

Price: £1.19/$1.99
Developer: Tony Smith

Instapuzzle For iPad

Absorbing virtual jigsaw game that uses Instagram images as the source of its puzzles. You can set the size and number of pieces and choose the image and background colour, then the timer starts and away you go.

Overall Rating ★★★★☆

Price: Free
Developer: Antecea Ltd

PhotoCaster

PhotoCaster turns your iPad into an image server, linking to nearby computers via Wi-Fi and allowing you to access the images and videos in your Photo Roll from your Mac. However, we couldn't get it to open the Saved Photos folder at all in our tests.

Overall Rating ★★☆☆☆

Price: £1.79/$2.99
Developer: JS8 Media Inc

PopArtX

If you've ever wanted to follow in the footsteps of Andy Warhol, now's your chance: *PopArtX* creates the classic pop-art look for your photos simply and effectively, with adjustable colour and texture controls. Just tap on an image to apply the effect.

Overall Rating ★★★★☆

Price: £2.99/$4.99
Developer: Nik Software Inc

Snapseed for iPad

Top class photo editing on your iPad. Feature-packed, intuitive and featuring some unique creative effects, like the Vintage, Drama and Grunge filters and Center Focus mode. Capable of some remarkable results, this could be the only image editor you'll need.

Overall Rating ★★★★★

Price: £1.79/$2.99
Developer: Spark So

FaceSpy for iPad

FaceSpy allows you to mount covert surveillance using the iPad 2's cameras. Images from them are fed through to a window on one of ten fake theme pages, making it appear to the casual observer that you're just catching up on the news or browsing Facebook.

Overall Rating ★★★★☆

Price: £1.19/$1.99
Developer: Psionic Creative

Light Box

As the name suggests, this is a virtual light box upon which your digital images can be viewed, moved around, rotated and resized. You can change the border style and colour, and the light box background colour, and that's about it, really.

Overall Rating ★★★☆☆

Price: Free
Developer: Het is Simpel

PicStroom

All about sparking inspiration, *PicStroom* lets you quickly browse image streams from the web in a smart and efficient interface, then either store the ones that inspire you most into your Photo Roll or share them via Dropbox with colleagues and friends.

Overall Rating ★★★★☆

Price: Free
Developer: Red Bull

Red Bull Illume HD

22,764 photos were submitted to the Red Bull Illume Image Quest contest in 2010. This app presents the 250 semi-finalist images, all with the common theme of extreme sports, in a slick interface complete with notes on how each shot was achieved. Inspiring stuff.

Overall Rating ★★★★☆

Price: £1.19/$1.99
Developer: Shawn Skinner

Touch Up Pro - Photo Editor

Sophisticated editing app with a stylish interface that does its best to keep out of the way as you work. Offering a fairly standard set of tools and filters, several effects can be stacked to produce multiple possible combinations.

Overall Rating ★★★☆☆

Social Networking

One of the iPad's strengths is the way in which it can help you stay in touch with a sprawling network of friends, family and acquaintances. So leave the calls to your iPhone and concentrate on these social networking apps to stay well in the loop of what's going on.

Top Paid Apps	Top Free Apps
Echofon Pro for Twitter ★★★★	Boxcar ★★★★★
Blogsy ★★★★	AIM for iPad ★★★★★
Tweet It ★★★★★	Pingster ★★★★

Staff pick of the section

DoodleToo Lite ★★★★★	Tap to Chat 2 ★★★★★

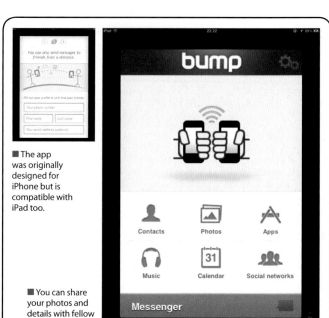

■ The app was originally designed for iPhone but is compatible with iPad too.

■ You can share your photos and details with fellow Bumpers…

Price: Free **Developer:** Bump Technologies LLC

Bump

Swap details instantly

 Bump is the deceptively simple brainchild of three ex-Texas Instruments employees who founded Bump Technologies to improve the ease of information sharing via mobile platforms. *Bump* was developed as a quick, easy alternative to typing new contacts into your iPad, instead offering an elegant solution: just 'bump' two phones together while running the app to exchange contact information.

The app works by sending data to a server across a wireless connection, be it Wi-Fi, 3G or Edge, using your location information and a clever algorithm to match your device to the device you bumped. Once both users confirm they want to exchange data, the server pairs the two devices. The result is one of the most effortless apps available, doing away with the process of setting up a wireless connection such as Bluetooth altogether – and apart from the occasional connection/detection issue, it works perfectly. Ideal for movers and shakers, or friends and family. Recent updates for *Bump* make it just as easy to select and share multiple contacts and photos, compare calendars and connect to social networking sites. Apps don't get more straightforward.

Rating

■ The app allows you to connect with a host of other social networking sites.

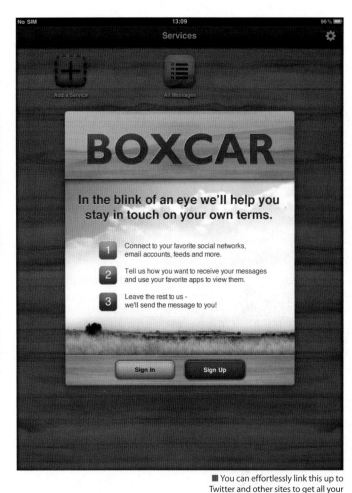

■ You can effortlessly link this up to Twitter and other sites to get all your feeds in one handy hit.

Price: Free **Developer:** Jonathan George

Boxcar

The news not when it happens, but as it happens…

Oddly, if you've no friends in this world whatsoever, *Boxcar* is certainly the app for you – though we sincerely doubt that was Jonathan George's intention in creating it.

More central to its existence is the plethora of social networking options available online nowadays. Whether it's through Twitter, Facebook, Foursquare, Google Buzz or any other portal, there's no shortage of places to keep up with current events of a serious or comedic nature. Trouble is, having so many sources can lead to mass confusion amid the bundles of data being cleaved out of the internet and thrown in the unsuspecting user's direction each day. *Boxcar* effectively addresses this situation by breaking down each of the above providers – along with email and RSS feeds – providing push notifications to your Apple device throughout the day the very instant one person or outlet updates. Rather tHAN than having to scroll through perhaps hundreds of Twitter feeds, or the brain-dead output of Facebook friends whose only concern is their next binge drinking session, it is now possible to cherry-pick the most valuable contacts across all fields, and be updated on

them instantly.

What's more, with specific relevance to Twitter, if you're interested in all the members of a particular band, magazine team or perhaps newsroom, the app makes slotting all of their Tweets together into an easily distinguishable whole just that little bit easier. It'll also open your preferred Twitter client, should you dislike *Boxcar*'s own interface for any particular reason. Naturally, if the idea of receiving push notifications every time an acquaintance has breakfast seems like some sort of living hell, rest assured you can restrict the app's functionality to certain times (though sadly not days of the week). The app did seem a little too prone to crashing upon various commands for our liking though, and this otherwise generous gesture does rely upon advertising support to survive (unless you're okay with the £4.99/$9.99 ad removal fee), but there's little denying *Boxcar*'s streamlining functions are pretty useful in this multi-multimedia world. Essential programming for the social network user who loves to network just that bit too much.

Rating

Price: £1.79/$2.99   Developer: Fomola

Blogsy

iPad blogging made easy?

 Blogging is currently one of the world's most popular technological hobbies – and has been for quite some time – with many ordinary people providing larger-than-140-character updates on how their life is going mixed in with inane and sometimes slightly disturbing rants. So it makes sense that purpose-built blogging iPad apps such as *Blogsy* exist.

When you first start the app up, you are greeted with what could well be considered a rarity in the App Store: a genuinely helpful welcome/tutorial page, which gives you all you need to start posting to your Wordpress or Google Blogger blogs. It goes into great detail about how you work the main mechanics of *Blogsy*, and by making it the first thing you see, you have no excuse not to know how the app works.

The first thing to note – and, indeed, the main gist of the aforementioned tutorial – is that the app has two 'sides' to it: the Rich Side and the Write Side, and throughout your blog editing/writing with *Blogsy* you will probably be using both in equal measure. The Write Side is by far the more technical of the two – it's essentially an HTML version of your blog's content – and, as the name suggests, it's where you write the blog. Of course, you use the iPad's on-screen keyboard to enter data,

and as usual the dreaded autocorrect is in full effect here, so be careful! If you don't catch your potentially embarrassing and costly mistake early, you may fall victim to one of *Blogsy*'s most annoying problems.

Fomola has designed its app so you simply switch from Rich to Write side with a horizontal swish of your finger. It's a great idea in theory, but you do a similar gesture when selecting the incorrect text, meaning that *Blogsy* will shift modes when you're trying to change a mistake – it's infuriating at best.

The Rich Side is where you can see how your blog entry looks so far, and take advantage of the app's best feature: integration. *Blogsy* allows files from Flickr, Picasa, YouTube and Google. Accounts are needed for all (except for Google), but if you have access to these sites, then *Blogsy* makes it very easy to use this content – it's just a case of dragging the video/image you want, and placing it into your blog. We'd like to see some music sites supported, but these will doubtless come from future updates.

It's definitely let down by a few almost fundamental control issues, but *Blogsy* is a decent blogging app with some potential. We recommended keeping an eye out for future updates.

Rating ★★★☆☆

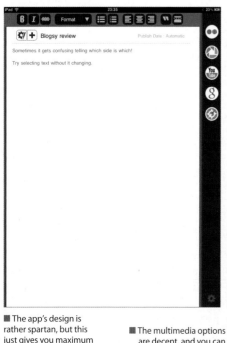

■ The app's design is rather spartan, but this just gives you maximum room to blog.

■ The multimedia options are decent, and you can attach YouTube videos.

AIM for iPad

Price: Free **Developer:** AOL Inc

Turn your iPad into a social lifeline

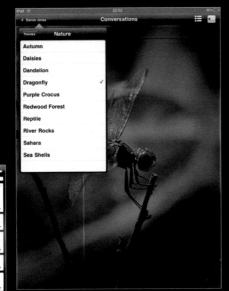

 Here's hoping the future releases will improve the app's stability.

The ability to receive multiple updates from many social-networking services is a real boon for AIM.

Being the social butterflies that we are, we were rather impressed with the idea of *AIM*. After all, what could be better than a cross-purpose app that allows you to chat on *AIM* while receiving updates from the likes of Facebook, Twitter, YouTube, MySpace and many more? Well an app that works consistently for starters.

Unfortunately, despite being a very solid app, this new version has continually crashed on us. It's a real pity that it's so flaky at the time of print, as there is plenty to enjoy here when everything is working properly, and we hope it's fixed soon.

Being able to get updates from a variety of different sources is incredibly handy, and really enables you to stay in touch with friends and family, while the whole interface system is relatively easy to navigate. If you're not a current member of *AIM* then setting up is a bit of a hassle, but it's a minor niggle and only needs to be done one time. Once registered you can sign in for a variety of other social network sites, switch between different identities at will and even post photos on your Lifestream blog.

Rating ★★★★★

Echofon Pro for Twitter

Price: £2.99/$4.99 **Developer:** Naan Studio, Inc

Tweet your life away

Echofon, the once-great official Twitter app, recently shot itself in the foot somewhat by introducing an update that integrated what has proven to be a universally detested trending bar into the main interface, thus ruining the overall experience for the vast majority of users.

Echofon Pro, on the other hand, remains slick and full of genuinely useful features, in the process providing a comfortable, well-rounded tweeting experience, with the added benefit of a useful timeline that always scrolls back to the last-read tweet on relaunch.

As such, *Echofon Pro* manages, very successfully, to be a better and more user-friendly experience than what using the standard Twitter app is. Whether you're a casual or regular user of the revolutionary social-networking program, you would be advised to download this if you're willing to pay the, admittedly not cheap, asking price.

It's relatively easy to share all your cute animal pics to your followers.

 The Echofon Pro Twitter interface will be familiar to most users.

Rating ★★★★★

Price: Free   Developer: DoodleToo

DoodleToo Lite
Bring out the artist in you

 As jaw-dropping social network apps go, this has to rank right near the top. We were presented with a blank screen and little idea of what we were supposed to do. So we scrawled a few lines. The next thing, something else was being drawn, accompanied by the word 'guest'. Someone who we have never met was doodling with us, and it was quite astonishing.

The app has two versions: a paid-for one a free one. And the free version suited us fine for what we wanted to do, which was play and interact (the full has more rooms, colour and better social facilities). You can invite friends to join you so that you're not randomly drawing with strangers and you can also snap your creation and send it via email or on Facebook, adding a message while you're at it.

DoodleToo Lite has a number of 'rooms' which offer various backdrops (the Photo Lite room, for example, has some scenic shots and White Lite is, as you would expect, just a plain white background). You can browse these, either looking for playmates or to find a different vibe. And if you want to communicate with anyone, you just tap 'Say It' and you have 120 characters for your message. It's great fun to use and well worth installing on your device.

Rating ★★★★★

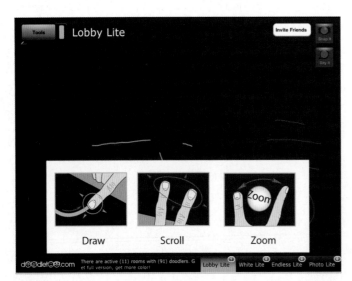

■ Some brief instructions are provided but it's all about the experience.

Price: Free   Developer: Osmosis Apps Limited

Tap to Chat 2 for Facebook Chat
Chat while you surf the net

 One of the most popular aspects of social-networking site Facebook, besides the status updates, is the chat facility. *Tap to Chat 2* draws this one particular feature out and wraps a standalone app around it, making it easier to converse with friends who happen to be online.

As soon as you log on using your Facebook details, the app will scour your account for any friends who happen to be online. So with this app, there is no need to jump to people's profiles and no messing around with tiny boxes on desktops. Once you're presented with your available friend, you can chat with one or more of them.

Although there is a separate app for GoogleTalk, it would be nice if these facilities were included in the one app for a better, more rounded experience. But that's not to say that *Tap to Chat 2* is any less of an app for concentrating on one chat facility at a time.

You can change your status from Online to Offline, Away or Invisible if you wish and you can toggle the sound effects and background alerts. The text can be enlarged if you wish it to be bigger. Finally, the app also runs on the iPhone and the iPod touch.

Rating ★★★★★

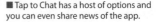

■ Tap to Chat has a host of options and you can even share news of the app.

■ The app searches for friends and, if there are none, displays this clearly.

■ You can see where you are on the in-built map which hooks into Google.

Price: Free **Developer:** TripTrace

Pingster
Be famous for 15 minutes

Pingster is a high-concept app. It presents you with a big red button and, when you tap it, you will become visible to anyone else using the app within your vicinity. You remain visible for 15 minutes, during which time people are able to locate you and attempt to contact you if they wish.

This may seem like a stalker's paradise but the key is that everyone remains anonymous, with only usernames visible to other people. You can probably see one flaw – you only get to see people if they are logged in and they have pressed the button too and so, like many social networks, it really does depend on the number of people who not only download it but use it as well.

But it's a very easy app to use. You can view a map to see exactly where you are on it and you can create emails and hook into Facebook as all social network apps worth their salt now do. Overall, it's an ambitious app that aims to connect people in real life using virtual means and without attempting to compromise your identity or safety.

Price: £0.59/$0.99 **Developer:** Andre Williams

Tweet It
It's yet another Twitter app

If you've ever used the brilliant *iA Writer* app, which aims to make word processing a far simpler affair, then you will take to *Tweet It* like a duck to water. The app strips away all but the ability to create a status update, which is mightily refreshing and also means you are going to be tweeting far more in the weeks and months to come.

The main screen is simply white. You can type your 140 characters into it and then press send and, given that you have linked a Twitter account to it, it will show in your feed. You can have more than one account too.

But it's not just a matter of writing a status and sending it. You will want more than that for your money. So *Tweet It* adds a few extra handy features such as a link to a web browser so that you can quickly find an internet address and cut and paste it into your tweet with just a couple of taps. And you can shorten web addresses by pressing the option to make it a bit.ly address.

If you have already been surfing the web and come across something worth tweeting, the app will pick up the last URL you were on before you opened Tweet It so you can effortlessly paste it in.

Rating ★★★★★

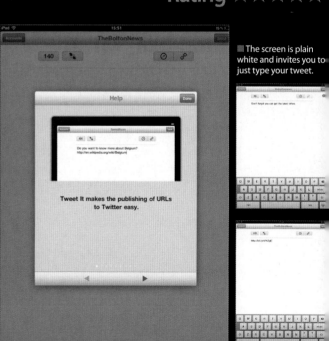

■ The screen is plain white and invites you to just type your tweet.

■ Publishing URLs is simple with the app pulling in information from your browser.

Price: £1.19/$1.99
Developer: Orjen Solutions

Signaller

In an area where you can't get a signal? Need to get your message across to somebody in double quick time? Just write a message using *Signaller*, hold your iPad aloft and your text will appear large. Great for use in a crowd or where you can't hear yourself speak.

Overall Rating ★★★☆☆

Price: £0.59/$0.99
Developer: Pavel Kanzelsberger

Upside down – crazy upside down sms, facebook

Turn messages on their head by writing some text, having this app flip them upside down and then pasting them into your social updates.

Overall Rating ★★★☆☆

Price: £0.59/$0.99
Developer: tao li

A Super Gtalk HD

This app works well as a way of isolating and using the Google Talk instant messaging service. You can send emails, set avatars and discover who is and who isn't online. It's a neat app but there are better and free alternatives around that are worth checking out.

Overall Rating ★★☆☆☆

Price: £0.59/$0.99
Developer: iApp Ventures LLC

Chat for Facebook (HD) with Push

As another Facebook chat client, this expands on the usual offerings with personalised themes and customised backgrounds as well as chat history. There are also emoticons and even pre-loaded status updates.

Overall Rating ★★★★☆

Price: £0.59/$0.99
Developer: Scott Kehrberg

Fotobooked

This arranges your Facebook photos into albums. It's simply a way of reorganising and displaying them so that you can view them more clearly. It allows you to see comments and tags and browsing through each one is made easier with a slideshow option.

Overall Rating ★★★☆☆

Price: £1.19/$1.99
Developer: Ka Man Fong

SMS & Messaging Glossary

Just about everyone's heard of Aesop's famous fables and this app is a commendable attempt at bringing these to your iPhone. The artwork and features aren't that great, but the stories are so entertaining you'll forgive the rest.

Overall Rating ★★★☆☆

Price: £0.59/$0.99
Developer: Matthew Chappee

HeyYou HD

Built for situations where lots of people will be in one room together – be it a business convention or a local bar – this uses wi-fi to exchange messages, photos and contact information, doing away with the humble business card in the process.

Overall Rating ★★★☆☆

Price: £1.19/$1.99
Developer: Irfan Farooqi

Persian Cookbook Pro

Mouth-watering recipes are brought to the social networking genre by *Persian Cookbook Pro*, allowing users to browse the foods on offer and share them with friends on Facebook and via email.

Overall Rating ★★★★☆

Price: Free
Developer: Hideki Kishioka

Stickam for iPad

Since it uses your camera, this is an app for iPad 2 owners only. It broadcasts live from your iOS device with just one click, letting others see what you are up to. People can watch you and communicate at same time. It works better over a wi-fi connection.

Overall Rating ★★★★☆

Price: £0.59/$0.99
Developer: iApp Ventures LLC

Q&A for Facebook

If you have a burning question and you need to ask friends and acquaintances for their valued contribution, you can use this app to communicate with your Facebook contacts. You ask a question and your friends can see and answer it. You can answer their questions too.

Overall Rating ★★★☆☆

Price: Free
Developer: Cheuk him LAM

Buyers' Conn

Given shopping is one of the most popular pastimes in the western world, it's nice to share information about the material goods you pick up. With *Buyers' Conn*, you can jot down what you bought, how much you spend and scan the barcodes of products for easier entry.

Overall Rating ★★★★☆

Price: Free
Developer: End of Time Studios

ShopFloorTalk

It's a social network for people who enjoy manufacturing. It gives welders, machinists and metal workers a platform to share tips and discuss their hobby or job and it is aimed at beginners, helping them to get the hang of the individual skills via a series of forums.

Overall Rating ★★★☆☆

Price: £0.59/$0.99
Developer: Heritage Academy

Smylies

Love them or loathe them, there's no getting away from the smilies. With this app, you can use them yourself, selecting a great selection of 460 colourful images for use in your emails, notes and text messages. It adds a new – fun - keyboard to your iPad.

Overall Rating ★★★★☆

Price: £1.19/$2.99
Developer: Scott Kehrberg

Starvator

Millions love to follow celebrities on Twitter but it's all a little, well, flat, isn't it? *Starvator* lets you select four cartoon personalities to who you can assign specific Tweeters. The characters open their mouths when tweets come through. Daft, but fun.

Overall Rating ★★★☆☆

Price: £0.99/$1.59
Developer: Kabir Nazmul

MoviesAndDates

If you are looking for love and adore the cinema then this app will combine the two. You can create and view profiles with the app searching for people nearby who best match you. It's only just got going so there aren't many people on there as yet.

Overall Rating ★★☆☆☆

Price: £1.79/$2.99
Developer: Wesson Systems

Friends Aloud HD

Gives your eyes a rest, sit back and relax. This app is going to get around the whole laborious process of reading status updates by reading them for you. It takes your Facebook feeds and converts them to audio so when they appear, you will be the first to know.

Overall Rating ★★★★☆

Price: Free
Developer: End of Time Studios

Property Community Forum

From the makers of the ShopFloorTalk app comes one aimed at people interested in property. It's primary focus is on property in emerging countries but it also includes the UK and US. It's a rather straightforward, specialised forum.

Overall Rating ★★★☆☆

Price: £0.59/$0.99
Developer: Alteru, Inc

Universal Translator

In the UN, people sit with headphones on interpreting the various languages. You don't need this. *Universal Translator* lets you use Google Talk with a person whose language you don't understand and translates it on the fly. And you get to see their responses in English.

Overall Rating ★★★★☆

Price: Free
Developer: Prodisky Inc

Checkin Photo

If you take a photo on your iPad 2, you can use this app to select a place, check in and upload the image to your Facebook account. The app used to take a short while to load but that has now improved. It's a one-trick pony but it works.

Overall Rating ★★☆☆☆

Price: Free
Developer: WorkVoices B.V.

Work Voices

To use *WorkVoices*, you need to have access to a work social intranet set up via the WorkVoices website. The app provides a way to hook into this network so that colleagues can keep abreast of whatever is happening and exchange information on projects.

Overall Rating ★★★☆☆

Price: Free
Developer: Invision Power

Volvospeed Connect

Car fanatics who adore Volvos will love this app. It lets them engage in a community of like-minded people, with the ability to upload photos and discuss all manner of subjects from mods to maintenance. There is also a section for sales.

Overall Rating ★★★☆☆

Price: Free
Developer: Javier Rayon

Friend Scanner

With Friend Scanner, you can access the Facebook webpage directly from your browser without having to go via Safari. The app goes beyond that too with a feature that lets you upload pictures from the Photos app to Facebook. The developer promises video uploading in future.

Overall Rating ★★★★☆

Price: £1.19/$2.99
Developer: Brockle Tech Corp

myNails for Facebook

If you want your nails done just right, play around with this app for a while. It lets you design your fingernails using more than 60 colours. The results can then be posted on Facebook and is great for checking out what others think of them.

Overall Rating ★★★★☆

Price: £1.19/$1.99
Developer: iRina Kun

1000+ 3D Animations Pro for iPad

Instead of using regular Joe emoticons, try out some 3D animated versions in your emails and instant messaging accounts instead.

Overall Rating ★★★☆☆

Price: Free
Developer: Taknology

Facedekk

Using just one Facebook account at a time may not suit you if you have others at your disposal. With Facedekk you can manage more than one at once, with magical features such as being able to send a single message to all accounts and posting status updates to Pages.

Overall Rating ★★★★☆

Price: £1.79/£2.99
Developer: Data Calibre

Social Login

It's difficult remembering all the different logins we have for sites. This app lets you use just one password to access a host of social networks from Facebook to Blogger, Twitter to MySpace. And it does it all simultaneously so it makes for very fast access.

Overall Rating ★★★★☆

Price: Free
Developer: AppIndustry

Stare

Billed as a live photo frame, Stare is slideshow of photographs pulled in from Facebook with headlines and comments placed randomly placed over the top, giving images a comic book feel of sorts. Favourites can be emailed direct from the app.

Overall Rating ★★★★☆

Price: £0.59/$0.99
Developer: Dating DNA

Christian Dating

Not so much a social network but a dating network, this app is aimed at Christians looking for love. But it does have integration with Facebook and MySpace and its match radar scours the real world for nearby matches. There are no subscriptions, which is a bonus.

Overall Rating ★★★★☆

Price: Free
Developer: End of Time Studios

Prison Talk Online Forum

This is not an app for prisoners but for their family and friends. It offers a support network for those who have a loved one in jail. It gives lists of subjects to which people can contribute and share help, tips and advice with each other.

Overall Rating ★★☆☆☆

Price: £0.59/$0.99
Developer: Amos Bianchi

InTouch for Facebook

This tailor-made Facebook app goes beyond the website in providing a handy user interface that makes navigation much easier. You can access most of the things you would expect via the web as well as watch videos.

Overall Rating ★★★★☆

Price: Free
Developer: William Bagshaw

FourSite Free

Users of Foursquare can see a map-based view of areas they are exploring. It uses Google's satellite view of the world and tells you who is in the local vicinity. You can also view tweets and see maps and venues. IT may not offer anything particularly new but what's here works well.

Overall Rating ★★★★☆

Price: £0.59/$0.99
Developer: Metehan Karabiber

Symbols 4 Facebook HD

If you are looking for a set of symbols to brighten up your Facebook postings (maybe a heart for your loved one or a telephone to show a number), then try this. It has 300 of them all positioned on an exhaustive-looking keyboard.

Overall Rating ★★★☆☆

Price: £1.19/$1.99
Developer: Dane Homenick

WakeUUUUP! Social Alarm Hub!!!

Mornings don't have to be anti-social. At least, that's the aim of this. It lets you find friends, create your own profile and send and receive messages. You can send audio and video that they can use as their wake-up alarm.

Overall Rating ★★★★☆

Price: £0.59/$0.99
Developer: Space-O Infocom

Chat Abbreviations

Search through this app and you see more acronyms than you can shake a stick at. But it will prove useful. You will soon be able to communicate with greater effectiveness when dealing with abbreviation lovers. The entries can be shared via social media.

Overall Rating ★★☆☆☆

Price:Free
Developer: Shimon Yannay

Ask Amigos

One of the benefits of social networks is the ability to ask questions of friends. Ask Amigos taps into that ethos but with an emphasis on questions that have just two answers. Question results can be posted on your Facebook wall.

Overall Rating ★★☆☆☆

Price: £0.59/$0.99
Developer: Saravanan K

The iBrowser

The unique selling point of iBrowser is its ability to take snapshots of the screen and make it available for instant emailing. The screen can be zoomed in and portions of the display can also be taken and there is integration with Facebook and Twitter.

Overall Rating ★★★☆☆

Price: Free
Developer: End of Times Studios

Tackle Box Forum

Fishing enthusiasts angling for a top forum should try Tackle Box with a bustling community sharing tips and hints on all manner of fishy things. Sign up is quick and easy and with all of the options running along the bottom it makes optimum use of the screen.

Overall Rating ★★★☆☆

Price: £0.59/$0.99
Developer: Mark Lussier & TapFactory

TweetyPop – Twitter, Reimagined

Rather than have Tweets in 2D, TweetyPop makes Twitter a 3D experience, giving the whole thing a fresh perspective and a cool shine that casual Tweeters will love. When you've finished with a Tweet just fling it off the screen.

Overall Rating ★★★★☆

Price: Free
Developer: NeuStar

Text Everywhere

This American service (that works only where a carrier offers Neustar Text Everywhere facilities) lets you send texts on your iPad using your carrier's phone number. The messages appear in exactly the same way as through the Messages app on the iPhone.

Overall Rating ★★★☆☆

Price: £0.59/$0.99
Developer: Nguyen Kent

Hello. App – Facebook for iPad

When apps appear in the App Store, we tend to like them to be complete. This app, which lets you view Facebook in a fresh way, keeps promises new features – chat and theme is due to arrive for instance – but this app does show promise.

Overall Rating ★★★★☆

Price: £0.59/$0.99 **Developer:** Jeremy Nixon

Tall Tales – Geolocation Spoofing

Tired of seeing friends 'check in' at exciting places on Facebook? Use *Tall Tales* to check in where you like: choose your own location or from a selection including 10 Downing Street, Las Vegas or the White House. The app doesn't use GPS or Location Services, but will fool Facebook, Twitter and more into thinking you're somewhere else.

Rating ★★★★☆

Price: £2.39/$3.99 **Developer:** Said Marouf

Osfoora HD, for Twitter

An easy to use Twitter client, *Osfoora HD* presents every Twitter feature plus more in an elegant interface. The app includes multiple user accounts, nearby tweets, customisable font sizes, an auto refresh, tweet timelines, subscribe and unsubscribe options and much more that the regular tweeter will love. In fact, rather bizarrely you'll find a whole boxload more tools and abilities here than in the official app. The price is a little steep but you get value.

Rating ★★★★★

Price: Free **Developer:** AircraftMerchants, LLD

Planes on Poles

This app enables users to post and share photographs of airplanes on poles – the kind usually found outside airports, air displays and aircraft manufactures. When photos are uploaded they're geotagged and appear on a world map for others to see. If you have a penchant for planes on poles, then this app is for you.

Rating ★★★★☆

Price: Free **Developer:** Yap.tv, Inc.

yap.TV

Keep up with TV schedules even when you're away from the gogglebox. A fantastic way to discover what's showing on TV, yap.TV displays the schedule for the week ahead with a unique and tactile interface. The app also integrates with Facebook and Twitter, enabling users to discover what friends are watching, creative interactive polls and more. The perfect app for those in the US who enjoy sharing TV show reviews and comments via Twitter.

Rating ★★★★☆

Price: £1.19/$1.99 **Developer:** Project Zebra Ltd

Dash Four

This is a map-based foursquare client. For those who haven't heard of foursquare, it's a location-based service similar to Facebook's Check-in. Simply check-in, leave comments and tips, and see where you're checked in. With its badges and mayorship system, this is a unique app with plenty of fun location-based antics.

Rating ★★★★☆

Price: £2.49/$3.99 **Developer:** Dilraba Ibrahim

U and Facebook for iPad

Unlike many Facebook apps for the iPad, U and Facebook includes support for video playback, live chat, a powerful rules engine, and also the ability to use two Facebook accounts at the same time - handy for those with business and personal accounts. It's marred by some terrible graphical choices however, including ugly background images and cartoon characters that litter the interface. A feature-packed app, but one with UI issues.

Rating ★★☆☆☆

Price: Free **Developer:** WordPress

WordPress

Manage your WordPress blog from your iPad. It's possible to create or edit posts and pages, moderate user comments, upload photos and insert links. Basically, everything you'd typically be able to do via the official website. However, the app is prone to crashing when inserting images, and on occasion doesn't save posts.

Rating ★★☆☆☆

Price: £1.19/$1.99 **Developer:** Christian Arild Strommen

Social for the iPad

This app gives full access to the Facebook website through your iPad, and we mean that literally – the app simply loads the Facebook site through a built-in browser and displays it with a custom skin. So for £1.19/$1.99 you can receive virtually the same Facebook experience by simply visiting the website through Safari or other browser, although the custom icons that appear in this app make the experience less fiddly.

Rating ★★☆☆☆

Price: £1.19/$1.99 **Developer:** Alekseev Vladislav

Jabba

This is a great instant messenger that supports Gmail, Facebook, Livejournal and Yahoo Online, enabling users to chat in real-time, send images, a map location and web link to chat buddies. It's tricky setting up accounts however, with authentication errors when trying to set up Gmail accounts not ending in .com

Rating ★★★☆☆

Price: £0.59/$0.99 **Developer:** Dev

Privacy Plus for iPad

A feature-packed browser for the iPad, *Privacy Plus* includes a number of useful tools including unlimited tabs that can be switched at the swipe of a finger, built-in brightness controls and a thorough privacy mode that enables users to browse the web without leaving any traces of search terms, cookies, cache files and passwords. The interface borders on cartoon-like in appearance, but look past this and you'll find one incredibly useful browser.

Rating ★★★★☆

Price: £2.99/$4.99 **Developer:** Dev

Cazcade

Cazcade enables users to share content from websites at the tap of a finger. The interface isn't exactly intuitive, it requires the user to browse a site, extract photos and RSS feeds, arrange them in a window called a pool and then share via Twitter. Once mastered Cazcade becomes a unique way to share content with friends.

Rating ★★★☆☆

Price: £0.59/$0.99 **Developer:** P.J. Tanzillo

Animoticons HD

Give your messages an emotional touch. Within this app are 680 smiley, grumpy, etc animations. For those unsure of what a smiley is, it's a small graphical icon representing an emotion. Originally they were cleverly made up of letters and punctuation, :o) for example, indicates smiling. Once a smiley has been chosen from within the app, it's possible to copy it to the clipboard for later pasting into an email, or send a smiley directly to the Mail app.

Rating ★★★☆☆

Price: £0.59/$0.99 **Developer:** Inyfx, Inc.

Whoodl

If you ever struggle to remember someone's name then this app is the perfect. Quickly jot down a name, and assign it to a location, such as 'coffee shop regulars'. Next time you visit the coffee shop, remind yourself of the those there, and you'll never forget their name. It's a more efficient process than adding details to the Contacts app.

Rating ★★★☆☆

Price: £1.19/$1.99 **Developer:** Levity Novelty

Alive Albums

Browsing Facebook albums using an iPad can be a chore. The next and previous buttons are small, and the page has to completely reload before another image appears. *Alive Albums* makes viewing multiple photos and albums incredibly easy. It's possible to select multiple albums from any source and then view them via an interesting animated slideshow. It works a treat, and is a great way to discover and browse new images.

Rating ★★★★☆

Price: Free **Developer:** Zuke Technologies

My Location – Social Edition

The ability to Check In at Facebook gives your friends an easy way to discover where you are. My Location – Social Edition enables any iPad user to upload their current location to Facebook with an image of a Google Map. Users can choose from a road map, satellite image or a hybrid of both, with a blue pin that indicates their exact spot.

Rating ★★★☆☆

Price: £0.59/$0.99 **Developer:** Dev

TweetPad

TweetPad enables users to create notepad-inspired blog posts using their iPad. The app includes the ability to import photos from the Photo Library, and include as much text as required (no 140 character limit here). Once a blog is completed it's saved to the iPad as an image file, enabling users to upload it as a single image. This is a handy app that makes blog posting easy, but bear in mind the notepad theme is the only one included.

Rating ★★★☆☆

Price: £2.39/$3.99 **Developer:** Richard Hyland

Tweetings HD for Twitter

A truly feature-packed Twitter app, *Tweetings HD* includes GeoLocation support, the ability to record and upload audio, tweet the current music track playing on the device, find nearby Tweeters and display them on a map, plus the usual Twitter features you'd expect. A great choice for heavy Twitter users, but one with a high asking price

Rating ★★★★☆

Price: £1.19/$1.99 **Developer:** Arramex

Dialogues

Once you've paid the download price, dialogues is a great way to chat with friends and family for free, enabling users to communicate with each other through the app. Your conversations are saved in full for later reference, and if the app is closed a Push Notification appears on screen when a new message has arrived for you to read. The app also includes a built-in browser that makes viewing web links a simple and quick process.

Rating ★★★★☆

Price: £0.59/$0.99 **Developer:** sobees Sarl

Sobees lite for Facebook

Sobees gives Facebook a newspaper-inspired appearance. It's an unusual approach that works to a degree, giving the news feed, user profile, photos and events sections of Facebook a professional look. The app also includes support for updating user status, commenting and liking posts and manage events and birthdays in a calendar view.

Rating ★★★☆☆

Price: £1.19/$1.99 **Developer:** TL Usher

Yo! HD

The iPad has a large 9.7 inch Multi-Touch display that's perfect for communicating across the web. But what if you want to send a message to someone across the room? *Yo! HD* enables the user to quickly type a message and then display it in massive letters across the iPad screen. It's perfect for cheering on friends, athletes and celebrities at public events, or sending a quick message across small areas. Shouting also works, but maybe not in your local library!

Rating ★★★☆☆

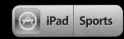

Sports

You either love sport or you don't and those that do are generally pretty obsessive about a particular team or event – and there is definitely an app to fuel such obsessions. The following apps allow you to embrace sport like never before, on your iPad.

Top Paid Apps	Top Free Apps
Tennis 109 With Jimmy Connors ★★★★	**Virtual Tennis Coach** ★★★★★
Golfplan ★★★★	**NBA Game Time** ★★★★★
Football Rumours ★★★★	**Eurosport for iPad** ★★★★★

Staff pick of the section

Sky Mobile TV ★★★	**Rules Of Golf** ★★★★

▓ Get the ball to the front man. There you go, lesson over.

▓ The app is designed to help with all sports.

Price: £2.99/$4.99 **Developer:** AlphaSprite Limited

Coachpad

Tips and tactics to manage a better team

 If you've ever fancied yourself as a football manager, play in a local sports team or just love discussing sports strategies with your mates then you're bound to be interested in this useful little app. *CoachPad* presents you with blank layouts of a number of different sports, ranging from football to basketball and tennis. Once you've chosen the template you wish to use it's possible to sketch all manner of different plays and formations on it.

Useful items ranging from different coloured pens to line tools and ball tokens are all available, you can choose from a variety of different icons to reflect balls and other sports tools and it's relatively easy to drag on-screen items over to new locations in order to better show off chosen tactics. You can go online to download additional templates, import backdrops and, best of all, link up to a larger screen to show off all of your final plans.

Despite its overall versatility, *CoachPad* is far from perfect. The inability to draw new plans while linked to a bigger screen frustrates, which is a shame as this is otherwise good.

Rating ★★★☆☆

Price: £5.99/$9.99 **Developer:** International Celebrity

Tennis 109 With Jimmy Connors
Get coached by a tennis legend

 While there are a few shortcomings with this tutorial-based tennis app, it offers a great way to learn fundamental tennis techniques from one of the game's biggest legends. With each tutorial delivered by the man himself, Jimmy Connors, this is no marketing cash-in, and through some neat features and comprehensive video tutorials, it hits the mark in all the right ways.

The app is broken down into four key areas, foremost of which is the 'Improve Your Game' section, where Jimmy provides introductions, tutorials, pointers and commentary on every part of tennis technique. From how to grip the racket, through to basic forehand and backhand strokes, and up to advanced shots such as drops, lobs and passes, Jimmy clearly and concisely shows you how to be successful and consistent.

For each element of the game, the app breaks down into a basic introduction to the shot, a video tutorial and a selection of key pointers to focus on. Each, while not overly short, are kept to a minimum in order to allow for quick courtside reference, with Jimmy's tutorial videos lasting a couple of minutes, and pointers broken down into easy-to-read bullet points. The efficiency in which Jimmy delivers the tutorials is definitely one of the app's best features, with no waffle and charismatic delivery.

The other notable areas of the app are 'Jimmy's World of Tennis', a selection of commentary by Jimmy on some of his greatest ever matches and toughest opponents. Veering away from a mere celebration of Jimmy's greatest moments, this section focus is centred on what techniques and tricks Jimmy and his opponents used to be successful, firmly grounding it as an addition to the tutorials. For example, when talking about his breakthrough, Jimmy highlights how his compact game and old playing style and grip allowed him to generate more power in his shots than players were normally used to.

Finally, the third and fourth key app sections are an integrated journal and in-built link to Jimmy's Twitter page. The journal really plays to the app's mobile, courtside nature, allowing users to mark-up notes on areas to work on, or set goals for future matches and training sessions. The Twitter link is designed to connect users directly with Jimmy, allowing them to ask questions about the game, or query pointers on technique.

Aside from a couple of minor niggles, such as videos repeating, this is a well presented and insightful app that anyone looking to improve at the sport will benefit from.

Rating ★★★★★

■ The options are fairly slim, the main onus here are the video tutorials that teach you the techniques.

■ Jimmy himself makes for a great teacher. He's been around the block a bit!

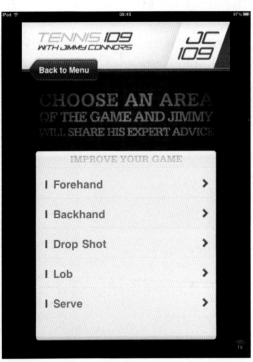

Price: £19.99/$32.99   **Developer:** Soft Pauer Limited

F1™ 2011 Timing App CP

Probably one of the best sports apps ever made

If you are a fan of F1 you will know that there is an incredible amount of data that helps enhance, excite and intrigue the fans. Everything from the obvious lap times and speed differences to the racing line, tyre types and pit stop tactics, to name but a few. If you want all of this information on the race you are watching or about to watch then this app is the one for you.

Its hefty price tag should be a signal of its depth and detail (this is no scam app, that's for sure). Should you take the plunge and invest you will be greeted by an app that befits the rich, slick world of F1 racing. The interface is cool but not over designed, functional but not dull. It probably wont win any design contests, but at no time will you look at it and think 'where do I go from here?' The amount of information available is deliciously deep. Of course, it depends on when the next race is, but if there is one imminently then you'll find all the qualification info and then even be able to do incredibly cool things like track car positions in real time, see corners being taken through the aptly titled corner camera section as well as being able to check live leaderboards.

In addition to the race data you can get news and standing information as well as a brief history of the teams and drivers. Each of the races has its own section and you can find out about the circuit and results if it's taken place. The only thing the F1 app lacks is any kind of video feed and we feel it would have been great to have some interviews or highlights package.

If you're a hardcore fan of Formula 1 the *F1 2011 Timing app* is going to be almost indispensable. If, however, you're just a passing Formula 1 fan it's probably a bit of over kill, but it's really an amazing app nonetheless. The level of detail is great and the ability to watch all the GPs whenever you want makes it really flexible. Some video footage would be nice, but even the animations manage to portray the action well.

What's quite amusing is that this app is so good that occasionally it will give you information before the TV updates so you will know what is going to happen before seeing it happen. If you are a real fan of F1 there are hundreds of good reasons to buy this app and we've not doubt that over coming seasons it will evolve as the iPad hardware does offering unrivalled content in the palm of your hand. A great app that other developers should be using as a benchmark for quality, features and focus. It really pushes the technology to the limit and delivers a stunning degree of detail that other apps could only hope to achieve.

Rating ★★★★★

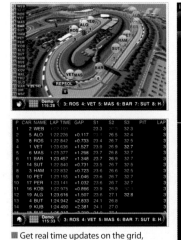

■ Get real time updates on the grid, lap times and all kinds of other stats.

■ Slick user interface invites exploration.

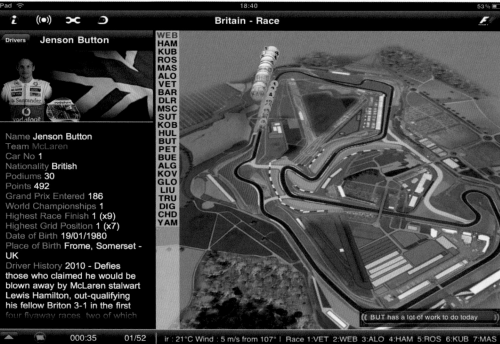

■ Pick the stake you can afford and the prize you want.

■ Watch as the system picks combinations of bets for you to try.

Price: Free **Developer:** WHG (International) Limited

Shake-a-Bet

Beat the bookies!

We've all dreamt of walking out of the bookies with a bundle of note shaving used divine inspiration to pluck the right horse, dog or goalscorer and win an unfathomable bet. Sadly, unless you are incredibly shrewd, spent a lot of time and money at the bookmakers already, or happen to be a walking four-leaved clover then it's an unlikely scenario. This app hopes to help you on that score by generating potential bet combinations that could net you a big payout. From William Hill, this app is a huge amount of fun, it's cleverly designed and will more than likely not only convince you to set up an account with them, but also to spend some cash too. The betting system is based on a great system and you can tailor the experience so it suits sports and events you are more familiar with, so you'll believe you have a greater chance of winning. You can sign into your William Hill account in the app and place bets directly, which is a masterstroke of technology. It doesn't even feel like gambling. A really good app that has been expertly crafted to help lighten your wallet.

Rating ★★★★★

Price: Free **Developer:** DBG World LTD

Haymaker

The app for your favourite fighter

This app is for fans of David Haye and although, as one would expect the information and news centres around him, there is a fair smattering of other interesting boxing news. It's interesting to get the opinion of the heavyweight fighter in the blog section of the app but the overriding problem that users face is the massive watermark-style logo that remains on every page.

It's so irritating that you may well leave the app. If you do decide to persist the Q&A section is worth a look. Here you can get an insight onto what the fans want to know and what David Haye is prepared to reveal. Some of the answers were disappointingly short but others were actually very insightful. If you are a real fan of his you'll no doubt enjoy them all.

As an app, it's nicely designed with some slick elements. We were impressed that it was free but don't worry, they've managed to sneak a David Haye Store into the mix so you can part with some cash if you really want to. If you are a boxing fan or just David Haye fan, this is worthy of an install for sure. A great free app with a lot of content that Haymaker fans and boxing enthusiasts alike can enjoy.

Rating ★★★★★

■ The watermark is really annoying.

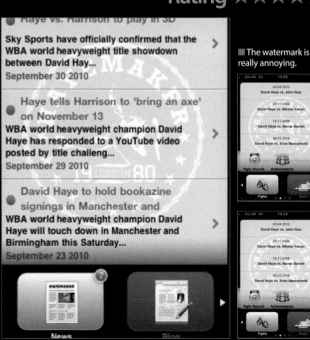

■ Simple clean interface makes the app easy to use and navigate.

Price: Free   **Developer:** Virtual Tennis Coach

Virtual Tennis Coach

A few hours with this and you'll give Murray a run for his money

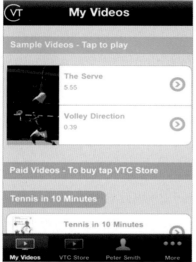

■ The videos are excellent. They're a really great way to learn the techniques needed.

■ The slick interface offers easy access to free and paid content.

If you want to learn how to play tennis, this app is almost as good as real, personal tuition. It contains lessons from the venerable Peter Smith, an Australian tennis coach who's renowned in the tennis world. Admittedly this free app is merely a vehicle for you to spend more money on more video lessons as in-app purchases, but one free video later and you'll be eager to part with some money. But the lessons are incredibly slick, easy to follow and leave no stone unturned. The sample video is on the serve and we've no doubt it will draw you in.

The rest of the app is equally well built, although pretty light on unpaid content – if you want quality tennis tuition then you're unlikely to find it for free. This is a great alternative to real coaching as it offers you the option to have the tuition at any time and you can go over the tips and advice over and over again.

We really rate this app and think that if you have even a passing interest in tennis then you should give this a look – it could well inspire you to pick up your raquet and hit the courts.

Rating ★★★★★

Price: Free **Developer:** NBA Digital

NBA Game Time

A stylish way to keep tabs on your favourite NBA team

This is one of those apps that you'll love to show to others. It's got everything you want and is a fantastic example of all the elements that make the iPad great. To begin with, it gives you incredible coverage of the NBA in a package that can be easily navigated. It makes use of news from the NBA website, video feeds that are regularly updated and great information on each and every team.

A nice touch that we think other sports apps could learn from is the inclusion of collated tweets from the stars of the game. Not only does this give users the opportunity to follow them themselves, but it also enables them to get involved in discussions with the players involved. It's a great addition to a scintillating app. Basketball fans have got a great portal to the world they love to follow and a true rival to the MLB app that tends to grab the headlines.

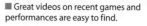

■ Great videos on recent games and performances are easy to find.

Rating ★★★★★

 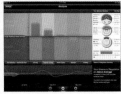

■ Easy-to-read updates come thick and fast every day.

■ Get links to full articles that offer more detail.

Price: £0.59/$0.99 **Developer:** Stephen Reynold

■ The videos will get you below par, but their quality is anything but.

Price: £0.59/£0.99 **Developer:** Shotzoom Software, LLC

Golfplan

A professional app for golfers with professional aspirations

Golfplan With Paul Azinger is a wonderfully well-crafted golfing app that means business. It has links to Golfshot accounts, so if you've already invested time in that system you can use this one too. You can also download the Golfshot app (although it's somewhat more expensive at a massive £17.99!) and the two will communicate to offer you the details of your swing and other training elements you've participated in.

But back to this app, and the instructional videos it contains are worth the already cheap cover price. They are very well shot, expertly delivered and will help you get to grips with a number of common techniques that most golfers crave the answers to. You can download more videos from within the app for free and of course there are number of in-app purchases too. If you are seriously into golf, beyond just popping down the pitch and putt, then this app is an exceptional example of great content being offered at a great price. A worthy instructional app for players of all abilities.

Rating ★★★★☆

Football Rumours

Don't flick to the back pages – this app will deliver all the gossip

If you're a football fan, the close season that runs from June until the middle of August presents a time where each and every story that is presented in the papers and on the TV, true or not, could seriously change the fortunes of your team as they prepare for the next season.

So to get your rumour fix, you could read a load of newspapers, visit a ton of websites and watch the same news reports all day long – or you could let the *Football Rumours* app do all of the hard work for you. Of course all the bigger teams get all the gossip – which is true of the papers and the websites, to be honest – but there is still a massive amount of content here, as there should be. And it's not just a boring RSS ticker.

You can of course filter the result so that you get just the news from your own club, but you may find that this filters too much and you're not getting your money's worth, even though you've only paid £0.59/$0.99. Besides, if you want to keep up with the banter you need to what's going on with all of your rivals too.

Rating ★★★★☆

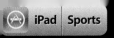

Price: Free **Developer:** Eurosport

Eurosport for iPad
Sports coverage from across Europe with all the latest news

Eurosport has done a great job of covering the less glamorous sports and catering for live events other than football since its inception. This iPad app doesn't include those same fringe sports, but there's a good selection of coverage.

There is a large choice of news, league standings and latest results from all over Europe. Those whose interests lie outside the Premiership and UK football leagues will find loads of results and news from Germany, Italy and Spain, not to mention other worldwide sports leagues too.

The interface is a bit busy and the way the breaking news sections and live sports results' panes whizz back and forth is a touch unsettling.

We like the way you can change the size of the text and even the font if you prefer, to tailor the app to your preferences. There are also handy share on Facebook or send by email options from within the app. The *Eurosport* app is great and has the added benefit of being free, but we'd have liked to see some video included and the layout could do with some polish.

Rating ★★★★★

■ The Eurosport app shows you an incredible range of sporting news though the layout could do with some polish.

■ You can see breaking news from sports leagues all over the world.

Price: Free **Developer:** Betfair

Betfair for iPad
Bet on just about any sport anywhere with this app

Betting on sport remains a very popular pastime and pitting your wits against the knowledge of the bookmakers can be a profitable exercise – when you're right that is. The *Betfair* app allows you to login to your account and place bets, view markets and assess the odds.

The interface is a touch bare and those not familiar with betting and how betting works will probably struggle to grasp the app quickly. Once you've go to grips with it all however it's a great way to place bets quickly and easily.

The range of sports you can bet on is dizzying. Obviously, you can bet on football and horse racing, all the usual suspects are there. In addition there are some sports markets you've probably never heard of, such as Pelota and handball. If sports are not your thing though it's also possible to bet on other subjects such as politics, The X Factor and the Turner prize, amongst others.

The *Betfair* app is a great way of placing bets and managing your account on the go is easy. There's a definite 1.0 feeling to the layout but in the main it's really clear and easy to use.

Rating ★★★★★

■ As well as the usual sports you can bet on lots of other non-sporting events.

■ Placing bets is simple just tap the odd next to your choice.

■ Picking a channel is simple, just tap on the one you want to watch and the line-up is displayed on the right.

■ You have to be a subscriber to a Sky package to get video on the iPad.

Price: Free (app requires Sky subscription)   Developer: BSkyB

Sky Mobile TV

Watch the very best sports coverage but at a price

You can't always be in front of a TV when the sports action is taking place so Sky has put its sports channels on the iPad for mobile viewing.

Although the app is a free download you have to pay for a subscription in order to receive the video feeds. However, if you're an existing Sky subscriber you get free access until January 2011. If you're not a subscriber the cost is £35 a month. That's a wallet-emptying £420 a year, but you do get Sky Sports 1, 2, 3, 4, Sky Sports News and Sky News. Unlike the iPhone version At the Races and ESPN aren't available on the iPad.

The layout of the app is really simple with the list of stations down the left and the 'what's on' menu to the right. You simply swipe the screen to view them all. Then it's simply a case of tapping 'Watch now' to view the live TV feed.

The app is great especially if you're a hardcore sports fan who can't miss live feeds of important fixtures, although you'd have to be to shell out the £420 a year. It's worth bearing in mind that video is going to chew through your 3G data allowance too so stick to Wi-Fi where possible.

Rating

■ The rules of golf can be complicated, but the app from the R&A hopes to clear things up

■ Videos are used to help clear up any complicated rules.

Price: Free Developer: The R&A

Rules of Golf

Get the rules book directly from the home of golf

Golf seems like an incredibly simple game; you hit the ball with a stick until it falls in the hole, the fewer shots you take the better. However, looks can be deceiving and golf has a number of complex rules and nuances that, if you're going to play properly you need to know.

The Rules of Golf takes you through all aspects of the game and the variety of rules and etiquette required. Illustrations help to clear up any confusion between things like loose impediments or movable obstructions.

As well as the instructions and illustrations there are videos to help you understand even more. You can set favourites for the rules you keep forgetting the exact wording on and there's a built-in quiz mode.

It's a great app for the golf lover and it's clear a lot of work gone in to it. The video elements help to clarify even the easily misconstrued points and the layout is easy to follow. The quiz is a bit of fun, but can genuinely help you learn the rules too. The app is made by the R&A so you can be sure of the quality and accuracy of the information.

Rating ★★★★★

Price: Free
Developer: YUDU Ltd

Adventure Kayak Magazine

Based on the print version of the same name, this app is a nice alternative and one that you could easily access while on a kayaking trip. There are a number of extras you can get like video, links and photo galleries.

Overall Rating ★★★☆☆

Price: Free
Developer: Adam Greenberg

GK Icon

If you're a goalkeeper and want an app to help you train and improve then this accompaniment to the GK Icon website is a great way to stay sharp and keep your mind on your game. A well made app that's full of information on football's hardest position.

Overall Rating ★★★★☆

Price: Free
Developer: Trueridge Ltd

Tee Hunter

Get great deals on golf and golfing equipment in the United Kingdom with this app. With over 650 courses to choose from, you can normally find a good deal near to you. *Tee Hunter* is a clever app that no serious golfer should ever be without.

Overall Rating ★★★★☆

Price: £3.99/$6.99
Developer: Andrew Aisbitt

Snooker Coaching School

Every aspect of snooker and all its nuances explained. It's basically a coach you can take anywhere. Everything is explained well and easy to follow. A must-buy for serious snooker enthusiasts.

Overall Rating ★★★★☆

Price: £3.99/$6.99
Developer: The Factor Network Limited

Lee Westwood (Athlete Factor)

The official app for former number-one golfer Lee Westwood, this provides essential content for fans. It includes photos, videos and tweets, of course, so you can get a daily fix of your favourite club swinger.

Overall Rating ★★★★☆

Price: Free
Developer: Adonai Kincaid

CricketWorld

Keep up with the latest news from all levels of cricket – from Test down to Village – with this well made, easy to navigate app. Follow your team, a league or even the international fixtures as well. Breaking news, videos, galleries and more.

Overall Rating ★★★★☆

Price: Free
Developer: South Coast Productions Limited

iBoxing Training

This app has even been approved by some boxing governing bodies, which means if you use it you will become hard as nails, right? Not really. But it does provide some expert training tips for would-be contenders and gets you in the right frame of mind.

Overall Rating ★★★☆☆

Price: £1.19/$1.99
Developer: Nick Brewer

Kick Class

So this app must be a guide to kicking people! Well, not quite. This is a serious app for serious martial artists looking to perfect their kicking style. It comes complete with great instruction from the very, very tough Nick Brewer. You don't want to see what happens if you don't buy it.

Overall Rating ★★★★☆

Price: £3.49/$6.99
Developer: Perish the Thought Ltd

EveryDay Golf Coach

EveryDay Golf Coach is a great little app that contains 32 videos designed to help you improve your game. The app is really well made and even includes a swing analysis element to boot. It may seem pricey, but we reckon it's well worth the money.

Overall Rating ★★★★★

Price: £3.99/$6.99
Developer: Moonstone Solutions Limited

Shooting Final

The *Shooting Final* app may be a little too niche as it's made for those training to complete in Olympic-style 10 and 50-metre shooting finals. Still, it's undoubtedly a well-constructed and official-looking app nonetheless – and could be handy for London 2012.

Overall Rating ★★★★☆

Price: £3.99/$6.99
Developer: ANT APPS Ltd

Field Designer

Yes, that's right, there's even an app for Paintball training and planning. If you have a regular paintball team that needs help getting organised then the *Field Designer* app is the final piece in your tactical armoury. It won't be able to find you any matches, though.

Overall Rating ★★★☆☆

Price: £0.59/$0.99
Developer: AndalueSoft

MMA Trivia

This incredibly inexpensive-looking app provides bags of stats and trivia on the bloody sport of mixed martial arts fighting. Impress your mates and learn all about your hard hitting heroes for a rather reasonable price.

Overall Rating ★★★☆☆

Price: £0.59/$0.99
Developer: Arthursoft studios Ltd

Fanzone

Covering every single professional football team in the country, and available for such a small price, the *Fanzone* app is a must for all serious football fans. Classically styled to great effect, this is a one-stop shop for the diehard fan. Brilliant.

Overall Rating ★★★★★

Price: Free
Developer: Eurosport SA

Eurosport Player

Officially endorsed by the ubiquitous sport channel, get your Eurosport fix at any time with this window into the channel. You will need a subscription for the month or year to get access. The rates are pretty good and the app's very slick.

Overall Rating ★★★☆☆

Price: Free
Developer: The Football Association Limited

Official England Football

If you're a fan of the England football team and want all the news from the horse's mouth, then this official iPad app is for you. As you'd expect, it's a well-made, slick offering that will keep you in the loop.

Overall Rating ★★★★☆

Price: £1.79/$2.99
Developer: Bright Artificial Intelligence Ltd

EPL Football LIVE

Get all the updates you need on the English Premier League and your club, if it's playing in it of course. The app contains links to news stories, transfer gossip, match reports, league standings and more. It's well presented with lots of content – a good effort.

Overall Rating ★★★★☆

Price: £0.59/$0.99
Developer: Bright Artificial Intelligence Ltd

MotoGP Total News

If you prefer your racing on two wheels and not four then this is an all-encompassing app for your needs. Great interface, great stories and a great price. A good all-rounder that motorcycle racing fans will get a kick out of.

Overall Rating ★★★☆☆

Price: £1.99/$2.99
Developer: upflatdown Limited

The Mountain Echo Guide To Val D'Isere - Ski Season

A guide to the Val D'Isere ski season that has everything from ski hire to entertainment venues. It's perfect if you're planning to hit those slopes.

Overall Rating ★★★★★

Price: £0.59/$0.99
Developer: Nick Brewer

Fight Class

The *Fight Class* app basically consists of video tutorials for kickboxers who are looking to improve their kicking, punching and those all-important combos. A cool app that will be put to good use by martial artists. We definitely recommend it.

Overall Rating ★★★★☆

Price: £0.59/$0.99
Developer: Tom Bates

Golf Scorecard

Taking a pencil and paper around the golf course simply isn't cool any more. You just need to let this app do all the work for you! You have to enter the info on par for the course, but once that simple task is done, *Golf Scorecard* is a great little app.

Overall Rating ★★★★☆

Price: Free
Developer: Mobile Software Design, LLC

Pocket Golf Pro

Mobile Software's *Pocket Golf Pro* is a great free resource for golfers looking to improve their long and short game. And it offers a lot more than a lot of paid apps do. Some useful tips will keep you on the up and using the app's useful tips to improve.

Overall Rating ★★★★☆

Price: £0.59/$0.99
Developer: Coffee Entertainment Inc.

Climbing Knots

Learn how to keep yourself safe and secure when partaking in the rather dangerous sport of scaling a mountain. It's a pretty easy-to-use app that could actually save your life. Therefore it's a must for all climbers, regardless of skill.

Overall Rating ★★★★☆

Price: £1.79/$2.99
Developer: Jeremy Debate

iFooty Plus

iFooty Plus is a one-stop shop for the avid football fan, with plenty of banter and personality added into the usual stats, results, news and other features that you would expect to see on perhaps more expensive apps. Another app worthy of your cash.

Overall Rating ★★★★★

Price: £0.59/$0.99
Developer: 84 World Ltd

Phil Neville - Football Training

Professional footballer Phil Neville is cashing in on his not-inconsiderable experience in the game. If you're a fan of his then maybe you should get it, if not then don't worry – you're not exactly missing much.

Overall Rating ★★☆☆☆

Price: £0.59/$0.99
Developer: Bikul Koirala

Live Football Score

A moderately good live score app with a host of options. The interface isn't as slick as some of its competitors, but it's a very cheap and very easy to use. We'd say it was only second to the free Sky Sports Football app for up-to-date scores. A great effort.

Overall Rating ★★★★☆

Price: £0.59/$0.99
Developer: David Miller

Football Ref

Football Ref is an incredibly simple but somewhat strangely fun app that turns your iPhone into a red or yellow card to brandish at football players or just friends when they bug you. It's certainly fun for five minutes, but probably not worth paying for.

Overall Rating ★★☆☆☆

Price: £1.79
Developer: zAppz Ltd

Street Skills Premium

Forget just playing on grass, the cool kids practise their skills anywhere and everywhere. If you're a street skills advocate, then this app is for you. Learn new tricks, be part of a community and more.

Overall Rating ★★★★☆

Price: £1.19
Developer: Clear New Media Ltd

Football On The TV

If you love football then you will always curse when you miss the opportunity to catch a live game on television, be it on BBC, ITV or Sky Sports. This clever little app will prevent that from ever happening again.

Overall Rating ★★★★☆

Price: £0.59/$0.99
Developer: Colin Vassallo

Wrestling Online.com News

Wrestlingonline.com's app enables you to keep tabs on all kinds of wrestling and mixed martial arts in this rather low-key app. We like that it's not too in your face (unlike the 'sport') and fairly easy to navigate.

Overall Rating ★★★★★

Price: £1.79/$2.99
Developer: Tri Active Media Ltd

Total Sea Fishing Magazine

A nice conversion of the popular fishing print magazine. A first purchase gets you a free issue of the mag and the rest are in-app purchases. A great buy for anglers who love the sea.

Overall Rating ★★★★☆

Price: £2.99/$4.99
Developer: Jeff Hall

Carp Lakes

Dedicated anglers in England will absolutely love this app as it provides a staggering amount of information on a staggering number of carp lakes. You won't just find directions and general information, but you'll find the biggest catch too.

Overall Rating ★★★★☆

Price: £0.59/$0.00
Developer: Simon Gladwell

F1 2011 Formula One News, Views And Media

Not the slickest of Formula One apps but easily one of the best for the money. All the info you could possibly want in one app. Well worth the cash.

Overall Rating ★★★★☆

Price: £0.59
Developer: Moonswing Ltd

The Bet Settler

The Bet Settler is probably the most comprehensive betting app around at the moment – although you will need to know your stuff to get the most from it. If you are a serious gambler then the odds are that you'll love this.

Overall Rating ★★★★★

Price: £1.79
Developer: Zachary Price

Kitesurf Instructor: Beginner

Instructor's a really competent portable resource for those interested in the extreme sport of kitesurfing. There are a huge number of elements covered, so if you're a beginner you'll have plenty to go on.

Overall Rating ★★★★★

Price: £4.99/$8.99
Developer: OneWhitePixel

The Stormrider Surf Guide

Offline surfing mapping is the main highlight of this very well-crafted surf guide. If you're out on the road looking for some great breaks then *The Stormrider Surf Guide* is one gnarly companion.

Overall Rating ★★★☆☆

Price: £0.59/$0.99
Developer: Matthew Jones

iSurfer - Surfing Coach

iSurfer's a really comprehensive surfing app for those with a passion for hitting the waves. There are way too many features to list here, but even if you have just a passing interest, you should get this app.

Overall Rating ★★★★★

Price: £1.79/$2.99
Developer: Cricket4Evry1 Pty Ltd

Cricket Coach Plus

Cricket Coach Plus is a sporting app that takes itself very seriously – and rightly so. It's a well-made cricket coaching app with bags of features that are perfect for the budding cricketer – young or old. It's well worth a download, and it's pretty cheap to boot.

Overall Rating ★★★★☆

Price: £0.59/$0.99
Developer: Datex Media, Inc.

The Horse Lover's Ultimate Horse Quiz

There really is an app for everyone – as this delightfully quaint equestrian app proves. If you wish to test others on their equine knowledge or even improve your own, it's worth a look for 59p.

Overall Rating ★★★★☆

Price: £0.59
Developer: Glimmer Design Limited

Kit Quiz UK

Test your knowledge of the football strips in the United Kingdom with the *Kit Quiz* app. It's definitely a fun app to pull out at the pub and test your mates with. To be fair, the team's badges give things away a little, but it's fun nonetheless.

Overall Rating ★★★★☆

Price: £2.39
Developer: Simon Hughes

Cricket Analyst

If you love cricket then this app will keep you entertained for hours. For the money this app offers real value and bags of opinion, and it's developed by Simon Hughes, who has featured on many cricket television broadcasts. Cricket fans should download today.

Overall Rating ★★★★☆

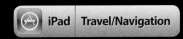
Travel/Navigation

With clever use of in-built GPS technology and, with iPad 2, Augmented Reality, the iPad is the perfect tool for finding places of interest and generally not getting lost. The following apps are designed to help you out of a tight spot and bombard you with things to do while out and about.

Top Paid Apps	Top Free Apps
Theodolite HD ★★★★	**Google Earth** ★★★★
Nav Trainer ★★★★	**Trip Viewer** ★★★★
Navigation Compass ★★★★	**Word Lens** ★★★★★

Staff pick of the section

 **MapOmatic** ★★★★		**Maps+** ★★★★	

■ Images can be grabbed straight from your photo album.

■ Symbols can be added to your postcards for a bit of fun.

Price: £0.59/$0.99   **Developer:** Natural Systems

E-CardCreator ShakaLife

Let everyone know how sunny it is

 Postcards are so last century. Today, it's all about the digital. With your iPad you can not only save on the cost of buying postcards and stamps but also all the legwork that goes with having to find the right shops and a postbox. Instead, you can sit on the beach, feet up with a cocktail or two and, as long as you have an internet connection, send your e-cards in seconds.

E-CardCreator allows you to produce and send personalised e-cards in next to no time. The card is split into three sections. One is the main image and the other two are smaller boxes which another pair of pictures can slot into. By tapping on each one of these sections, you can grab an image which is then placed on your card.

In many ways, this app works better if you have an iPad 2 because you can then take pictures on your device and have them ready for importing into this app. But you can still take images from your album and, if you have an iPad 1, you'll just have to be a little more creative.

Rating ★★★☆☆

Price: £2.39/$3.99 **Developer:** Craig Hunter

Theodolite HD

The professional's choice for real-time navigation stats

For most people, Augmented Reality offers the opportunity to create a cool game or help users find local services, Hunter Research has found an incredible way to combine several navigation instruments in one app. Features include a camera overlay in real-time showing information about position, altitude, bearing, range, and inclination. The instruments respond to touch, and although to most they better represent what Iron Man might be seeing in his heads-up display, they actually offer a perfect set of tools for engineers, geologists, architects and military personnel.

The ability to track the exact position of the device using GPS is combined with the ability to take readings of the exact angle of the iPad both relative to the horizon and the floor, as well as calculating the axis angle at which the iPad is leaning. A practical use for this would be the measurement of the inclination of a hill for surveyor. What's more,

There are probably a thousand and one uses for this app, not least it's great to play around with.

the app can measure two points in relation to each other so that users can use the reference to make detailed calculations about the relationships between those two points.

Serious users will no doubt find the information very useful, but there is a limitation to the iPad 2 as a potential precision instrument. It's not fixed and will require a tripod for any really technical work so that exact angles can be worked out and measured. In the interim before the iPad is mounted, users can use the horizon gauge to get accuracy on a 90 degree plane, but more detailed angles may be difficult to achieve. Other features that may entice those who don't wish to cart a bag of instruments around them include a GPS reading and its presentation relative to a map on a separate screen. You can, of course, use the nautical bearings on the Heads up display, but the Map view has obvious benefits. The ability to alter the settings is a plus, as is taking screenshots for future recall.

This is a specialist app, and as a result one would expect a price tag that would reflect this. However, *Theodolite* is well worth the investment. While the information may not suit all, its ease of use means anyone can enjoy it. Of course, if you have the money to hand then it is worth investing in just to impress your friends down the pub. No other app does Augmented Reality quite as good as this at present and to have such quality graphics layered over the viewfinder screen of your iPad 2 is very impressive.

Rating ★★★★☆

The app also uses GPS technology to great effect.

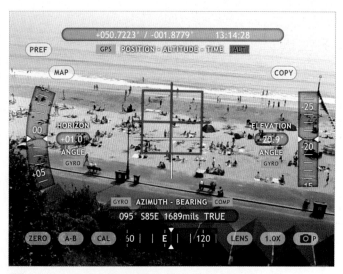

The screen comes alive with readings, gauges and measurements…

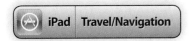
Price: Free **Developer:** Google

Google Earth

Explore the world from the palm of your hand

Google Earth was one of the key applications in driving consumer interest in geo-mapping/location software following its desktop launch in 2005. Essentially a three-dimensional virtual globe, *Google Earth* enables users to instantly search or spin their way around the planet, zooming in on points of interest illustrated via up-to-date satellite imagery. When the application launched there was a tremendous novelty factor in finding your house, or surveying global landmarks and other aerial sights, but with the same satellite data now easily overlaid on Google Maps, the app is now starting to feel somewhat obsolete.

Presentation is generally excellent – start the app and you're presented with the Earth sat serenely in space, before it spins and zooms cinematically to your last location. Navigation is simply a case of dragging your finger to spin the Earth around, while tapping the screen zooms in on a point. Using two fingers on your multi-touch screen enables you to zoom out, or spin the planet on a different axis. Google Maps-style icons enable you to search and pinpoint your location, but with the ability to rotate your view there's also a handy compass to remind you where magnetic North is.

Google Earth has been available on mobile platforms since way back in 2008, and although the mobile version doesn't include anything like the number of features included with its desktop equivalent, Google has attempted to integrate as many as possible. Layers were omitted from the launch version of the *Google Earth* app, but have since been included via updates. Overlaying a variety of online information onto maps, the optional layers available on iPhone cover basic data from borders and place names, to businesses, relevant Wikipedia links and images on photo site Panoramio. Roads have also been included in Version 3.0.

The terrain layer that renders certain environments in 3D is an interesting addition, but let down by the clunky and kind of unnecessary tilt functionality. The only other addition to Version 3.0 is iPad-specific support, which ups the resolution. *Google Earth* already looked fairly polished on the iPad, though, with only occasional sluggishness letting it down, and although the app is serviceable over 3G, unsurprisingly, it's most impressive when it's used with Wi-Fi.

Although it's not particularly useful as a navigation tool, *Google Earth* is still a fun and educational way to traverse the globe.

Rating ★★★★☆

■ The maps include tube station locations, among plenty of other things.

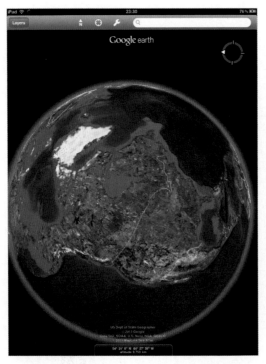

■ The 3D rendered environments are awesome; the tilt functionality not so much.

Price: Free Developer: iQuest Technologies

Trip Viewer

Bring your holidays to life

Once upon a time, people would invite others around to view their holiday slideshows. Then folks had video parties, showing off their latest camcorder escapades in a caravan park. But these 'experiences' are nothing when compared to the interactive way people can view your trips on the iPad with this new app.

iQuest Technologies' *Trip Viewer* lets you chart a route through your holiday destination, adding images and video to maps. It works in combination with the Trip Journal app on the iPhone or Android, enabling you to import any trips you have documented on your handset. The *Trip Viewer* app then plots your route and includes all of the multimedia content for each specific location.

So if you took many images of New York outside the Empire State Building, tapping on that location will show up the variety of pictures as well as any video you may have gathered. But that's not all. If you tap the Play function in the top-right-hand corner of the iPad display, it will take you on an air balloon ride through the location.

As the balloon passes over area of key interest, it will display your photos in a slide show before moving on to the next set of images. Images show up as green blobs on the map and videos are blue. By tapping on an image, you can see them in a larger size and you can use your fingers to zoom in. Beneath the image is a selection of other photos which can also be tapped and viewed.

Tapping on the notes option brings up information that has been taken from Wikipedia. So, you may be in the vicinity of the Eiffel Tower within the app. You can view the images and any video, but also tap the notes icon and find out more about it.

What *Trip Viewer* does is bring a destination to life and, more importantly, it shows your perspective on it. With the ability to use Flickr photos in real-time, you can combine your experience with other people's. Not only can you then share your trips but see other's too, and you can do so in your own time and in comfort rather than feeling you have to gush when your friend is explaining the great time they had.

This is the first version of the app, which will surely only get even better as time goes on, and the fact that it is free is a bonus. Do be aware, however, that there is a cost for Trip Journal (£1.79/$2.99) but that's also worth the cost when you consider the package you have here.

Rating ★★★★☆

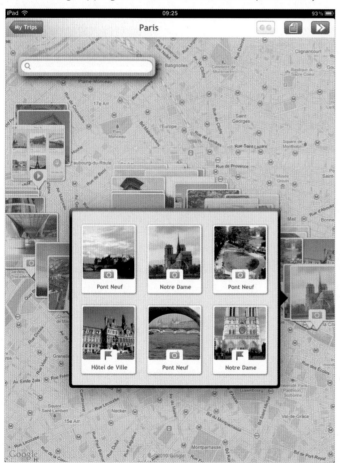

By tapping on an image, you can bring up your photos and view them neatly.

Trips can be imported from the Trip Viewer app on iPhone and Android.

All of your images and video are displayed on a map so you can see where you have been.

Price: Free **Developer:** Quest Visual

Word Lens

Instant language translation

Word Lens takes Augmented Reality apps to a whole new dimension by translating text via your iPad 2's camera in real-time. You simply point the camera at foreign text – be it a signpost, book, noticeboard, absolutely anything – and the text will be magically translated into English as you stare at it through the iPad's viewfinder.

The magic doesn't happen instantaneously with this free download though. Once downloaded, what you essentially get is a demo that enables you to play around with the technology without utilising any useful features. The only features you are initially privy to are the 'Erase Words' option, which will remove chunks of text from wherever you point the camera and 'Reverse Words'. The latter is slightly more enjoyable to play around with as you can point the camera at logos and suchlike then marvel as it reverses the words in the viewfinder.

Where this app really excels though is text translation and for that you have to spend and additional £2.99 apiece for the Spanish to English and English to Spanish add-ons. More languages are promised in time but for now this is very impressive.

Rating ★★★★★

■ Point the iPad 2 camera at Spanish text and it will instantly be translated into English.

Price: £2.99/$4.99 **Developer:** Amir Fleminger

Nav Trainer

Instrument navigation for pilots and nerds

This app is aimed specifically at people who are learning to fly, flight instructors or anyone who wants to practice the use of aviation navigational equipment on their mobile device.

With this app you can improve your situational awareness under IFR, prepare for your instrument rating or proficiency check, test your progress with the various test modes and save time and money on your initial instrument training.

If you are preparing to take a pilots exam then this app should prove to be something of a god-send. It's very technical, easy to navigate and even comes loaded with test modes so that you can pit your wits against the computer.

If you aren't a trainee pilot and have no real interest in flying then it will be a complete waste of time and effort, though even the most grounded of app air-heads should marvel at the technology involved and applaud the developer for being able to put the iPad to such a good practical use. So while this has limited appeal, as an app it is very well put together and comes highly recommended to anyone in the field of flying.

Rating Rating ★★★★★

■ *Nav Trainer* will test your skills to the limit.

■ This app is a useful learning tool for pilots.

Fuel Station United Kingdom

For when you run out of gas

Price: £0.59/$0.99 **Developer:** Martin Bovan

■ The app finds your location and shows you fuel stations nearby.

■ When you tap on a pin, you can some information and a number.

We have often wondered just how far we could get when the fuel light comes on in our cars. Usually it is tinged with slight panic as we look in vain for a petrol station to loom on the horizon and put us at ease. That's where apps such as this come in. It takes a Google map and overlays it with loads of pins, each one denoting the location of a petrol station. It uses your location in order to find the ones nearest to you and by tapping on the pin, you can see the road it is on and have the ability to email it to someone else (maybe a friend who has called you in a panic).

The locations are updated daily, according to the developer, although we don't see petrol stations springing up that often. It's just a shame that the app doesn't go on to direct you to the petrol station you wish to use, leaving it to you to map read and figure it out yourself.

The problem is this kind of thing is done better elsewhere and, for the price, we'd expect a bit more. That said, it could help you out in an emergency.

Rating ★★★★★

Restaurant Finder

When hunger hits, you just gotta eat

Price: £0.59/$0.99 **Developer:** Aliphonse Yaro

The location feature built into the iPad has thrown up many navigation tools such as this one. Catering for people who are looking to eat out, *Restaurant Finder* for iPad is actually very comprehensive in its search results, finding not only the finest places to dine but the local takeaways too.

The results are displayed as lists with the address and telephone number. Tapping the address shows you the location on a map but very annoyingly, once you have been taken to the Google Map, there is no option to then go back to the lists unless you tap the Home button and relaunch the app. We also found that it would say there were no results when we knew of restaurants nearby and there is no way of setting the locality parameters. This app could also do with reviews or a ratings system to justify having to pay for something that can be found for free elsewhere. We're not entirely sure where the information is coming from either – in the American restaurant search, one result was a firm called the Anglo American Electrical Company.

Rating ★★★★★

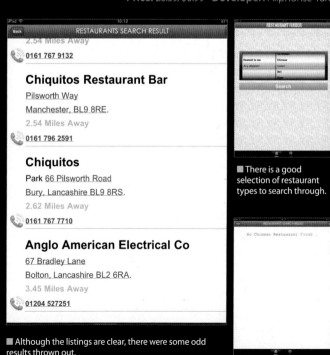

■ There is a good selection of restaurant types to search through.

■ Although the listings are clear, there were some odd results thrown out.

Price: Free **Developer:** Alan Paxton

The Complete National Cycle Network

It's time to get on your bike

With more than 25,000 miles of cycle paths documented in this app, keen cyclists will certainly be overjoyed. It suggests recommended routes and is perfect for quiet Sunday afternoons or even trying to work out a better way through the hectic traffic on the way to work. You can even draw your own route on the map.

■ Suggested routes are shown on a map, which can be zoomed in.

Overall Rating ★★★★☆

Price: Free **Developer:** TripTrace

mapOmatic

You'll never walk alone with this app

Ask *mapOmatic* for directions and it will draw the result on your own private map, storing it in your history folder for future use. It also hooks into Facebook and Foursquare, with a heart button showing all the places in your vicinity where your friends have checked in, meaning you could hotfoot it to where they are for an impromptu meet-up. The app also integrates Pingster.

■ The directions are drawn on the map for you, and they're stored in your history.

Overall Rating ★★★★☆

Price: Free **Developer:** Pear Logic

Maps+

Taking mapping to another level

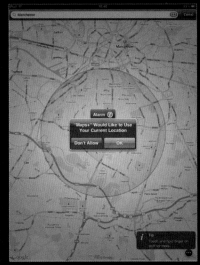

This app's free but it does have limitations. You can only place pins on the map a limited number of times; if you want more, you must pay £1.79/$2.99 for unlimited access. Is it worth it? Well, Maps+ takes the traditional Google map and extends it capabilities. It searches for local Tweets, lets you track your location, and it can set location-specific alarms.

■ You can set an alarm for a specific location.

Overall Rating ★★★★★

Price: £0.59/$0.99 **Developer:** Piet Jones

Speed App

Avoid getting an accidental ticket

Roads today have many speed cameras, and we all know it's very easy to find your foot pressing on the accelerator without realising and just accidentally edging over the speed limit. With *Speed App* in your car, you can see just how fast you're going at all times, either in mph or kph. While you may think you have this facility on the dashboard of your car, what the app does is change colour when you go at a certain speed. So you can see out of the corner of your eye if you are going too fast.

■ The colour changes depending on your speed.

Overall Rating ★★★★★

Price: Free **Developer:** mxData Limited

Manchester Metrolink

Don't get mad when in Manchester

Manchester's extensive tram system can now be navigated for free by using this new app from mxData Limited. It lets you plan your route across Greater Manchester, find tram stations and view a map of the network. Many improvements have been made since the first version. You can squeeze the map for an overall view, and the iPad makes good use of the display with live information in the left panel. You can quickly calculate your route through the city too. The share option doesn't let you send on route information but it's certainly getting better. We look forward to similar apps for more cities.

■ The layout is neat with live information in the left panel.

Overall Rating ★★★★★

Price: Free **Developer:** Tishman Hotel Corp

Westin New York

Book a meeting in the Big Apple

It's good to see hotels getting in on the app act. The Westin in New York's app is a simple offering, with a large image of the hotel and a menu that allows you to take a look around. You can view the guest rooms with quality images that can be slid through and you can see floor plans of the meeting areas. Not only can you see the restaurants, but you can view the menus too – there's even a brief guide to New York here.

■ It's got a useful guide to New

Overall Rating ★★★★★

Price: £1.19/$1.99 **Developer:** Alexy Pankov

Earthquake Alarm

Make sure you don't become shaken

There could be little more scary than being caught up in an earthquake. We have all seen the devastating results, most recently in Japan, and so with this in mind, we checked out *Earthquake Alarm*, which claims to be able to warn you if you are near an earthquake. The app can be updated in real time and it is based on your location. It doesn't offer advice on what to do if there was a quake, however, and we doubt you'd always have this app turned on when you actually need it, but perhaps that is the cynic in us.

■ Earthquake data is refreshed with the tap of a button.

Overall Rating ★★☆☆☆

Price: Free **Developer:** Starburst Software

Days Out In Sussex

Get the iPhone to work out tips for you

It starts with a big, bright intro, but when it comes down to it, *Days Out In Sussex* is yet another Google-mapped app, albeit a Google-mapped app with lots of location information. You can see all of the major attractions in the area and clicking on each one throws up a full page of information with a link to the website and the ability to suggest updates to the details via email. It gives a brief description, opening times and full location info including the all-important postcodes of each of the Sussex attractions.

■ A Google map displays lots of Sussex attractions

Overall Rating ★★★★★

Price: £0.59/$0.99 **Developer:** Ying Liu

Navigation Compass

If you need to get your bearings, then a compass comes in handy. The *Navigation Compass* app runs in two modes: one which has a full screen compass and another split-screen mode which also includes a map. The map can be zoomed in and out of with a pinch of the fingers and the compass itself looks brilliant and classy. It would serve you well if you were stuck in the wilderness and it is very easy to use, finding your current location and basing map readings on it. By pulling on the full page, you can scroll to reveal the map.

Rating ★★★★☆

Price: £0.59/$0.99 **Developer:** Martin Bovan

Hot Spot United Kingdom

Wi-fi is increasingly important nowadays, especially with data caps on mobile phones and with many iPad's being wi-fi only. If you are out and about, though, it's not always easy to discover where you can tap into a wi-fi hot spot. This app aims to change that by showing a map littered with wi-fi symbols. Tapping on one will show you the name of the place on the map. You can also check the map for fuel too.

Rating ★★☆☆☆

Price: £0.59/$0.99 **Developer:** Fransisco

Distances from here

For what this app does, there really shouldn't be a charge. It essentially takes Google map, lets you find a location, works out where you are and then tells you how far away you are from that destination. And yet it is something you could do with no problem by firing up Google and doing a search. For the number of times you will most likely use this, it is not really worth the hassle of the download, even if we are talking mere pennies and a small footprint. The good thing is that your destinations are saved for future.

Rating ★☆☆☆☆

Price: Free **Developer:** bonJones

Oi! PingMe! - Locate friends on map

You can use *Oi!* to find friends who are close by. It works by sending requests to mates to follow you and by allowing you to locate them on a map. With the ability to text message them for free and in real-time, and with push notifications letting you know when you are being contacted, it's a good social tool that makes navigating to your friends a piece of cake. The app needs to be on for it to work which is fine until you want to do something else.

Rating ★★★★☆

Price: £0.59/$0.99 **Developer:** Irfan Farooqi

Clap Night Lamp and Clock

When you are on your travels, it's nice to have a clock to hand. This app lets you control its night lamp and clock by voice so whenever you whistle or clap, the screen changes to a soothing pictures and helps to illuminate the room. It certainly works but the clock is rather small. The screen doesn't revolve and we found there were dead ends. We couldn't work out how to change and image and then go back to the clock.

Rating★☆☆☆☆

Price: Free **Developer:** Theis srl

SanLorenzo

We can but dream. So when we saw an app for San Lorenzo yachts, we thought we would give it a go. It's a catalogue which lets you browse through preowned yachts and read up on the very latest news on this most aspirational of purchases. The app's navigation revolves around a series of icons along the bottom of the screen and clicking on the yachts brings up good descriptions, but in tiny text that you can't enlarge. Then again, when you see the prices of some of the yachts, your eyes are likely to bulge to compensate.

Rating ★★★☆☆

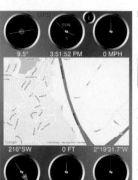

Price: £0.59/$0.99 **Developer:** Timothy O'Malley

NavPad

Using this app can tell you how fast you are travelling, the time of day and you longitude and latitude. You can also see an artificial horizon and an altimeter. In the middle of all of this is a map of your current location. As far as navigation goes, you've pretty much got the whole lot nestled in one cheap package that looks neat and tidy, makes good use of the iPad display and will have some solid real-world applications as well as act as an awesome plaything. The app also hooks into the GPS and you will be made aware of this when it flashes.

Rating ★★★★☆

Price: Free **Developer:** All4IP Technologies

mapZero

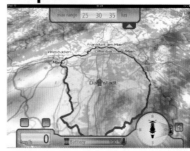

It's such a shame that *mapZero* is in German and so aimed purely at a German audience because it has real potential. It estimates how long your battery-powered car will last while you drove, giving you the number of kilometers and the limits. Future updates promise the ability to select your vehicle for greater accuracy. It's a good idea crying out for translation.

Rating ★★★☆☆

Ontario

Price: Free Developer: Ontario Tourism Board

The iPad has always been great for reading magazines on but sometimes a dedicated app is preferable. When we were planning our trip to Ontario, we thought this app would give us a quick lowdown on the various sites. Instead, it is essentially an app which asks if you want to download a French or English version of the Ontario Tourism Magazine.

Rating ★★★★☆

Zipcode Finder HD

Price:£0.59/$0.99 Developer: Amy Faulkner

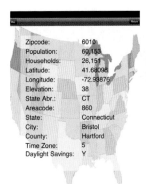

Delivering information on more than 80,000 zipcodes across America, this easy-to-use app gives you the lowdown on population size, number of households, county and timezone among many other attributes. You can search by city or zipcode and the information is provided clearly on top of colourful map of the United States. You can also view a street map via Google of the area in question. There's a free version available which has ads and that is a better download than the paid-for one, given you probably wouldn't use it often.

Rating ★★☆☆☆

Disney World Resort Menus

Price: £1.19/$1.99 Developer: Flora's Secret

Before you set out of your hotel room for a restaurant, it is sometimes nice to see what may be on offer before you get there to ensure you're not wasting vital energy. With this you can check out what nosh you can eat at some of Disney's parks. Navigating the app caused frustration at first when we realised you had to tap in a specific place on the main menu to access the categories but if you can justify the cost of the app, then you'll find it useful.

Rating ★★☆☆☆

Family Travel Notes

Price: £1.19/$1.99 Developer: Said Asad

It's one of the least pleasant apps to look at but this does have its uses. You can input the records for six family members and include information about their prescriptions, notes and Travel history. It's a database at heart, storing vital information about you and your loved ones that can be saved and updated. Decent enough, but there are better apps out there.

Rating ★★☆☆☆

MyTravel Singapore

Price: Free Developer: Ruperto de Guzman

This free guide to Singapore shows you the city's key attractions, a selection of hotels which can be booked online, maps and information about this fascinating location. The interface is clean and simple to navigate with key features presented in a left-hand menu sidebar and the content shown in the right-hand window. Simple but effective.

Rating ★★★☆☆

Complete Weather

Price: Free. Developer: John Lyons

One of the most important aspects of getting away is the weather. There are loads of weather apps available on the iPad and Complete Weather is just one of the latest offerings. It doesn't do anything particularly spectacular other than display a pretty picture, give you the time, date, and temperature in any one of 100,000 different locations. In that sense it is a disappointment because such things are done elsewhere with more besides. If it was real-time image of your destination, we'd be impressed. Alas it is not.

Rating ★★☆☆☆

Hemispheres

Price: Free Developer: Pilkington Bedwell

At first glance it appeared as if Hemispheres was just taking the United and Continental Airlines magazine, converting it to PDF and throwing a navigation tool around it. We were wrong. The app adds video and audio content and you see this starkly on the front page. The image zooms out showing just how dynamic this offering is. The same trick is repeated inside the magazine on a photo spread. There are live weblinks and interactive advertising too. And, most importantly, it's a decent enough read.

Rating ★★★★☆

Disneyland Park Hours

Price: Free Developer: VersaEdge Software

If you're planning to visit Disneyland Park and you need to know what times they are open, then look no further – this delivers up to two months worth of information. As well as openings, it also tells you when certain events are on and it also works with VoiceOver Accessibility for those who are blind. You will soon get to grips with the navigation which is essentially about tapping the screen in order to draw up the information.

Rating ★★★☆☆

Price: £1.19/$1.99
Developer: taghg McKenna

HolidayItinerary

This most simplistic of apps will allow you to plan and record your holidays but it won't particularly hold your interest or provide an astonishing journal of your travel. It looks rather uninspiring and the entries fields don't allow for much in the way of expression.

Overall Rating ★★☆☆☆

Price: £1.79/$2.99
Developer: Tobin Fisher

Beijing on a Budget

Cutting through the expensive stuff, this shows you how to have a great time without splashing too much cash with step-by-step instructions and the ability to sort by price. It is written by a travel writer and is packed with hundreds of photos and reviews.

Overall Rating ★★★★★

Price: Free
Developer: Locatify ehf

SmartGuide Germany

You can take historic trips to Germany with the aid of an app which makes use of GPS and automatically plays audio whenever you reach a particular destination. It means you don't have to have a physical guide with you.

Overall Rating ★★★★☆

Price: £1.19/$1.99
Developer: NKR Innovations

Find Campgrounds

American travellers can use this app to find the location of various campgrounds around the States. You can search by name, city or zip and the app not only maps it for you but gives you directions too. An email or SMS can be sent with the details.

Overall Rating ★★★★☆

Price: Free
Developer: Teknit

Travelgate

Use *Travelgate* to search for flights and hotels. This well laid out, smart app looks identical to a regular webpage but navigation is easy to follow and you can search destinations across the world and bookmark the pages that are of particular interest.

Overall Rating ★★☆☆☆

Price: £0.59/$0.99
Developer: Jetpack Studios

Tube Tracker

Offering information on live departures for every tube train that is updated every five seconds (which is its unique selling point because others usually update less regularly), you should never miss a train again. It tells you exactly when a train is due at a station.

Overall Rating ★★★★☆

Price: £0.59/$0.99
Developer: Otto Chan

Country Flag Glossary

We may well be showing our age but lots of flags we were familiar with at school don't exist any more. Keep yourself up to date with current flags using this app. As well as displaying flags, it also has information about public holidays.

Overall Rating ★★★☆☆

Price: £1.19/$1.99
Developer: The App Ranch, Inc

Winery Locator

Wine buffs will enjoy discovering the locations of various wineries. The app lets you search by city and zip code (it's American) and you can also check out the availability of tours and find out whether picnic areas are available for some sandwiches and a nice glass of red.

Overall Rating ★★★☆☆

Price: £0.59/$0.99
Developer: Otto Chan

The Tapas and Spanish Cuisine Bible

Not strictly a travel app (despite being listed under travel), you can get a real flavour of Spain with this cuisine guide. It's not a recipe book – it's a guide to the types of food around, complete with English names.

Overall Rating ★★☆☆☆

Price: £2.99/$4.99
Developer: sebastian juarez

Bruges Travel Guide

Coming from a developer which has a wealth of travel guides for many other destinations, this guide to Bruges looks professional and slick and it has options to view maps, galleries and nearby activities. You can also play useful audio phrases.

Overall Rating ★★★★☆

Price: £1.79/$2.99
Developer: Columbus Travel

World Travel Atlas - Premium

It's hard not to fascinated by an atlas but when you've got one that shows you maps and divulges lots of information on countries, complete with traveller advice and the ability to save, you can easily see yourself whiling away time.

Overall Rating ★★★★☆

Price: £1.79/$2.99
Developer: Tobin Fisher

London's Backyard

This is a London guide with a twist. Instead of concentrating on the capital itself, it looks at areas around and about with photos and maps of nearby towns and suggested walking tours. Many attractions are listed and it is full of ideas and suggestions for eating.

Overall Rating ★★★★☆

Price: Free
Developer: Thomas Hicks

DogFriendly.com Mobile

Ensure your pampered pooches will be given a great welcome in America and Canada by firing this up and tapping into the app's website to find out which destinations will allow dogs. You can discover off-leash parks and more.

Overall Rating ★★★☆☆

Price: £0.59/$0.99
Developer: Paul Kramer

Travel Expense Wallet

Stick to your travel budget by making a note of everything you buy when you are abroad so ensure you don't suddenly find yourself incredibly short when you get back. Reports can be emailed and you can take receipts pics on an iPad 2.

Overall Rating ★★★☆☆

Price: Free
Developer: Gemini Solutions

iSee for iPad

One of the nicest things about travel is being able to share your experiences. This app lets you place review notes on Google maps and add pictures so you can tell others what you think. The app makes use of the iPad's GPS but you can turn this off.

Overall Rating ★★★☆☆

Price: Free
Developer: Masakazu Matsuyama

PackList Free for iPad

Many of us find packing a major chore and you usually think you've left something behind. Advert-driven *PackList Free* will allow you to list the items you are taking on your trip and note details such as size and weight of each item. You can then use it as a checklist.

Overall Rating ★★★★☆

Price: £0.59/$0.99
Developer: Kiran Reddy

Tip Calculator Lite

Although this app works – in that it allows you to work out how much a tip should be and how much each person should pay – the maths involved is so simplistic that you really shouldn't need an app for it. And how many take an iPad to the restaurant with them?

Overall Rating ★★☆☆☆

Price: £2.99/$4.99
Developer: Angel Santiago

ONtrack

A number of world airlines and hotels have signed up the *ONtrack* rewards programme and with this app you can keep a check on your entitlements. It's packed with information about the various rewards and there is a blog with lots of friendly advice.

Overall Rating ★★★☆☆

Price: £2.99/$4.99
Developer: Allstays LLC

Camp and Tent

Another camping location map, this tracks more than 13,000 campsites in America and Canada, showing private and public areas where you can bed down for the night. The map uses GPS to plot camps in relation to your current destination. You don't need internet access.

Overall Rating ★★★☆☆

Price: £3.49/$5.99
Developer: Paragon Technologies

VOX Spanish-English Phrasebook

You don't need an internet connection in order to make a translation. But what else do you get for this pricey app? You can view all sorts of phrases placed in categories but there are just over a thousand words overall.

Overall Rating ★★★★☆

Price: Free
Developer: David Vernon

Resort Maps

It claims that it will deliver a range of maps showing you where you can eat, ship and play in 100 resorts across America but we couldn't even get past the bit which asked for us to submit a passcode "for secure access" which made it frustratingly impossible to progress.

Overall Rating ★ ☆ ☆ ☆ ☆

Price: £1.19/$1.99
Developer: Audama Software

GPS & Map Toolbox

Building upon Google and Bing maps, *GPS & Map Toolbox* lets you map locations, compare map and satellite data between the two and produced location lists than be loaded into Google Earth and GPS devices. It's a sterling effort that makes navigation a breeze.

Overall Rating ★ ★ ★ ★ ☆

Price: Free
Developer: Sergiy Fesenko

Traxxit HD

Using *Traxxit HD*, you can discover where your cars, pets, friends and family are in the world. How? It works in tandem with a GPS tracking chip called the Traxxit360. When one of those is fitted to something or someone, it beams information back.

Overall Rating ★ ★ ★ ☆ ☆

Price: £0.59/$0.99
Developer: Kai Aras

AirLocation

By tethering the iPhone and iPad together, you are able to use this app to track your location using the GPS data on your phone. It means you can utilise the personal hotspot on your iPhone in order to make full use of the GPS function that Apple promised.

Overall Rating ★ ★ ★ ★ ★

Price: £0.59/$0.99
Developer: Intersog

Get Directions

Having a map to yourself is all well and good but sometimes you want to be able to share information. With *Get Directions* you can. It lets you share route information and give directions via email using, as most apps of this type do, Google Maps.

Overall Rating ★ ★ ★ ☆ ☆

Price: £0.59/$0.99
Developer: Martin Bovan

Hot Spot France

France is one of the most popular holidaying destinations in the world but you don't want to waste your time scouring the land for wi-fi hotspots. This app provides a map together with the nearest internet points.

Overall Rating ★ ★ ★ ☆ ☆

Price: £0.59/$0.99
Developer: Martin Bovan

Store USA

Desperately need to find a Walmart store in America? Fire up this app and you will get the location of dozens upon dozens of them with your own current location mapped too. It taps into a Google map and places pins seemingly everywhere. Better if it was free.

Overall Rating ★ ★ ☆ ☆ ☆

Price: £0.59/$0.99
Developer: Marin Bovan

Hotels USA

One name crops up time and time again: Marin Bovan. This developer has been producing numerous apps based around Google maps. This one finds the location of Marriot hotels in America just in case you can't find anywhere else to stay or just love the chain.

Overall Rating ★ ★ ☆ ☆ ☆

Price: Free
Developer: iTravel Tech Co inc

Compass Map

If there was ever an app that described exactly what it was in two words, this is it. It's a compass and a map. Together. It places a compass in the right hand corner of a Google map so you can ensure you know exactly which way you are facing as you navigate.

Overall Rating ★ ★ ★ ★ ★

Price: £0.59/$0.99
Developer: Sean Griffin

Where's the Route New York

Visitors to NYC can see all the bus routes for the City using this mapping app. Catching a bus can be much more of a headache than a taxi or subway but it can be much cheaper. Knowing where the routes are make it a no-brainer.

Overall Rating ★ ★ ★ ★ ☆

Price: £2.39/$3.99
Developer: Jose Maria Quevedo Mate

Real Course

If you have an iPad 3G, you can make use of the GPS when firing up this app designed for recreational sailing. It will allow you to plot a course and check out your speed in both miles and kilometres per hour. Although it's a little pricey, it is certainly precise.

Overall Rating ★ ★ ★ ★ ☆

Price: £2.99/$4.99
Developer: Luis Gargate

AviMapsGPS

If you are a regular pilot, this app is aimed at you, delivering up aviation specific maps that show your speed and location while you are in the air. You can display routes and store them too. The apps warns you not to use it as a primary means of navigation.

Overall Rating ★ ★ ★ ★ ☆

Price: £1.19/$1.99
Developer: Changrong Yao

UK Tides

UK Tides will allow you to see predictions of the heights and times of the tides around the United Kingdom and parts of Ireland. It features 500 locations and will make predictions over 28 days. The results make use of the full display, broken down day-by-day.

Overall Rating ★ ★ ★ ★ ☆

Price: Free
Developer: Flourishworks

yippt

Let people know exactly where you are by sharing your location automatically using *yippt*. Other users will be able to see when you check in and out of various locations, with messages even being sent via Google Chat. It uses GPS which can drain the battery.

Overall Rating ★ ★ ★ ★ ☆

Price: £0.59/$0.99
Developer: Kristian Kraljic

Fastfood (United Kingdom)

Ensure you never go hungry again and use this to discover the nearest McDonalds, Burger King, Subway, KFC, Pizza Hut and many more fast food restaurants. It finds your location, lets you share locations and includes opening times.

Overall Rating ★ ★ ★ ☆ ☆

Price: £0.59/$0.99
Developer: HALIL I KUCUKKURT

Speedometer Plus HD Video Camera with Auto Splitter

Although the legalities of this app are a bit on the grey side, it's certainly intriguing. You can pop your iPad 2 on the dash and video the traffic.

Overall Rating ★ ★ ★ ☆ ☆

Price: £0.59/$0.99
Developer: Leland Roys

EZCarFinder

Losing your car is an annoyance. Just make sure you don't lose your iPad too. With this app you can tell the app where you have parked so that you can get back to it with little hassle. It's bold, colourful display will guide you back to your car via a Google map.

Overall Rating ★ ★ ★ ☆ ☆

Price: Free
Developer: Syzygy Research

Mapster

You can download maps direct to your iPad with *Mapster* which means you don't need an internet connection to use it once you are out and about. The maps are stunning in their detail and boast loads of topographical information drawing on OpenStreetMap.

Overall Rating ★ ★ ★ ★ ★

Price: £0.59/$0.99
Developer: AOBO Co. Ltd

Navigator 360 for iPad

Make your iPad run like a GPS navigator. Type in the name of the place you wish to go and see what else is around. The iPad will help you get to your destination and it will sound an alarm when you get near.

Overall Rating ★ ★ ★ ★ ☆

Price: £0.59/$0.99
Developer: Visual Info

Map Editor

Using *Map Editor* allows you to draw up your own routes which can then be emailed. You can add 38 type of map features and produce labels. Maps can be created using GPS and distances and areas can be measured. You end up with some very colourful maps.

Overall Rating ★ ★ ★ ★ ☆

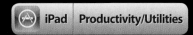
Utilties

There are thousands of apps on the App Store that are designed to save you time, make life easier or just help you maximise your efficiency. Here we showcase the useful iPad apps that serve very specific purposes to assist you in your day-to-day routine.

Top Paid Apps	Top Free Apps
Storyboards Premium ★★★★	**D-Desk** ★★★
Pages ★★★★	**Offline Reader+** ★★★★★
GeoBoard ★★★★	**Maven Web Browser** ★★★★

Staff pick of the section	
Mannequin ★★★	**Speak It!** ★★★★

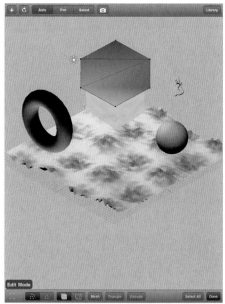

■ The developer certainly hasn't held back on the amount of options available…

■ There's a sizeable array of texture mapping and editing tools…

Price: £4.99/$7.99 **Developer:** Michael Farrell

Verto Studio 3D

A new 3D design studio that's heading in the right direction

 Verto Studio 3D is, in essence, a sandbox design studio that intends to replicate what other programs already offer on the PC. It brings a whole new level of functionality to an otherwise untapped market, but, as is the case with new apps, there are teething issues which need to be ironed out.

The first thing that's apparent when loading up a new document is the amount of options that are available. Although it's fairly cheap, the developer really hasn't held back. There's a sizeable array of texture mapping and editing tools, from 360 degree camera control to individual object mesh manipulation. You can import your own textures and objects, or use the stock ones available, all performed with a user-friendly interface and some basic touch screen controls.

Once in a scene, the app runs smoothly for the most part, and editing or moving the scenery is a breeze. The utilities available for object editing purposes are considerable, but no doubt some designers will be left wanting more options in future versions. A great starting point but it needs a few tweaks if it is to ever be deemed an essential app.

Rating ★★★★☆

Price: £8.99/$14.99 **Developer:** Tamajii Inc

Storyboards Premium

With this scene-crafting iPad app, Hollywood's red carpet starts at the tips of your fingers...

Storyboards Premium offers somewhat self-explanatory help to budding writers, comic-book creators and movie directors in order for them to form a more clear picture in their mind of a narrative before committing it to paper, or indeed celluloid. Unlike its free counterpart, this paid-for edition allows a whole manner of techniques to be employed, smoothing the transition from the artist's initial conception though to the final product. Though some additional functionality is left to be desired, such features would tread on the toes of regular image manipulation software were they to be included, meaning that expert users may well wish to become familiar with an app of that kind before putting Storyboards Premium to active use. Amateurs and professionals hoping to offer a brief narrative outline, though, should find the options on offer to be more than adequate.

Creator Tamajii allow users to create an unlimited number of storyboards, each composed of a theoretically infinite total of individual frames. After selecting an appropriate background (which could naturally feature a simply manipulated photo from one's library), users are free to populate each panel with their choice of dozens of incidental objects, ranging from heavy goods vehicles and the humble club sandwich, to, naturally, human figures. Each on-screen actor can be customised via a simple single tap, switching between a handful of costume ideas and a rainbow of fabric colours. Naturally too, this principle cast can be rotated over eight compass directions, allowing users to expand and contract their size to be shown from every conventional camera angle. So, bad news if you like your actors shot from below through a sheet of glass. There's good news if you're the kind of individual that prizes ergonomics over finer details, though. Simpler panels can be completed in well under one minute, thanks in part to a handy ability to favourite items used with greater frequency.

Similarly to their human counterparts, each in-app prop can be rotated, scaled and made transparent to each user's content, allowing for swift placement of auxiliary objects inside a room, even at the last possible minute. Though pixel perfect accuracy naturally isn't quite achievable with such a limited set of tools, especially given that the app won't permit figures to be cut out from pre-existing digital camera images, a rough approximation of the scene is always possible here. Though more artistic visionaries may feel the need to import background images drawn by their own hand, the level of integration on offer here makes an occasional painstaking frame more than worthwhile.

A lavishly produced and easy-to-use app that is sure to inspire you to start mapping out your own movies.

Rating ★★★★★

■ The app is so easy to use that you'll be drafting out you own storyboards in minutes. But when do the cameras start rolling?

■ Objects can be scaled, rotated and placed within your scenes to help you visualise how each scene will look.

Price: £5.99/$10.99 **Developer:** Avatron Soft

Air Display

Double up your desktop display space with a second screen

Two displays are better than one and the *Air Display* app is here to make the scenario a reality without the added expense of a second screen. But unfortunately, *Air Display* did not take off with the instant impact we had hoped for, which instantly shattered some of its appeal.

Connection was simple enough: install the software, start the app, connect. But our tests via Windows Vista and XP were drawn out and not completely successful, particularly with Vista. However, this could be down to other factors such as the hardware used and connection issues, and we did have more success via a Mac – so it's not all doom and gloom.

Air Display uses the same Wi-Fi network as the desktop so the quality of service can be dependent on the quality of the connection. If the connection does drop out there is the option to connect automatically, but we only had occasional success with this. Once connected and into action it's all about the moving windows and apps to arrange. The mouse moves right and makes an appearance on the iPad screen, but when dragging a window from desktop to iPad there is a delay.

Using the mouse across two screens takes some getting use to and – somewhat annoyingly – it occasionally disappears when making the transfer. Swapping windows also didn't see any auto resize for the different resolutions, meaning the user needs to perform the action. Swapping more dynamic content, ie video, saw a poor frame rate and jerky video.

So while it worked on a basic level, there were many issues that slowly become apparent that made the app more trouble to use than it is ultimately worth. The need to transform your iPad into an extension of your PC monitor will undoubtedly only appeal to a minority group but for it to do so in a cumbersome and disjointed manner will only alienate those who actually have a need for it. And the price you're paying doesn't exactly put it into the impulse 'worth a go' category.

The app is much cheaper than a second screen, but it just doesn't fulfil its potential just yet. This could be a great app for those who need two screens, but it just needs to be made more foolproof. Hopefully future updates will allow it to run smoother but for now this is hard to recommend.

■ The app transforms your iPad into an extension of your PC monitor, but there are certain problems with it…

Rating ★★★☆☆

■ Here we can see the image as it appears on your desktop computer monitor, but when you start to drag it across on the iPad certain problems arise…

■ The app doesn't auto resize to the different resolutions, meaning that the user has to manually perform the task.

Price: £5.99/$9.99 **Developer:** Apple Inc

Pages

A full word processor at your fingertips

It makes sense for Apple to deliver the superb *Pages* on iPad thanks to how well the device is suited to word processing on the move. It has a large, clear screen, plenty of space for a chunky on-screen keyboard and it boasts a wealth of connectivity options. When creating their first document, users are greeted with 15 preset template options to suit many needs. Starting from scratch with a blank spread and turning it into a custom document is as simple as using Word or the OS X version of Pages, thanks to the wealth of formatting and file embedding options available.

Typing at speed is as intuitive as using a physical keyboard with no lag between input and page display. Text can be aligned, formatted, tabbed and manipulated at speed using custom toolbars at the top of the screen. Viewing pages in both portrait and landscape is superb and while landscape may give users a bigger keyboard to play with, portrait mode works just as well. Correcting formatting mistakes is a simple case of tapping or dragging over the area of interest and hitting the Inspector tab, which then displays the full range of formatting options available for that region. Additionally, text errors can be corrected using the iPad's native dictionary function. Once users are happy with their finished documents, they can be saved into an on-board document folder that can also be emailed to contacts or exported to your desktop Mac or iWork.com account. It's simple and it works a treat, however, there are some glaring feature omissions that

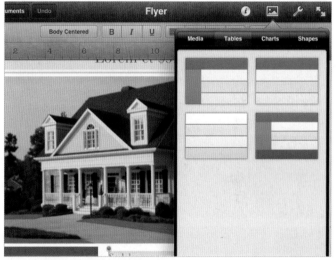

■ You can create work quickly and efficiently with this app…

■ The app includes a selection of templates for you to use.

hold the *Pages* app back. For starters there are no character or page count trackers. Users are also unable to print documents due to a lack of device connectivity, and finally, Pages comes without the option to track changes. Although it is missing a few key features, users are unlikely to find a more powerful word processor available for iPad. The range of features the app does offer more than justifies the price, but we expect future updates to rectify the shortcomings of this most recent build. Largely powerful, the *Pages* app sadly misses features that other word processors deliver as standard.

Rating ★★★★☆

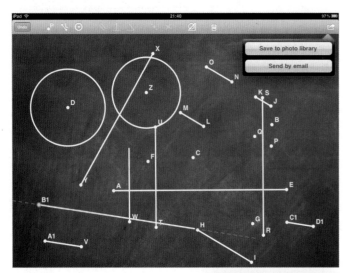

■ You simply move your finger around the slate to create perfect geometrical shapes in an instant.

■ All that's missing is an option to instantly (and quite literally) wipe the slate clean.

Price: £1.19/$1.99 **Developer:** zheng min Wei

GeoBoard
Geometry at your fingertips

Being able to draw a perfect circle generally isn't a skill possessed by many people. Regular folk have to use a tool like a compass, but on *GeoBoard* you just need a single finger. Drag a fingertip across the blackboard-style screen, and it'll make a perfect circle appear precisely to the size you like. Why? Because *GeoBoard* is a drawing tool for nerds, allowing you to create all kinds of geometrical illustrations by hand. In addition to circles, they include straight, parallel and perpendicular lines. There's also the ability to draw a line at any angle you like relative to another point, the option to create a point exactly mid way between two others, and slightly more complicated things we don't understand, like creating an intersection for lines and circles.

What's the use of all this? As mere intellectual mortals, we're not really sure, but *GeoBoard* seems to be only suited to geometry students or teachers, and is very popular with said users if the user reviews are anything to go by. Without that specialist knowledge, all we can say is that *GeoBoard* is a smart and well-made app, albeit one for a very specialist field.

Rating ★★★★✩

Price: £1.79/$2.99 **Developer:** Fabrication Games

Mannequin
Strike a pose with this virtual 3D artists' mannequin

On the face of it, the app is a simple and straightforward: there is a plain textured background, a fully poseable 3D figure, and a modest array of controls. However, it is the 3D lay figure that holds the interest. It's fully controllable using an array of finger gestures. Users can take any joint and twist and bend into the desired position, turn the model is various directions and rotate 360 degrees. In fact, the figure can be manoeuvred into almost any position simply using swipes, taps and gestures. It is worth noting that there is no way to save poses, and no zoom.

Beyond finger control, the app has a host of buttons and sliders to get more precise positioning. There is a chain function which allows users to move whole limbs in unison or at least more than one part together. Tap to switch off and each individual element is free to move.

More recent additions to the app include a very useful reset button that takes the 3D figure back to its original state. For those feeling uninspired there is the a random pose button and for those who have made a wrong move there is an undo and redo button to save the day. The ideal app for budding artists, a lay figure that fits in a pocket or bag. It certainly won't interest everyone, but still worth a look.

Rating ★★★★✩

■ Move him how you like and then tap a button to reset his position.

■ This is perhaps only really of interest to artists and animators.

■ You basically use your finger as a stylus to draw on the screen. Basic stuff, but it works.

■ A tutorial will show you around the app, not that there's anything too complicated to grasp.

Price: £1.79/$2.99   **Developer:** Time Base Technology Limitedt

eNote Taker

If you're not a fan of keyboards, this does the job

eNote Taker lets you use your finger or a stylus to add notes to pages. It gives you control over the scale of the notes so you can write big letters or cram in small print, and also choose the thickness of your pen. You have the choice of paper types, and can re-arrange pages and projects with the utmost ease. What's more, you can add a wrist rest so that you don't accidentally add random inputs.

In practice, this app is mildly useful. If you have a decent stylus, then it's a completely different app. Its controlled, easy to use, and lot more effective. In terms of build and ease of use, this app trumps many more expensive note-taking apps that are available. Its excellent instructions see to it you know exactly what to do once its downloaded. An enjoyably simple notes app that's best suited to use with a stylus. Without one, it's only average. An enjoyably simple notes app that's best suited to use with a stylus. Without one, it's only average.

Rating ★★★★★

Price: £2.99/$4.99   **Developer:** Addition Lda

I'm Downloading

All the downloads and links that you could possibly want

One of the major complaints about the iPad as a viable replacement for a desktop computer is that it doesn't have the file hierarchy to support normal computer behaviour online. This comes in many forms, one of them being an inability to download files from the web, as there is nowhere to put them.

Luckily, clever developers exist to think of ways around such problems. *I'm Downloading* offers a limited but useful option for those that wish to grab files from online and save them to the iPad. In most cases, the files you download aren't useable on the iPad, but they can be later transferred to a main computer through iTunes. The main element of the app is a browser where you can search for those files you want to download. You have the choice of search engines, and can of course go direct to a URL. Once you've got to a page that contains the download file, a message pops up once you tap the button, and your download is added to a queue. Once it's safely landed in the app, you can view it, save it and edit its name. It can then be exported during the next sync for proper use. A very well-made, easy-to-use app.

Rating ★★★★★

■ The main element of the app is a browser where you can search for files you want to download…

■ Once in the app, you can view the file, save it and edit the name.

Dropbox

Price: Free   **Developer:** Dropbox

■ You can open any of the files in your Dropbox with an appropriate app on your iPad

■ Store and open all sorts of file types on your Dropbox

Online storage, for free!

The iPad doesn't have a built-in file manager and therefore it can be a bit of a pain to transfer your files to it from a computer. It means that you have to open iTunes and manually drag files across, then sync to get them onto your iPad.

Dropbox for iPad integrates with the free online storage service of the same name to give you a better method of managing your files. It's not quite a fully fledged file manager, but it allows you to easily use documents on your iPad.

Dropbox gives you 2GB of free online storage and you can copy any file that the iPad understands to the service. Open *Dropbox* for iPad and you can see all the files and use them as you wish. You can even stream video content too.

With many other iPad apps allowing you to save to or read from your Dropbox, it's a great tool for managing documents. For a free app, the *Dropbox* app is excellent and getting 2GB of free online storage is great too. If you need more space, you can upgrade to 50GB or 100GB options.

Rating ★★★★★

iAnnotate PDF

Price: £5.99/$9.99   **Developer:** Aji, LLC

Mark-up and edit your files

iAnnotate PDF is a tool that allows you to mark up and edit standard PDF files on your iPad. There are a full range of tools available that enable you to highlight elements, cross out text and add your own comments.

The range of options is really flexible and the annotations that we tested worked exactly as expected when opened on Macs and PCs – in both Preview on the Mac and Adobe Reader on the PC. Annotating PDFs is one of those tasks that seems built around a mouse and keyboard, but *iAnnotate* really does make it possible to annotate a PDF on the touch screen of the iPad.

Each PDF opens in a tab, enabling you to quickly jump between documents. You can also email annotated PDFs from within the app, so it's a fully featured tool that's perfect when you're on the move. For £5.99 this is a great app and if you annotate PDFs on a regular basis it'll soon become indispensable.

Rating ★★★★★

■ Add all the usual lines, highlights and notes to your PDFs…

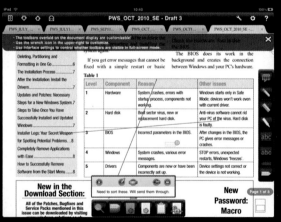

■ You can mail your marked PDFs directly from the app…

MobileMe iDisk

Price: Free   **Developer:** Apple, Inc

Take the world's largest hard disk with you, anywhere you go!

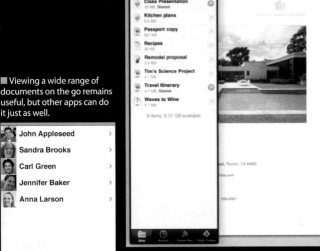

■ Viewing a wide range of documents on the go remains useful, but other apps can do it just as well.

■ If the services were provided at a fraction of the cost, the convenience just might beat more traditional file-transfer systems…

Have you ever entered into a conversation with somebody at work about this commercial issue or that, desperate to have a certain set of figures to hand, or perhaps an appropriate graph? Well, thanks to Apple's MobileMe service, this is now perfectly possible. After installing this app on their iPad, workers can gain access to their own MobileMe account remotely, and with it pretty much everything contained therein. Be it JPEG images or PDF documents – everything will be available to call up from the palm of your hand, ready to influence that crucial decision or simply settle a particular argument.

What's more, once the document in question has settled whatever discussion was taking place, it can easily be shared from within the app; a download link being sent to whatever contact is in need of the information, direct from MobileMe itself. It's possible, too, to time limit or password-protect this information, ensuring it doesn't fall into the wrong hands. Enjoy this app now because when iOS 5 arrives it this be consigned to the scrapheap.

Rating ★★★★★

Speak It! Text To Speech

Price: £1.19/$1.99   **Developer:** John Stefanopolos

Talk is cheap

We suppose many aspects of modern life would have astounded us, ten or 20 years ago. Live online gaming, for instance, or how terribly expensive things are. Topping the list, though, come apps like *Speak It!*, which allows a device in the palm of your hand to speak for itself near-perfectly.

It's not quite as simple as that, naturally. Though its sales blurb suggests the ability to read PDF files, it can only do this insofar as it can read any copied and pasted text from any document. So, before having the device spell out any text, users must delve into the source document as they would have done anyway, which is a shame but doesn't kill off the app's purpose entirely.

It's possible, for instance, to send a spoken message to others via email, just through the entry of text. Naturally, too, it may prove of use to those unwilling to strain their eyes through the viewing of large text documents to have one of this app's four automatons speak it to them while either browsing other apps or doing nothing at all. The interface isn't great but this is still a triumph.

■ Emailed sound files are sent directly from the app itself.

■ The sound files can be tweaked, forming more widely used MP3s, the app would be better still.

Rating ★★★★★

Price: Free **Developer:** Christopher Weems

Jumbo Calulator

t tackles the biggest sums

While some apps fail to make use of the iPad's large display, others, such as *Jumbo Calculator*, are simply re-sized versions of existing apps. It's hard to expect much more – after all, it simply exists as a clear, chunky calculator. The buttons are satisfyingly large and the display is clean, and the fake solar panel and button tap sound are nice touches. A super-sized version of what you already own, but it's free.

■ Even the fattest fingers will be able to use this beast.

Overall Rating ★★★★★

Price: £2.99/$4.99 **Developer:** Nikita Lutsenko

GoDocs for iPad

Bringing Google Docs and the iPad together

As the iPad lets you sync email accounts from multiple service providers, it makes sense that Google Mail users can have access to Google Docs as well. Unfortunately, this isn't the case. Enter *GoDocs*, a handy app that gives you direct, secure access to your Google Docs at speed. On downloading the app, all you need to do to sync accounts is enter your Gmail username and password, and then you'll be connected in a matter of seconds.

■ Get fast and secure access o your Google Docs in econds…

Overall Rating ★★★★★

Price: £0.59/$0.99 **Developer:** Savage Interactive

Sorted

Keep track of your hectic life in colourful style

While there is a glut of task management apps doing the rounds on iPhone, it's clear that the iPad's crisper display is more suited for creating complex, easily navigated lists. *Sorted* from Savage Interactive is a bright and colourful app complete with fully customisable task schedules. Users can create multiple lists packed with chores, including specific pages for multi-tiered projects. Creating new tasks and lists is simple thanks to Sorted's large, clear display. Events can be prioritised using a sliding colour scale, queued up by date and time to create accurate schedules, as well as emailed to multiple addresses.

■ Add a little colour to your day with this delightful app.

Overall Rating ★★★★☆

Price: £1.19/$1.99 **Developer:** Sud Soft System

I Will HD

Stay focussed and organised at work

Whether you're self-employed or working in-house, iWill HD is a superb app geared towards helping you stay organised in the workplace. More than just a standard task manager, developer Sud Soft System has created a colourful, clean interface that houses a plethora of useful tools. Thanks to superb functionality and presentation, it really can make a difference to your working day.

■ The attracive interface makes this app stand out from the crowd.

Overall Rating ★★★★★

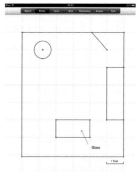

Price: £2.99/$4.99 **Developer:** Robert Shawhan

GraphPad

GraphPad is, quite simply, virtual graph paper. Designed specifically for technical drawing, it allows you to create plans by hand, and automatically adjusts your wonky lines into perfectly straight ones. There's also a 'points' feature that allows you to tweak your designs by manually dragging parts of the drawing until they're exactly where you want them. You can then add arrows and annotations until you've got a plan you're happy with, and then… well, there doesn't seem to be an option to print or email yet,

Rating ★★★★☆

Price: £0.59/$0.99 **Developer:** Isaac D. Lim

Radial Keyboard

Radial Keyboard is intended to make typing much easier, but actually achieves the opposite. Typing with two thumbs involves a certain period of adjustment, and much worse, there's no way to use it in conjunction with other apps. So, you have to type into the Radial Keyboard app, copy the text, and paste it into the app you want to use.

Rating ★☆☆☆☆

Price: Free **Developer:** Vijay Anand

Offline Reader+

An app that may be useful for owners of Wi-Fi-only iPads, *Offline Reader+* allows you to browse the internet and save any page for future reading without needing to be connected to the internet. Aside from this basic function, it allows you to switch the web page to a more readable version containing only the text and main images, as well as print the page via a wireless connection. It's really quite simple, but brilliantly useful nevertheless. If you like to read a lot of online articles, or save important ones, then it's indispensable.

Rating ★★★★★

Price: Free **Developer:** Paolo Bottigliero

D-Desk

If the iPad is the lazy person's mobile device, then D-Desk is the lazy iPad owner's app. Designed to keep meetings quick and convenient, it features a notepad, calculator and a mini web browser all on the same screen. It may seem a little pointless when all three apps already exist separately on the iPad, but there is something to be said for all-in-one.

Rating ★★★☆☆

Price: £0.59/$0.99 **Developer:** Paul Abraham Jaimovich

Easy Converter Pro

This sells itself as the only all-in-one conversion calculator you'll ever need, and it certainly seems up to the task, at least at first. The menu offers a staggering 22 different types of units to convert, including currency, temperature, and radioactivity. It sounds great, but the user interface is so cumbersome – thanks to an unreliable unit selection menu.

Rating ★★☆☆☆

Price: £1.79/$2.99 **Developer:** Yuri Selukoff

GoodReader for iPad

Already hailed as the daddy of document readers because of its ability to display and annotate large size files in a dazzling array of file formats, a recent update for the *Good Reader* iPad app added VGA output support. Now, you have another option for presentations — convert an existing Keynote or PowerPoint presentation to PDF or Word format, hook your iPad up with a VGA cable and use *Good Reader* to run the presentation. A very good app that, thanks to updates, now offers great presentational potential.

Rating ★★★★☆

Price: Free **Developer:** Dropbox Inc

Dropbox

Dropbox enables you to store your files, and in the process sync them between your iPhone, iPad, Mac or PC. It's possible to save photos and videos, including HD videos, on the iPhone. Files can also be exported to other apps from within Dropbox. The iPad app fares better for office work, with native support for exporting files to iWork, and a larger landscape keyboard for easier typing. Perhaps the most important aspect of Dropbox is that many office-based apps such as Quickoffice support syncing files via a Dropbox account.

Rating ★★★★★

Price: £2.99/$4.99 **Developer:** Cory Powers

Whiteboard HD

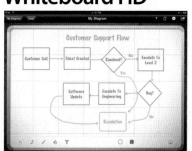

Whiteboard HD lets you connect your iPad to an external display or projector using an Apple VGA or composite/component video-out cable, and transmits directly to an external display using the iPad's touch screen. Freeform drawing with a fingertip is possible, and it's also easy to add pre-drawn shapes and lines using multi-touch gesture controls.

Rating ★★★★☆

Price: £79.99/$139.99 **Developer:** TeamViewer GmbH

TeamViewer PRO HD

TeamViewer takes the approach of offering a free version alongside a Pro version that doesn't add any further features, but is licensed for commercial use. Once the desktop client has been installed on your computer, it's a doddle to log in via the app. It works over both 3G and Wi-Fi connections, so wherever you are you can access your office computer.

Rating ★★★★★

Price: £0.59/$0.99 **Developer:** Vision Maker UK Limited

Rota Ruler

Rota Ruler replaces the more traditional ruler/tape measure for those who don't have one to hand. The title gives a clue as to how the app works. The iPad is lined up against the start point, and then rotated on its edge until it reaches its destination. In principle this works well, but relies on the user not making any mistakes. When a measurement is complete, a tab is added to the history with the option to add a title, photo and email. Does its task reasonably accurately, but it's hard to see how much use it will be.

Rating ★★★★★

Price: £0.59/$0.99 **Developer:** HandyPadSoft

Converter Touch HD

Convert currency easily and quickly with what claims to be the fastest converter on the iPad. The drag-and-drop interface makes it a breeze to pick up – it's much more intuitive than tapping and scrolling through the typical currency conversion websites. This version adds the ability to manually update the current exchange rate for added accuracy when you need it. It's ideal for traders and finance professionals, but also good for those who regularly purchase goods online from abroad. A handy currency converter.

Rating ★★★★★

Price: Free **Developer:** Insphere Software

MyDidiWallet

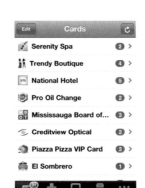

Digital wallets are hugely popular in Asia, with consumers using their phones and tablets for everything from store purchases to discount cards. Will it be as popular in the West? *MyDigiWallet* takes only the loyalty card aspect of the idea, setting itself up as an organiser for all your various money-off cards. In the coupon-clipping USA, this is appealing; most of the businesses that offer discounts are US-based. Over here the offers are thinner on the ground, however. UK consumers may be happier sticking to their Nectar card.

Rating ★★★★★

Price: £4.99/$7.99 **Developer:** Richard Silverman

10 Key 1:1 Calculator

This app has an old-fashioned feature that's actually really useful – the digital equivalent of a paper tape, on which your sums are noted down in order. This really comes into its own when you're working with complex equations – whether that's quantum physics or your VAT bill – but it's also handy as an educational tool, and when doing your household budget. You can clear the tape when you're done, although exporting it would be handy, especially to a spreadsheet. Especially useful for checking your working process.

Rating ★★★★★

Price: £0.59/$0.99 **Developer:** DJ Kang

Maven Web Browser

If you've stuck with Safari, you might wonder why you should bother changing, but this browser has some beguiling features. A pleasant interface with a digital jog-dial for your bookmarks is quick and easy to use, and dual panels mean you can look at two pages at the same time the way you would on a larger screen. Keychain support saves passwords for you, and a Reader serves up RSS feeds. It's let down only by some barely noticeable linguistic quirks. An improvement on Safari, with a great user interface and a good level of usability.

Rating ★★★★★

Price: £2.99/$4.99 **Developer:** Ice Cream Studios

Writings

In the increasingly competitive market of text editors on the iPad, *Writings* aims to stand out from the crowd by offering simplicity in place of features. While it's a nice idea, there are other apps that have the same approach for a lower price. The best thing about *Writings* is the ability to inverse the colour scheme to write white-on-black, which is perfect for writing in the dark when the colours might otherwise strain your eyes. More neat little touches like this in future versions would make *Writings* a 'must-buy' writing app.

Rating ★★★★★

Price: £0.59/$0.99 **Developer:** John Millhouse

Roman Calulator

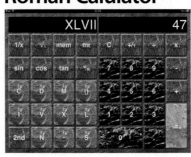

Roman Calculator lets you perform fairly detailed mathematical equations with Roman numerals. It includes a converter to switch to regular numbers, and the option to turn your device on its side, and have both numerical options next to each other. If you're struggling with your Roman denominations, there's a handy help screen. Good, if a little pointless.

Rating ★★★★★

Price: Free **Developer:** SpinThought Inc

SoundSlateLT

Soundslate is a customisable soundboard, and the LT version is the free option of the app. To get started, users create a new page with title and notes, which in turns creates a new soundboard. This is a grid of 20 sound buttons across a single page, with a maximum of two pages and 40 buttons in the LT version. To assign a sound, it's a simple matter of holding down a button and selecting. The library of sounds is limited, though there is a record option, but offers enough variety for users to appreciate the app.

Rating ★★★★★

Price: Free **Developer:** You Jinwen

USBSharp

USBSharp is a free app that turns the iPad into portable file storage. The app uses Wi-Fi to connect to a browser via a simple interface for file transfer. The one niggle here is that only one file at a time can be transferred. File format support includes plain text, popular document extensions, image files and video (MP4), HTML and zip. The files are organised via name, date or type, and a quick tap will open to view. New folders can be added, plain text files created, and photos from the Camera Roll added to File Explorer.

Rating ★★★★★

Price: £2.99/$4.99 **Developer:** Bonfire Dev Advisors

I Can Do It for iPad

The sentiment of this app is admirable, attempting to turn negative and feelings into something more positive. However, the execution is limited, and doesn't offer much more than a formatted notepad. Users can add a new event, what they need to do, and their current feelings and 'blocking thoughts'. A list of emotions with a slider to register how acute an emotion is about as technical as this app gets. Events can be saved and altered, which is effectively editing the original event. *I Can Do It* has good intentions, but it is technically limited.

Rating ★★★★★

Price: £1.79/$2.99 **Developer:** G Marangoni

Notesizer

Notesizer is a multi-talented app dressed up as a real-life notebook with tabbed pages. The virtual notebook allows the user to add a profile, add notes, paint and browse the web. The tabbed page premise works reasonably well, and the individual components are simple but effective. However, it is difficult to see what the benefits are.

Rating ★★★★★

Price: Free **Developer:** Orchestrator Inc

OrchMail

OrchMail is an email manager on one level and a competent organiser on another. The standard mail window offers categories which can be applied when sending a mail, providing extra organisation. It gets more interesting after mail is sent, as the user receives the standard email, but the sender gets a breakdown of the email sent. Very clever.

Rating ★★★★★

Price: £2.99/$4.99 **Developer:** Steve Sprang

Inkpad

Inkpad is a high-end paint tool that comes at a low cost considering the technical clout beneath its simple exterior. With ease and precision, you can create complex visuals using a wide range of paint, line and shape tools, as well as text editors, droppers and image pasting options. Creating files is simple, and if mistakes are made the undo option offers a long memory, allowing you to go back several steps if need be. There are also a number of fill patterns and gradients, brush shapes, and custom sizes for each tool.

Rating ★★★★★

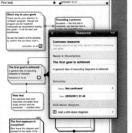

Price: £2.99/$4.99 **Developer:** Jury Shortki

inShort

Intended as a task manager for those looking to visualise the completion of their goals and create a to-do list for huge work projects, *inShort* is a powerful tool, if not a little daunting. Using the tutorial, you can get a feel for how complex flow chart tasks can be created, complete with branching paths for different outcomes and sub-levels for multi-tiered tasks. It may seem over the top for a task manager, but if a goal is technical in nature, requiring more than a text list, then *inShort* can help you create a personalised road map to success.

Rating ★★★★★

Price: £2.99/$4.99 **Developer:** Appigo Inc

Corkulous

Corkulous is a collection of virtual pinboards for every occasion or category. Users can create as many new corkboards as they want. Just add a title and it's ready to go. Access to a pinboard is a single tap away, which expands to reveal a neat little filing cabinet at the bottom of the screen. Tap to open and tap again to add notes, labels, photos and tasks.

Rating ★★★★★

Price: Free
Developer: Ben Johnson

Free-Time

 Free-Time is a neat little app that lets you keep track of how much free time you have in a day by inputting your work and social commitments. It's a good idea and, apart from a few niggles here and there, it's definitely worth downloading and adding to your app collection.

Overall Rating ★★★★☆

Price: £2.99/$4.99
Developer: David Findlay

Notesy for Dropbox

 If you're a frequent note taker and also use Dropbox, then you might want to consider this app. As you might expect, you can share all your note content over Dropbox for other devices, but the design is unfortunately a bit plain and boring for our liking.

Overall Rating ★★★☆☆

Price: £1.79/$2.99
Developer: Spore Tools Ltd.

Idea Store

 Here's yet another note-taking app for your iPad. This one aims to set itself apart from the pack by letting you group your notes to more easily search through. If you take a lot of notes then you'll surely welcome this feature, although it's not cheap.

Overall Rating ★★★★☆

Price: £2.99/$4.99
Developer: bitolithic

ThinkBook – Write, Plan, Outline

 This note-taking app has a nice interface that makes switching between notes and documents a breeze. There's a number of tools to edit your notes, you can link documents together and there's Dropbox integration.

Overall Rating ★★★★☆

Price: Free
Developer: FutureMedia Studio

PerfectReader – PDF Reader For iPad

 This app is a really clean and fluid way to view PDFs, as they are displayed in a 'book' format for you to browse through. Dropbox, GoogleDocs and other external app integration make this a decent choice.

Overall Rating ★★★☆☆

Price: £1.79/$2.99
Developer: Hand Carved Code, LLC

Priorities

 Priorities is a quick and easy way to manage your life on your iPad. It joins a host of similar 'reminder' apps but it has tons of functionality including alerts and syncing with other devices, and it's all executed brilliantly. Excellent stuff.

Overall Rating ★★★★★

Price: £0.59/$0.99
Developer: Moshen Chan

Living Earth HD – World Clock

 With *Living Earth HD* you can get the time and weather for cities around the world by interacting with a visually stunning globe. Real-time satellite cloud data and an alarm clock are just some of the features on offer.

Overall Rating ★★★★★

Price: £11.99/$19.99
Developer: The Omni Group

OmniOutliner For iPad

 OmniOutliner is a highly advanced and feature-rich writing tool, letting you design entire pages with a variety of styles and content. It's expensive, but if you're serious about presentation then it might just be worth it.

Overall Rating ★★★★☆

Price: £0.59/$0.99
Developer: Emerald Sequoia LLC

Emerald Observatory For iPad

 Casual and serious astronomers alike will get a kick out of this app. With astronomical information, including the motion of the Sun and the planets, presented in a visually appealing way, this is a brilliant app.

Overall Rating ★★★★☆

Price: £8.99/$14.99
Developer: CounterPath Corporation

Bria – Mobile VoIP SIP Softphone

 Bria lets you make calls over the internet for free and includes a variety of features and functionality. However, it requires some external server set up to be of any use, so if you don't know what you're doing then you might struggle.

Overall Rating ★★★☆☆

Price: £2.99/$4.99
Developer: Junecloud LLC

Notefile

 There are so many 'note-taking' apps on the App Store that it's hard to tell one from another. *Notefile* definitely isn't unique but it's got a nice clean UI, syncs to all devices and is simple to use. Could maybe do with some other features, but otherwise good.

Overall Rating ★★★☆☆

Price: £0.59/$0.99
Developer: Recession Apps

System Activity Monitor

 With this app you can see what programs are taking up the most memory on your iPad, as well as additional information about running processes. It doesn't look great and doesn't have a huge number of uses.

Overall Rating ★★★☆☆

Price: £1.19/$1.99
Developer: Simzart

Heart Writer

 This text editor brings to the table a wide range of functionality to vie for your attention over its competitors. With the ability to interact with Dropbox and Google Docs, along with a clean and simple layout, this is a well-done app overall.

Overall Rating ★★★★☆

Price: Free
Developer: Condé Nast Digital

Idea Flight

 This is a really neat idea that's hindered by some hidden costs. Basically, you can share information such as PDF files across a network instantly with others using the app, perfect for staff meetings or otherwise. Good, if you don't mind shelling out a bit of money.

Overall Rating ★★★☆☆

Price: Free
Developer: SciMobile.com

Crystal Calculator Free – Scientific

 This app lets you input and solve detailed calculations thanks to a neat paper-tape feature. It's relatively simple to use, although some of the visual effects can be a little distracting when typing a complex calculation.

Overall Rating ★★★☆☆

Price: £0.59/£0.99
Developer: Intridea

Car Finder

 It's sometimes easy to forget where you've parked amid hundreds of other vehicles, so is way apps like this exist. Just take a photo on your iPad 2 and the app will use Augmented Reality to keep tabs on it, complete with handy maps and a timer to say when your parking expires.

Overall Rating ★★★☆☆

Price: £0.59/$0.99
Developer: Gee Whiz Stuff

Use Your Handwriting GOLD

 This is a good idea for an app that lets you write notes in handwritten format. It works well and is fairly simple, although it's all a little plain and if you don't have a stylus, you might not find it that easy to write on.

Overall Rating ★★★☆☆

Price: £2.99/$4.99
Developer: The Skins Factory, Inc.

Zen Viewer HD

 Zen Viewer HD lets you view and edit an impressively large array of file types including audio, video, image and document formats. If you like all your stuff in one place then check this out, and it's got plenty of other features to keep you busy.

Overall Rating ★★★★☆

Price: Free
Developer: acrossair

AirBoard

 AirBoard is basically an instant-messaging chat application but, in place of a text box, you're given a blank white canvas to draw on and share with others. It's good for messing around on but probably not that practical for any serious work.

Overall Rating ★★★☆☆

Price: £2.99/$4.99
Developer: 9 Square Workshop

DocAS – Docs Organizer

 If you ever feel that there are too many apps for too many different things, then this might be for you, combining a PDF reader, document viewer, note taker and more into one app. It doesn't come together seamlessly but it's not bad.

Overall Rating ★★★☆☆

Price: Free
Developer: iBear LLC

Notes On The Fridge Free

This app is a fun little idea that mimics the sorts of notes you'd leave on a fridge. You can write and draw with a variety of different styles and themes, and there's plenty of colourful graphics. More fun than practical, but still quite good.

Overall Rating ★★★★☆

Price: £1.19/$1.99
Developer: Hesham Wahba

Tracing Paper

Tracing Paper is a fun idea that, rather unsurprisingly, lets you trace over images in your library, altering the level of translucency to improve your drawing skills. It could do with some more drawing tools and some additional features, though.

Overall Rating ★★★☆☆

Price: £1.79/$2.99
Developer: AlwaysOn Technologies, Inc.

Cloud Browse

This is a brilliant example of how not to design an iPad web browser. With a style reminiscent of early 90s Internet Explorer, this is a simply a horrible browser that, although it touts Flash and Java support, lacks any usable functionality. Avoid.

Overall Rating ★☆☆☆☆

Price: £5.99/$9.99
Developer: iTech Development Systems Inc.

PDF Reader Pro Edition for iPad

This is an average PDF reader that doesn't bring much to the table at all. It's light on features and functionality, and there's plenty of other apps out there that do the same or a better job for a cheaper price. Very bland, this one.

Overall Rating ★★☆☆☆

Price: Free
Developer: Eggman Technologies Inc.

Live Cams Pro

This is a neat app that allows you to check in on a personal CCTV camera or otherwise when you're on the go. Potentially useful if you're someone who already uses several cameras, it all works together rather nicely indeed. Worth a punt.

Overall Rating ★★★★☆

Price: Free
Developer: BestApps

theVault – Secure Storage of Passwords

If you've ever needed to store info on your iPad but you don't want it to fall into the wrong hands, then consider this. The ability to hide photos, documents and text with 256-bit AES encryption will be welcomed by many.

Overall Rating ★★★★☆

Price: £1.79/$2.99
Developer: voi nguyen

The Elements Pro HD

If you need to study the periodic table, or just want to know more about it, and don't mind paying for the information then check this out. While you might find similar free stuff elsewhere, there's enough content here to almost justify the price.

Overall Rating ★★★☆☆

Price: £0.59/$0.99
Developer: Smart Solutions

Weather Forecaster Pro

This is an excellent and simple weather app that eschews some of the flashy graphics its competitors offer in favour of a visually appealing UI. There's a variety of functions included and the whole thing works really coherently. Brilliant.

Overall Rating ★★★★★

Price: £1.79/$2.99
Developer: SimoApps

All Cell Phone Tracker 2011 HD

Apps like these need to be showcased for the scams that they are. This one claims to be able to track any phone in the world from only its mobile number. Does it work? No. It just tells you your own location. Don't be fooled.

Overall Rating ★☆☆☆☆

Price: £1.79/$2.99
Developer: Zeng Rong

Remote Mouse For iPad

If your computer is lacking a wireless mouse then this app wouldn't be a terrible way to go. Your iPad becomes one giant trackpad, with mouse buttons and a keyboard, making navigation a breeze. The price is a bit steep, however.

Overall Rating ★★★☆☆

Price: £6.99/$11.99
Developer: Hoang Le

CalPad

If you want an easy and simple way to manage your social life and calendar then this app might not be for you. There's a huge amount of detail and features on offer, but it's all a bit clunky and hard to read. Still, if you stick with it you'll get used to it.

Overall Rating ★★☆☆☆

Price: £1.79/$2.99
Developer: Smart Solutions

World Atlas For iPad

This is pretty much a Google Earth clone but with some additional features. That's not necessarily a bad thing, as the level of detail is good and you can view a variety of different types of map, such as time zones and political ones. Not bad.

Overall Rating ★★★☆☆

Price: Free
Developer: Ishaan Gandhi Studios

Calculator HD – Free and Ad Free

Oh dear. Dear, dear, dear. A strong contender for the worst app of all time, *Calculator HD* improves upon the iPad's built-in calculator by offering a changeable background and… that's it. Completely and utterly pointless.

Overall Rating ★☆☆☆☆

Price: Free
Developer: Linkus

Private Photo

Private Photo is a fairly efficient and easy way of storing and organising your photos on your iPad. It also gives you the ability to lock certain folders with a password so prying eyes can't see them. It works. Certainly useful for managing photos simply.

Overall Rating ★★★☆☆

Price: Free
Developer: Ussy

FlipClock65

This is a very aesthetically pleasing app that provides a nice visual clock. It doesn't offer much in the way of features or interactivity, but if you want a simple desk clock for home or at the office then you might as well give it a try – it's free.

Overall Rating ★★★☆☆

Price: Free
Developer: AppXpress

Sunrise Clock+

If you've ever wanted to know the exact times for sunrise and sunset in cities around the world, and you don't have the energy to perform a simple Google search, then *Sunrise Clock+* has got you covered. We can't see this appealing to too many people.

Overall Rating ★★☆☆☆

Price: Free
Developer: Diigo Inc.

iChromy – Chrome Style Web Browser

If you're a fan of the Google Chrome web browser then this is the closest you'll get to it on the iPad. It's still got a few niggles, such as the navigation buttons disappearing when you scroll down a page, but it's certainly promising.

Overall Rating ★★★☆☆

Price: £1.19/$1.99
Developer: LY MobileSoft

Bluetooth Share HD – Sharing Photos

This is an excellent app that makes sharing via Bluetooth or USB quick and painless. Simply set up a connection and then select which of your iPad's media you'd like to share with another device. A welcome alternative to using iTunes.

Overall Rating ★★★★☆

Price: £1.19/$1.99
Developer: Fakhr

My Translator Pro UK

This is a nice idea in principle, letting you translate between 52 different languages. However, when the Google Translate app is free, and this one doesn't offer much else in the way of features for a price, you have to wonder if it's really worth it.

Overall Rating ★★☆☆☆

Price: £3.99/$6.99
Developer: m3me, Inc.

Remote Conductor HD: Track

This app lets you control your Mac or PC remotely with your iPad. A variety of swipes and gestures make it fun and easy to use, and overall the experience is smooth. While it's a little complex at times, it's great once it's running.

Overall Rating ★★★★☆

iPad 2 App Directory *Index*

Your at-a-glance guide to what's inside...

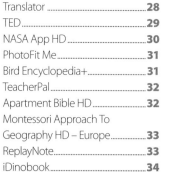

App Store | Entertainment

App Store | Games

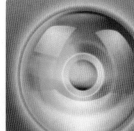

App Store | Health/Medical

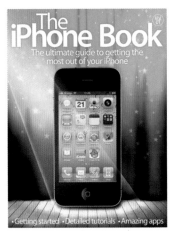

The iPhone Book vol 1
Whether you are new to the iPhone or have had one for a while, **The iPhone Book** is the ultimate resource for getting the very best from your Apple device.
SRP: £9.99

iPhone App Directory vol 7
The latest collection of iPhone apps are reviewed right here, including the very best available for iPhone 4.0, with every single App Store category featured inside.
SRP: £9.99

Mac for Beginners 2011
Starting with the basics, this essential guide will teach you how to master all aspects of switching to Mac including OS X, Snow Leopard, Mail and Safari.
SRP: £12.99

Retro Gamer Collection vol 5
An unmissable selection of in-depth articles featuring timeless games and hardware. From Zelda to Asteroids, this book covers all the classic games from days gone by.
SRP: £9.99

The world's best cre
to collect and keep

iPhone for Beginners
Everything you need to get started on your iPhone. With step-by-step tutorials, the 100 essential apps and a troubleshooting guide, this is a must-have for iPhone owners .
SRP: £9.99

The iPad Book
The ultimate guide to iPad and iPad 2, this comprehensive book brings you a wealth of productivity, entertainment and lifestyle tips, along with all the top apps to download.
SRP: £9.99

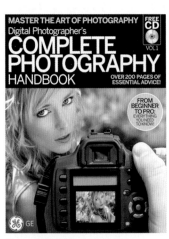

Complete Photography Handbook vol 1
With fantastic shooting ideas and a wide variety of practical tips, this tome is the only resource for digital photographers.
SRP: £12.99

iPhone Tips, Tricks, Apps & Hacks vol 4
Step-by-step tutorials and in-depth features covering the secrets of the iPhone and the ultimate jailbreaking guide make this a must-own book.
SRP: £9.99

Prices may vary, stocks are limited and shipping prices vary

Order online www.im

Photoshop CS5 Genius Guide
Over 200 pages packed full of advice for Photoshop CS5 users, including tool guides, step-by-step workshops and a free CD with over 60 minutes of top video tutorials.
SRP: £12.99

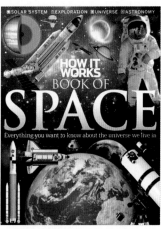

Photoshop Creative Collection vol 7
This latest addition to the Photoshop Collection includes excellent guides to improve your image editing skills whether you're a beginner or expert.
SRP: £14.99

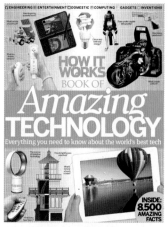

How It Works Book of Space
Feed your mind and fuel your imagination with this amazing guide to space and the universe from **How It Works** magazine.
SRP: £9.99

How It Works Book of Amazing Technology
Taking a look into the workings of some of the hottest gadgets and everyday appliances, this is the perfect guide for all tech-lovers.
SRP: £9.99

3D Art & Design vol 2
Covering characters, environments, architecture and transport, there is something for everyone interested in 3D design in this book. Become a 3D master in no time at all…
SRP: £14.99

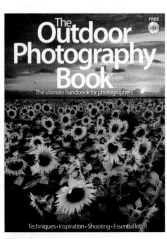

The Outdoor Photography Book
Enhance your photography techniques and learn a range of brand new skills with this essential guide to outdoor shooting.
SRP: £12.99

Web Design 6
The ultimate guide to creative cutting-edge web design. Discover how to produce next-generation web design projects using some of the hottest technologies…
SRP: £14.99

The Mac Book vol 6 Revised
256 pages of practical and creative tutorials and in-depth features that will take you through all areas of OS X, iLife, iWork, Mac App Store and third-party applications.
SRP: £12.99

Go creative with your Mac, iPad & iPhone

Upskill today with the very best creative bookazines and DVDs

Mac for Beginners vol 3
Starting with the basics, this essential guide will teach you how to get to grips with every aspect of your Mac, from iLife and iWork to iTunes, Safari and Mail.

SRP: £12.99

iPhone Tips, Tricks, Apps & Hacks vol 4
Step-by-step tutorials and features covering the secrets of the iPhone and a jailbreaking guide make this a must-own.

SRP: £9.99

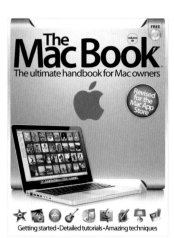

The Mac Book vol 6
256 pages of practical and creative tutorials and in-depth features that will take you through OS X, iLife, iWork and even third-party applications.

SRP: £12.99

iPhone App Directory vol 7
The world's best iPhone applications are reviewed here including the very best for iPhone OS 4.0, with every App Store category featured inside.

SRP: £9.99

iPhone for Beginners
Everything you need to get started on your iPhone. With step-by-step tutorials, the 100 essential apps and a troubleshooting guide, this is a must-have for iPhone owners .

SRP: £9.99

The iPad Book
The ultimate guide to iPad and iPad 2, this book brings you a wealth of productivity, entertainment and lifestyle tips, along with all the top apps.

SRP: £9.99

iPhone Games Directory vol 2
The world's most comprehensive guide to iPhone, iPod touch and iPad gaming apps, with all gaming genres reviewed and rated.

SRP: £9.99

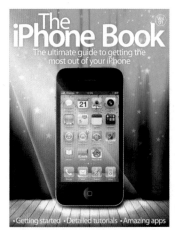

The iPhone Book vol 1
Whether you're brand new to the iPhone or have had one for a while, this book is the ultimate resource for getting the best from your favourite device.

SRP: £9.99

IMAGINE PUBLISHING

Prices may vary, stocks are limited and shipping prices vary depending on destination

Order online www.imaginebookshop.co.uk